Al-Qaida after 9/11

Al-Qaida after 9/11

The War on Terror and the Decade of Demise

Anne Likuski

I.B. TAURIS

LONDON • NEW YORK • OXFORD • NEW DELHI • SYDNEY

I.B. TAURIS

Bloomsbury Publishing Plc, 50 Bedford Square, London, WC1B 3DP, UK
Bloomsbury Publishing Inc, 1359 Broadway, New York, NY 10018, USA
Bloomsbury Publishing Ireland, 29 Earlsfort Terrace, Dublin 2, D02 AY28, Ireland

BLOOMSBURY, I.B. TAURIS and the I.B. Tauris logo are
trademarks of Bloomsbury Publishing Plc

First published in Great Britain 2026

For legal purposes the Acknowledgments on p. vii constitute an extension
of this copyright page.

Cover design by Paul Smith
Cover image © John Moore/Getty Images

A catalogue record for this book is available from the British Library.

Library of Congress Cataloging-in-Publication Data

Names: Likuski, Anne, author.
Title: Al-Qaida after 9/11 : the war on terror and the decade of demise / Anne Likuski.
Description: London ; New York : I.B. Tauris, 2026. |
Includes bibliographical references and index.
Identifiers: LCCN 2025030829 (print) | LCCN 2025030830 (ebook) | ISBN 9780755648566
(hardback) | ISBN 9780755648573 (paperback) | ISBN 9780755648597 (epub) |
ISBN 9780755648580 (pdf) Subjects: LCSH: Qaida (Organization)–History. | Terrorism–
History–21st century. | Terrorism–Religious aspects–Islam. | Afghan War, 2001-2021. |
Iraq War, 2003-2011. | Middle East–Politics and government–21st century.
Classification: LCC HV6432.5.Q2 L55 2026 (print) | LCC HV6432.5.Q2 (ebook)
LC record available at https://lccn.loc.gov/2025030829
LC ebook record available at https://lccn.loc.gov/2025030830

ISBN: HB: 978-0-7556-4856-6
          PB: 978-0-7556-4857-3
          ePDF: 978-0-7556-4858-0
          eBook: 978-0-7556-4859-7

Typeset by Integra Software Services Pvt. Ltd.
Printed and bound in Great Britain

For product safety related questions contact productsafety@bloomsbury.com.

To find out more about our authors and books visit www.bloomsbury.com
and sign up for our newsletters.

Contents

Tables

Acknowledgments

I would like to express my sincere gratitude to my employer, the Norwegian Defence Research Establishment (FFI), for granting me the time and space necessary to complete this book. Moreover, I wish to thank my colleagues at FFI's Terrorism Research Group (TERRA), with whom I have had the privilege of working for nearly two decades, for fostering an intellectually stimulating and collegial environment in which this work could take shape.

Special thanks are due to Professor Brynjar Lia, whose expert reading of earlier drafts and incisive feedback significantly improved the quality and clarity of this manuscript. I also wish to thank Dr. Erik Skare for his valuable comments during the manuscript's final stages. I am especially indebted to my editor at I.B. Tauris, Ms. Sophie Rudland, for her constant encouragement and support throughout the publishing process.

This book has benefited from the contributions of countless individuals who, in ways both large and small, helped piece together the puzzle at the heart of this story. Their assistance in locating key primary sources, sharing oral histories, and offering interpretations of difficult material was invaluable. While I am unable to name them all—out of respect for anonymity or the limitations of memory—I am deeply thankful for every contribution.

Needless to say, all errors and shortcomings remain my own.

Oslo, June 17, 2025

Note on Transliteration

The transliteration of Arabic words into English has been simplified by making no distinction between emphatic and non-emphatic consonants, and between long and short vowels. When ayn and hamza appear at the beginning of a word they have been omitted. In other positions they are represented by the signs ' and '. English names and words occurring in Arabic texts have been transliterated back to their original form. Arabic names follow the same transliteration rules as above, except for names that already have a widely used spelling in English (e.g., Osama bin Laden).

Note on Sources

To reconstruct al-Qaida's history after 9/11, I mainly relied on collections of private communications to and from al-Qaida's senior leadership, internal reports, personal memoirs, and diary notes. Most of these documents were captured during the raid on Osama bin Laden's house in Abbottabad, Pakistan, on May 2, 2011, and this collection is commonly known as the "Abbottabad documents." The documents were de-classified and released online in four batches between 2015 and 2017. The three first batches were released by the Office of the Director of National Intelligence (ODNI), and the last, and by far the largest collection, was released by the CIA on November 1, 2017.[1] The documents published by ODNI were given file names that are sometimes quite descriptive (i.e., "Letter to Shaykh Abu Abdallah dtd July 17, 2010"); other times, the file names are generic (e.g., "Kind Brother" or "Letter re Afghanistan"). As for the batch of letters released by the CIA, the filenames are nondescript and the collection has not been organized in any meaningful way, except that there is a folder with "Converted Materials" that contain files that had to be converted from MS Office format to PDF, and these contain many (but not all) of al-Qaida's private correspondence. Other than this, the materials have been sorted into folders for audio, documents, images, and video. A large majority of the materials in these folders are not private al-Qaida communications, but files expected to be found on anyone's computer, along with a large number of materials downloaded from the internet, such as e-books, news articles, and the like.

To establish a chronology of al-Qaida's internal communications, I decided to make my own archive of al-Qaida communications. The reason was threefold: (1) due to the need to consolidate the ODNI and CIA collections into a single, chronologically ordered archive; (2) because most of the files published online currently lack descriptive file names; and (3) because both the ODNI's and CIA's online archives have been subject to intermittent unavailability, making direct URL citation unreliable. I intend to make this chronological archive available online when this book is published in 2026.

The Abbottabad documents quoted in this book are referenced as personal communications with information about the sender, receiver, and date. When dates of letters are given in the Hijri calendar, I have converted these to the Gregorian calendar using the *IslamiCity* online date converter.[2] When the sender, receiver, or date is unknown, I have made qualified guesses based on the content of the letter, of other letters in the same time frame, and of the historical context. I have also used the various metadata that are available for documents downloaded from the CIA. In cases where there is some doubt, I have put the information in brackets, e.g., "[Mullah Omar], letter to Osama bin Laden, n.d. [ca. August 28, 2010]."

When quoting names of sender and receiver, I have used the real names of Osama bin Laden and Ayman al-Zawahiri, although in the letters they commonly use nicknames such as "Abu Abdullah" or "Azmaray" for bin Laden, and "Abu Muhammad" or "Abu Fatima" for Zawahiri. For other individuals, I have used the name they most commonly use in their letters, e.g., "Hajji Uthman" for Mustafa Abu al-Yazid (Sheikh Saeed). At the start of this book, there is a list of Dramatis Personae explaining the various nicknames used.

The Abbottabad documents collection covers al-Qaida's history between 2002 and 2011, but it is far from complete. There are large gaps in the private communications between Osama bin Laden and other al-Qaida leaders, especially in the period 2002–6, when Osama bin Laden moved several times. Moreover, it must be assumed that an unknown number of documents remain classified. Therefore, I have been somewhat careful reading too much into the documents, especially into missing information, because the Abbottabad documents do not represent the full extent of communication between the al-Qaida leaders.

To fill the missing gaps, I have used other archives of internal al-Qaida documents, primarily the collection known as the "Harmony Program" hosted by the Combating Terrorism Center at West Point.[3] This program was launched in 2005 and includes documents captured during the wars in Afghanistan and Iraq from 2001 and 2003, respectively. Moreover, I have relied on other sources such as jihadist propaganda, court documents, journalistic sources, and leaked intelligence documents. During the research for this book, I was fortunate to have access to a large archive of jihadist propaganda from the early 2000s, which is located at the Norwegian Defence Research Establishment (FFI) at Kjeller, Norway. During my own career as a researcher at FFI from 2006 onward, I collected and stored sources about al-Qaida, Afghanistan and Pakistan, referred to in the footnotes as "author's collection."

All the above-mentioned sources have weaknesses which must be taken into consideration. I consider al-Qaida's own, internal documents to be the most reliable and accurate source, but like all other sources, they must be interpreted in light of the context in which they were written. We sometimes know little or nothing about the context of the letter, which is a weakness. However, I generally rely on Abbottabad documents as a single source of information if the sender, receiver, and intent of the document seem clear and unambiguous. As for autobiographical accounts, I have evaluated the consistency and accuracy of various authors by comparing their writings across time and by comparing accounts by different authors that overlap thematically. For all other sources, I have assessed their accuracy by comparing information from multiple types of sources whenever possible.

Dramatis Personae

Abd al-Hadi al-Iraqi, see Nashwan al-Tamir.

Abd al-Rahman al-Muhajir, Egyptian, real name Muhsin Musa Matwalli Atwah (1964–2006). Explosives expert and old-time member of al-Qaida. Helped organize the bombing of the US Embassies in Nairobi and Dar es-Salaam on August 7, 1998. Worked as a bomb-maker for al-Qaida in the Tribal Areas of Pakistan after 2001.

Abu Bakr al-Baghdadi, Iraqi, real name Ibrahim Awwad Ibrahim Ali al-Badri (1971–2019). Leader of the Islamic State in Iraq (ISI) from 2010. Self-declared "Caliph" of the Muslims from 2014 to 2019.

Abu Abdullah al-Shafiʻi, Iraqi Kurd, real name Wirya Rasoul Salih Hawleri. Emir of the Iraqi insurgent group Ansar al-Islam, later Ansar al-Sunnah.

Abu Basir, see Nasir al-Wuhayshi.

Abu al-Faraj al-Libi, Libyan, real name Mustafa Faraj Muhammad Masud al-Jadid al-Uzaybi (b. 1970). Believed to be in charge of al-Qaida's activities in Afghanistan and Pakistan in the early years of the Taliban insurgency, from about 2002 to 2005. He was arrested by Pakistani authorities on May 2, 2005, in Mardan, Pakistan, and handed over to US authorities. As of 2025, he remains imprisoned without charge at the US Naval Base at Guantánamo Bay, Cuba.

Abu Hamza al-Muhajir (aka Abu Ayyub al-Masri), Egyptian, real name Abd al-Munʻim Izz al-Din Ali al-Badawi (1967–2010). "War minister" of the Islamic State of Iraq (ISI), 2006–10.

Abu al-Layth al-Libi, Libyan, real name Ali Ammar Ashur al-Raqiai (1967–2008). Field commander, member of the Libyan Islamic Fighting Group (LIFG). Fought on the Kabul frontline prior to 2001, leading commander at the Battle for Shah-i-Kot (Operation Anaconda), fought in the Afghanistan-Pakistan border areas post-2001.

Abu Musab Abd al-Wudud, Algerian, real name Abdelmalek Droukdel (1970–2020). Emir of al-Qaida in the Islamic Maghreb (AQIM).

Abu Musab al-Suri, Syrian, real name Mustafa Setmariam Nasar (1958–?). Jihadist theoretician—author of several books on the history and strategy of the jihadist movement. Arrested in Quetta, Pakistan, in 2005, later transferred to Syria and imprisoned by the Assad regime. His current whereabouts are unknown, but he is rumored to have died in prison prior to the fall of the Assad regime in 2024.

Abu Musab al-Zarqawi, Jordanian, real name Ahmad Fadil Nazal al-Khalaylah (1966–2006). Veteran of the Afghan-Arabs movement, fought in the Iraqi insurgency from 2003. In spring 2004, he announced the formation of his group, Monotheism and Jihad (al-Tawhid wal-Jihad), which in October 2004 switched names to al-Qaida in Iraq.

Abu Ubaydah al-Masri (aka Abdul Hafiz), Egyptian, real name unknown. Chief of al-Qaida's External Operations from *c.* 2006–7. Died of natural causes in Pakistan in late 2007 or early 2008.

Abu Omar al-Baghdadi, Iraqi, real name Hamid Dawud Mohamed Khalil al-Zawi (1959–2010). Emir of the Islamic State of Iraq, 2006–10.

Abu Yahya al-Libi, Libyan, real name Mohammad Hassan Qa'id (1963–2012). Islamic scholar, member of Libyan Islamic Fighting Group (LIFG), merged formally with al-Qaida in 2008, head of al-Qaida's Sharia Committee.

Adnan al-Shukrijumah (aka Ja'far al-Tayyar, Tufan), Saudi Arabian, born Adnan Gulshair el Shukrijumah (1975–2014). Grew up in Florida, United States. Left the United States in May 2001 and spent time in Afghanistan, then Pakistan after 2001. Wanted by the FBI since 2003 for terrorism-related offenses.

Atiyah Abd al-Rahman (aka Atiyatullah, Sheikh Atiyah), Libyan, born Jamal Ibrahim Ashtiwi al-Misrati (1969–2011). Islamic scholar, mediator in the Algerian Civil War in the mid-1990s, online activist in the mid-2000s writing under the pen name "Atiyatullah." General manager of al-Qaida from 2010 to 2011.

Ayman al-Zawahiri (aka Abu Fatima, Abu Muhammad), Egyptian, born Ayman Muhammad Rabi' al-Zawahiri (1951–2022). Doctor, founding member of *Jama'at al-Jihad*, or the Egyptian Islamic Jihad (EIJ). Joined the Global Islamic Front of Osama bin Laden in 1998; merged his group with al-Qaida in June 2001. Deputy Emir of al-Qaida 2001–11; Emir of al-Qaida 2011–22.

Baitullah Mehsud, Pakistani militant (1970–2009). Commander in South Waziristan, later Emir of the Pakistani Taliban Movement (Tehrik-e-Taliban Pakistan).

Bekkay Harrach (aka Abu Talha al-Almani), Moroccan-German (1977–2010). Traveled to Pakistan around 2006, worked in al-Qaida's propaganda and external operations, carried out a suicide attack against Bagram Air Base in 2010.

Gulbuddin Hekmatyar, Afghan (b. 1949). Engineer and politician, leader of Hizb-e-Islami, one of the seven official mujahidin parties that fought in the Afghan-Soviet war in the 1980s. Fled the country when the Taliban came to power in the 1990s, returned to participate in the anti-US insurgency after 2001 with his group, now often referred to as Hizb-e-Islami Gulbuddin or "HIG."

Hajji Uthman, see Mustafa Abu al-Yazid.

Hamza Rabia (aka Abu Hamza al-Rabia), Egyptian (*c.* 1960–2005). Member of Egyptian Islamic Jihad (EIJ) and old-time associate of Ayman al-Zawahiri, chief of al-Qaida's External Operations from *c.* 2003 to December 2005.

Hafiz Sultan, see Mustafa Abu al-Yazid.

Hamid al-'Ali, Kuwaiti (b. 1960). Salafi scholar and former professor of Islamic Studies at Kuwait University. Known in the 2000s for issuing a handful of fatwas in support of al-Qaida ideology. In 2007, he publicly denounced the establishment of the "Islamic State in Iraq."

Khalid Habib, Egyptian, born Shawqi Marzuq Abd al-Alam Dabbas (?–2008). Tank driver, veteran of the Afghan-Arabs movement, participated with al-Qaida in the 1989 Battle for Jalalabad, and the 2001 Battle for Kandahar. In 2004, he was appointed Emir of al-Qaida's frontline in Afghanistan.

Khalid Sheikh Mohammed (aka KSM, Mukhtar). Pakistani of Baloch origin (b. 1965) who grew up in Saudi Arabia. Veteran of the Afghan-Arabs movement. Mastermind of the 9/11 attacks. Arrested in Rawalpindi, Pakistan on March 1, 2003. Currently imprisoned at the US Naval Station at Guantánamo Bay, Cuba, awaiting trial by a military tribunal.

Karim, see Abu Hamza al-Muhajir.

Mansour Dadullah, Afghan, real name Mullah Bakht (1972–2015). Taliban commander mainly active in Helmand, half-brother of Mullah Dadullah. He was expelled from the Taliban in 2008 due to disobedience, and later arrested in Pakistan.

Muhammad Tayib, see Tayyib Agha.

Mukhtar Abu al-Zubayr, Somali, real name Ahmed Abdi Godane (1977–2014). Emir of al-Shabaab in Somalia.

Mullah Dadullah Akhund, Afghan (1966–2007). Famous Taliban commander who lost a leg fighting in the Afghan-Soviet war, but who remained active in the Taliban insurgency after 2001, and who rose to the rank of highest military official in the Taliban before he was killed by British Special Forces in Helmand, Afghanistan, in 2007.

Mullah Muhammad Omar, Afghan (1959–2013). Mullah from Kandahar who fought in the Afghan-Soviet war in the 1980s. Founder and leader of the Taliban from 1994 to 2013. He was awarded the title Emir al-Mu'minin (Leader of the Faithful) in a ceremony in Kandahar in 1995.

Mustafa Abu al-Yazid (aka Sheikh Saeed, Hajji Uthman), Egyptian, born Mustafa Ahmed Muhammad Uthman Abu al-Yazid (1955–2010). Member of al-Qaida since the late 1980s or early 1990s. Known as "bin Laden's accountant," was in Sudan with bin Laden in the 1990s and went with him to Afghanistan in 1996. General manager of al-Qaida from *c.* 2006 to 2010.

Mustafa Hamid (aka Abu Walid al-Masri), Egyptian (b. 1945). Journalist, writer, and intellectual and veteran of the Afghan-Arab movement. Old-time acquaintance of bin Laden and author of numerous books about al-Qaida's early history. Since 2006, he was owner and main contributor on the Arabic website *Mafa al-Siyasi—Adab al-matarid.*[4] Father-in-law of Sayf al-Adl.

Nashwan al-Tamir, Iraqi (b. 1961). Fled Saddam Hussein's Iraq in 1991 and settled in the Afghanistan-Pakistan region. Worked as a commander for the Taliban after 1997. In 2001, he was appointed as Deputy Emir for the Taliban's Foreign Brigade, led by the Uzbek Juma Namanjani. After 2001, he was a commander for Arabs and other foreigners fighting the United States in Afghanistan. He was arrested in Turkey in 2006 and transferred to the US Naval Station at Guantánamo Bay, Cuba, in 2007. He was convicted by a US military tribunal in 2024.

Nasir al-Wuhayshi (aka Abu Basir), Yemeni, born Nasir Abd al-Karim al-Wuhayshi (1976–2015). Leader of al-Qaida on the Arabian Peninsula (AQAP) from 2009 to 2015.

Osama bin Laden, Saudi millionaire (1957–2011), veteran of the Afghan-Arabs movement. Founder and leader of al-Qaida from the late 1980s until his death in May 2011.

Rashid Rauf, UK-Pakistani (*c.* 1981–2008). He left Great Britain in 2002 for Pakistan, joined the Pakistani militant group Harakat ul-Mujahidin, before starting to work with al-Qaida in *c.* 2004. He participated in organizing the July 7, 2005, London bombings in addition to other plots in the UK.

Saleh al-Somali (aka Abu Salih, Abd al-Hafiz al-Muhajir), prob. Somali, real identity unknown. Chief of al-Qaida's External Operations in 2008–10.

Sayf al-Adl, Egyptian, real name Mohamed Salah al-Din al-Halim Zaidan (b. *c.* 1963). Member of al-Qaida since late 1989. Son-in-law of Mustafa Hamid. In 2001, he was chief of al-Qaida's Security Committee. Fled to Iran in 2002, current whereabouts unknown.

Sheikh Saeed, see Mustafa Abu al-Yazid.

Tawfiq, an alias most likely used by Abu al-Faraj al-Libi.

Tayyib Agha (aka Muhammad Tayib, Sheikh Tayyib), Afghan (b. 1976). Senior member of the Taliban, with personal links to Mullah Omar. Known as "Mullah Omar's secretary." He was responsible for Taliban's foreign relations from *c.* 2009, head of the Taliban's delegation to Qatar from 2012 to 2015.

Uthman al-Shihri, prob. Saudi Arabian, real identity unknown. Supporter of Gulbuddin Hekmatyar after 2001, repeatedly sought to solicit bin Laden's support to Hekmatyar's group.

Yunus al-Mauritani, Mauritanian, real name Abd al-Rahman Ould Muhammad al-Husayn Ould Muhammad Salim (b. 1981). Former member of al-Morabitoun, an armed rebel group led by Mokhtar Belmokhtar based in Mali. Wanted on terrorism charges by Mauritanian authorities since 2006. Spent some time with al-Qaida in the Islamic Maghreb (AQIM), possibly around 2006–7. Member of al-Qaida's Sharia Committee in Waziristan since at least 2008. Appointed by Osama bin Laden to lead part of al-Qaida's External Operations activities in 2010. Arrested in Quetta, Pakistan, in late 2010, expelled to Mauritania in 2012. Currently imprisoned in Mauritania.

Maps

Map 1 *Map of Afghanistan.*

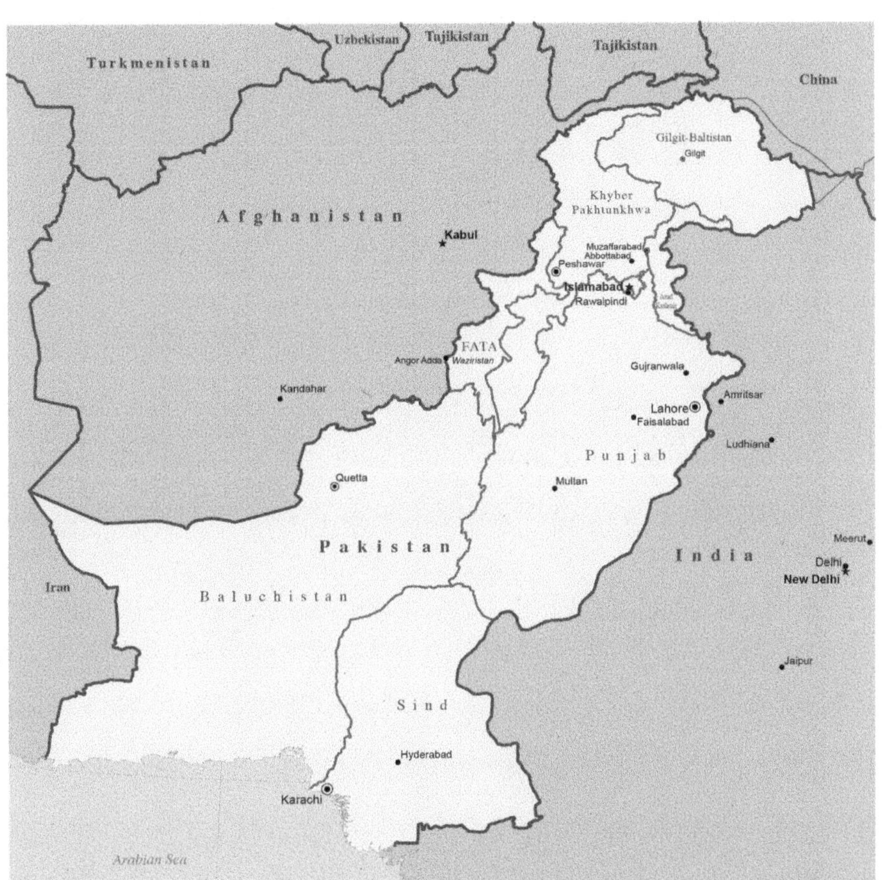

Map 2 *Map of Pakistan.*

Introduction

This book is about the history of al-Qaida in the decade after 9/11. The reason for writing it might not be obvious. Al-Qaida was surpassed in 2014 by the so-called Islamic State in Iraq and Syria (ISIS), and the original group, which grew out of the Afghan-Soviet war of the 1980s, is now largely a thing of the past. Even al-Qaida's own propaganda reflects this fact. Al-Qaida's official media agency, *al-Sahab*, which once had the exclusive rights to bin Laden's newest speeches, has in recent years been more resemblant of a history channel dedicated to re-issuing old videos and commemorating past events.[1]

At the same time, we are today in a unique position to study al-Qaida. Never before have we had access to so many primary sources about the group's inner workings. In addition, we have witnessed another decade of history in the Middle East. We therefore know more about what happened to the ideological movements of Salafi-jihadism and revolutionary Islamism, of which al-Qaida was a part. This means we can start to assess al-Qaida's ideological and political legacy. In spite of this, al-Qaida's history in the decade after 2001 has overall received little attention among scholars.[2] The reason is perhaps that after Osama bin Laden was killed in 2011, other seminal events happened in the Middle East such as the Arab spring and the rise of the Islamic State in Iraq and Syria (ISIS). Afterward, the world moved on to worrying about issues other than terrorism.

This is a book about how al-Qaida shaped the world after 9/11 and how the world, in turn, shaped al-Qaida. Before going any further, a short definition is in order. There are many ways of understanding al-Qaida. It can be viewed as an organization, a network, or a social movement bound together by a common ideology. In this book I use a narrow definition of al-Qaida, referring to the historical organization around Osama bin Laden, which after 2001 has been referred to as al-Qaida's "central leadership" or "central organization."[3] Initially, these were terms used by Western media to refer to the remnants of bin Laden's organization that had fled to Pakistan after the fall of the Taliban regime in late 2001. Later, the term "al-Qaida Central" became a standard way of distinguishing al-Qaida's branches from the core organization in Pakistan.[4] As for the al-Qaida leaders themselves, they sometimes used the term *al-qiyada al-'amma* (General Command) in their propaganda and, inspired by the media, also started using the term *al-qa'ida fil-markaz* (a direct translation of "al-Qaida Central") in internal communications in 2010.[5] In this book, I generally use "al-Qaida" for short when I mean al-Qaida's senior leadership in Pakistan, and when I discuss al-Qaida's regional branches I use their full names, like al-Qaida in Iraq (AQI) or al-Qaida on the Arabian Peninsula (AQAP).

As for the definition of who is an "al-Qaida member" and who is not, this is a tricky question because the answer depends on who is asking, and for what purpose. The only thing that seems fairly certain is that al-Qaida was historically a fluid organization, with blurred boundaries between who is regarded as a member and who is not. Al-Qaida's leader, Osama bin Laden, probably did not emphasize formal membership criteria, although there was a membership ritual based around the *bay'a* (Islamic oath of allegiance) that some eyewitnesses describe as secret, others as voluntary.[6] In any case, social networks appear to have been more important than formal membership in shaping the inner dynamics of the group. In Afghanistan prior to 2002, it was common for a number of individuals to "work with" or even "advise" al-Qaida without being a member of the group.[7] One could also work with al-Qaida while at the same time being a member of other groups, although some restrictions may have been put on individuals working in al-Qaida's "external operations" department (i.e., international terrorist planning) in 2004.[8] Overall, al-Qaida appears to have had a pragmatic approach to membership, which I believe was one of the reasons the group survived so long.

Despite the fluid nature of al-Qaida, we can assume there was a core membership or a close circle of associates who enjoyed the trust of Osama bin Laden and of his lieutenant Abu Hafs al-Masri, the chief of al-Qaida's Military Committee. Some of these individuals were responsible for international terrorist planning and other sensitive tasks, which, due to their nature, had to be compartmentalized from al-Qaida's other activities.[9] This would be nothing unique if one compares with, for instance, the Muslim Brotherhood which had several layers of members or associates, including a secret paramilitary wing known as the Special Apparatus (*al-nizam al-khass*), for periods of its existence.[10] At the same time, al-Qaida ran an organization in Afghanistan that was set up to serve the wider Arab community there, a sort of "Services Office" modeled after the organization set up by Abdullah Azzam in Pakistan during the 1980s Afghan-Soviet war.[11] This part of al-Qaida ran guest houses and training camps for newly arrived recruits, offering basic military training for individuals who wanted to fight jihad whether in Chechnya, on the Taliban's frontlines, or elsewhere. Thus, a large number of Arabs who came to Afghanistan came into contact with al-Qaida at some point, but only a fraction went on to become part of Osama bin Laden's trusted inner circle. As we shall see in this book, most of the individuals, who held senior positions in al-Qaida after 2001, had historical ties to bin Laden going back to the late 1980s or the first half of the 1990s, when al-Qaida was based in Afghanistan and Pakistan, then Sudan. After 2001, this core group of individuals ended up in Pakistan and played an essential part in shaping al-Qaida after 9/11.

Existing Literature, Scope, and Argument

One of the common arguments in existing literature about al-Qaida after 2001 is that it went from being a hierarchical organization to a networked structure comprised of "franchises."[12] Based on new primary sources about al-Qaida, we can conclude that this is a simplification at best. Al-Qaida's organization always had elements of informal networks and partner organizations, as well as rules and hierarchies incorporated into its structure. This is partly because al-Qaida sprang out of the social movement known as the "Afghan-Arabs," with its eclectic mix of personalities from various social, organizational, and cultural backgrounds.[13]

Instead of simply arguing that al-Qaida changed from hierarchical organization to network, I suggest that al-Qaida's organization and ideology were in continuous development, molded on the one hand by internal dynamics and on the other hand by the local environment. Here, I draw some inspiration from Raphaël Lefèvre's case study of the Islamist group Tawhid in the 1980s Lebanese city of Tripoli. However, while Tawhid operated before the age of the internet and within a confined geographical space, al-Qaida evolved into a center-periphery type organization with branches on several continents and with access to modern communications technology. I have therefore adopted in this book a wider definition of "the local environment" that includes the local operating contexts of both al-Qaida central and its affiliates. This was necessary because the affiliates came to play a central part in al-Qaida's ideological evolution, and indeed in al-Qaida's definition of itself, in the late 2000s.[14]

In exploring the importance of the local context, I also built upon my previous book, *Al-Qaida in Afghanistan*, which covered al-Qaida's history from the 1980s until 2001. In that book, I made the observation that al-Qaida was involved in a wide range of activities in Afghanistan that were not directly related to international terrorist planning, although the book stopped short of connecting any of the empirical findings to broader theoretical discussions within social science or conflict studies.[15] The aim of the present work is therefore not just to continue writing the history of al-Qaida from 2001 onward, but to explore how a case study of a clandestine organization like al-Qaida can enhance our understanding of how the interaction between local space and ideology shapes organizational behavior.[16]

Another, common debate about al-Qaida since 2001 is whether the group grew weaker or stronger as a result of the War on Terror.[17] In this book, I take for granted that al-Qaida grew weaker, but this is bearing in mind my narrow definition of al-Qaida as the "core organization" around Osama bin Laden in Pakistan. After bin Laden was killed in Abbottabad, Pakistan, in 2011, this core group's ability to lead a global network of affiliates was significantly weakened, signified by the dominance of ISIS over al-Qaida in the 2010s. On the surface, one could argue that the weakening of al-Qaida's core leadership was the direct result of US-led counterterrorism operations, including years of meticulous intelligence work, arrests in Pakistan, drone attacks, and ultimately, the US Special Forces raid that killed Osama bin Laden. In this book, I provide anecdotal examples of how the US-led War on Terror affected al-Qaida, but it is not the main focus of the book. The reason is that such a question would be limited to considering only one out of many factors that contributed to al-Qaida's demise. Instead, I look at the whole range of factors affecting al-Qaida on the macro-, meso-, and micro-levels.[18]

Macro-level factors include the US-led counterterrorism campaign, but also the activities of states with an ambivalent relationship to al-Qaida, such as Iran and Pakistan, and transnational networks of religious scholars who supported or contested al-Qaida's ideology. On the meso-level, I primarily look at the local environments that al-Qaida interacted and cooperated with, either in Afghanistan and Pakistan or via one of the regions in Iraq, Yemen, Somalia, or Algeria. On a micro-level, I consider the internal dynamics among al-Qaida's senior and mid-level leaders, which we now can study in detail thanks to the Abbottabad documents found in bin Laden's house in 2011. Throughout the book, I ask two overarching questions: How did al-Qaida react to the constraints and opportunities brought about by the

War on Terror? And how did al-Qaida's organization and aims change in the process?

The main argument is that al-Qaida changed fundamentally as an organization in the decade after 9/11. Al-Qaida started out as an organization focused on "global jihad," but after the US-led invasion of Iraq, al-Qaida became associated with the idea of establishing Islamic states across the Middle East. This idea was introduced and implemented by al-Qaida's affiliate in Iraq, which declared the establishment of an "Islamic State" in 2006. Al-Qaida's leaders were not consulted beforehand and were too far away to influence events on the ground. The best al-Qaida could do was to endorse the "Islamic State in Iraq" (ISI) in public while working in secret to mend the internal divisions that the announcement of ISI had caused within the Iraqi insurgency. Meanwhile, other insurgent groups in Algeria, Yemen, and Somalia turned to al-Qaida's leadership in Pakistan for support to their own state-building projects. By the end of the decade, al-Qaida thus found itself in a new role—that of being looked to as *"al-markaz,"* or the center, of a future Caliphate. This was very different from the first vision for al-Qaida as a purely military organization that had been prevalent prior to 9/11.

In the end, al-Qaida's demise happened because the organization was too weak to handle the role that was thrust upon it, which was to be a group focused on state-building rather than jihad. Al-Qaida struggled in particular with controlling excessive use of violence (*takfirism*) in its ranks. In an attempt to distance itself from takfirism, al-Qaida moved closer toward non-Salafi activist groups, such as the traditionalist Afghan Taliban or the Brotherhood-affiliated Hamas. In the end, the death of bin Laden and the dilution of al-Qaida's methodology caused the group's descent into irrelevance, and its remaining activists were soon absorbed into the support networks of other and more powerful groups.

Chapter Outline

The book has seven chapters and a conclusion. Chapter 1 tells the story of al-Qaida's exit from Afghanistan in 2001, and the purpose is to place al-Qaida within the larger environment of Arabs and other foreigners in Afghanistan. Chapter 2 evaluates al-Qaida's role in the nascent Afghan insurgency. I argue that al-Qaida in 2002–3 was dysfunctional as an organization, but leaders like bin Laden continued their activism as individuals, and around 2004, al-Qaida started working as an organization again.

Chapter 3 tells the first part of the story of al-Qaida's international terrorist campaign. Al-Qaida struggled to operate from Pakistan, due to Pakistani counterterrorism operations which intensified around 2004. In this context, al-Qaida contemplated moving their international terrorist planning to Iraq. Al-Qaida nevertheless managed to carry out the London bombings in 2005, which were a result of opportunity owing to the presence of a network of British-Pakistani jihadists in al-Qaida. This network was disrupted in 2006 when key operatives were arrested.

Chapter 4 explains how al-Qaida sought to exploit the Iraq War for the purpose of spreading its agenda of global jihadism. Iraqi groups also sought to exploit al-Qaida's name to gain status and power locally. This was the basis for the alliance between al-Qaida and the Jordanian Abu Musab al-Zarqawi, who in 2004 formed al-Qaida's first regional branch. In 2006, this Iraqi branch declared the establishment of an Islamic state without al-Qaida's approval. After a long internal discussion, bin Laden decided to endorse the Islamic state, which over time changed al-Qaida's image from a group focused on jihad, to a group supporting "jihadist" state-building.

Chapter 5 discusses al-Qaida's relationship to Afghanistan and the Afghan Taliban. In late 2007, some al-Qaida leaders suspected that several high-ranking Taliban leaders were under the influence of Pakistani intelligence. Al-Qaida discussed how to cope with this suspicion, but in reality, they had no choice but to stay and work pragmatically with the Taliban. I argue that this local context was one among several factors that encouraged al-Qaida's leaders in 2009–10 to intensify their efforts at building up alternative sanctuaries in countries such as Yemen and Somalia.

Chapter 6 continues the history of al-Qaida's external operations office, which experienced a lull in activities in 2007. In 2008 the activity re-started, but was severely weakened by drone strikes, and this forced al-Qaida to experiment with low-cost and ineffective ways of terrorizing the west. The death of al-Qaida's external operations manager in December 2009 spurred an internal discussion in al-Qaida about the future of al-Qaida's external operations. All of al-Qaida's senior leaders, save for bin Laden, believed that attacks on the United States were no longer essential, because the United States was being depleted economically in the wars in Afghanistan and Iraq.

Chapter 7 covers what bin Laden called al-Qaida's "new phase of correction and development." This phase marked a fundamental shift in al-Qaida's self-image, because al-Qaida started to think of itself as a "center with regions" and a template for the future Caliphate. However, al-Qaida was too depleted by the War on Terror to carry out the plan in practice, and in the end, al-Qaida's caliphate project was hijacked by the larger and far more bureaucratically competent Islamic State in Iraq and Syria (ISIS). The public split between al-Qaida and ISIS in 2014 pushed al-Qaida to align their propaganda more closely with that of non-Salafi groups such as the Taliban and Hamas, which caused ideological fragmentation and ultimately, al-Qaida's descent into irrelevance.

1

The Fall of the Emirate

*The Crusader war was very intense, beyond the imagination of most of us, and
there was a rapid collapse, dispersion, confusion, and complete chaos, in which
souls, money and other things were lost.*[1]

—Letter from an al-Qaida member, describing the collapse
of the Taliban in 2001

This chapter describes the battles in Afghanistan where Arabs participated in
October to December 2001. The purpose is to set the stage for understanding
what kind of organization al-Qaida was and the local context in which they
operated. Al-Qaida and "the Arabs" in Afghanistan are two categories that
have commonly been conflated. In Afghanistan, al-Qaida mainly played a
lead role in two battles, at Kandahar and Tora Bora in December 2001. The
other battles, in particular in Northern Afghanistan and Kabul, were led by
Taliban commanders and involved a mixture of groups. When the Taliban
surrendered, Arabs in the North were trapped, while in Kandahar, Kabul, and
Tora Bora, they were generally able to flee toward Pakistan. In this process,
there was a mixture of Arabs and other foreigners, of al-Qaida members and
other groups, and active fighters and civilians. Al-Qaida was without a leader
in this chaotic period, because bin Laden and Zawahiri were on the run,
and bin Laden's military chief, the Egyptian Abu Hafs al-Masri, was killed
in the US bombardment. In other words, al-Qaida did not withdraw in a
military sense, but its members were tossed into a stream of refugees as they
became refugees themselves. This context sets the stage for understanding
al-Qaida's history after 2001, when the group slowly managed to rebuild itself
in Pakistan.

The Battle for Northern Afghanistan

On October 7, 2001, President George W. Bush announced that the US military had begun striking targets in Afghanistan.[2] On the ground in Afghanistan, not much happened for the next month. The US strikes were random and ineffective. Then, at the beginning of November, things started happening in rapid succession. That's when US Special Forces on the ground, embedded with Afghan militias, started calling in concentrated airstrikes on Taliban positions.

The US strategy was to target one frontline at a time. First, they supported the Afghan militia commanders Abdul Rashid Dostum, Atta Mohammad Noor, and Mohammad Mohaqqeq in capturing the northern city of Mazar-e-Sharif. The three local commanders were part of what would become known as the Northern Alliance. They were based in the mountains south of Mazar-e-Sharif and had been waging guerrilla war against the Taliban for some time. When 9/11 happened, the war was at a standstill. Dostum, ever the opportunist, had called his old friend Zalmay Khalilzad shortly after 9/11. Khalilzad lived in Washington and was the US envoy to Afghanistan. "Tell the American friends that as far as they have hard enemies, they should know that they have hard friends, too. And that they are us."[3] The first US Special Forces team arrived at Dostum's guerrilla base on October 16, 2001.[4] Dostum was waging a type of war that was exotic to the American guests: His army rode horses to battle, something the Americans had not done since the Second World War. The scene seemed like something out of Hollywood. In fact, the US Special Forces who accompanied Dostum were later portrayed in the 2018 blockbuster movie *12 Strong*.

On the other side of the frontline, among the Taliban forces, was a mid-level commander named Mullah Abdul Baqi.[5] He had traveled to the north from Kandahar, where he had helped the Taliban organize their defenses. Then, the Taliban had received reports that the Americans were preparing to attack Mazar-e-Sharif, and reinforcements, including Mullah Abdul Baqi's group of two hundred men, were sent to the North. He worked there under the overall command of Mullah Fazl, the Taliban's division commander for Northern Afghanistan.

There were two frontlines in Northern Afghanistan. The first was south of Mazar, where Mullah Abdul Baqi was stationed and where Dostum was preparing to attack. The other frontline was 130 miles to the east and formed a vertical line that went from the Uzbek border in the North to the Hindu Kush mountains in the south. The line cut through the north-eastern provinces of Takhar and Baghlan, which covered the foothills of the Hindu Kush mountain range, as well as the main road to Faisalabad, the seat of power for the former president and mujahidin commander Burhanuddin Rabbani. Rabbani was now a member of the Northern Alliance which also included Ahmed Shah Massoud's forces. Over the summer they had been fighting the Taliban there, on the Takhar-Baghlan frontline.

This fighting season, the Taliban had reinforced the frontline in Takhar with a newly formed brigade called the Mujahideen Brigade (*Liwa al-Mujahidin*), which I will refer to here as the Foreign Brigade. It was comprised of around 1,200 Pakistani, Uzbek, and Arab fighters and led by an Uzbek commander from the Islamic Movement of Uzbekistan (IMU) named Juma Namangani. In earlier years, various foreign groups had fought on the Taliban frontlines through local arrangements. Over time, it led to competition and some outright conflicts between the foreigners. That is why Mullah Omar established the Brigade in early 2001. From now on, all Arabs who wanted to fight for the Taliban had to be part of the brigade and fight under the command of Juma Namanjani, who answered to the Taliban's chain of command.

In the summer of 2001, the Northern Alliance and the Taliban fought each other at the Takhar-Baghlan frontline without much result. The situation was the same there as on the Mazar frontline, and on the frontline north of Kabul. Each party was entrenched on their side, occasionally advancing to capture a hilltop or a village, only to retreat from it again later. When the US Air Force entered the battle, everything changed.

The Americans started on the frontline south of Mazar-e-Sharif, by ordering a massive air bombing of Taliban positions during the first week of November. The overall strategy was to first capture Mazar-e-Sharif, followed by an immediate attack on the Takhar-Baghlan frontline, while at the same time blocking the escape routes south. If the plan worked, Mullah Fazl's Taliban division, including all its foreign fighters, would be trapped in the North and forced to surrender. After that, the United States would start pounding Taliban positions north of Kabul, which would then allow Massoud's forces to capture Kabul itself.

From around November 1, 2001, Dostum and Atta's forces started advancing from their valley strongholds and toward Mazar-e-Sharif. On November 5, they carried out a major, coordinated assault on a village called Baloch, which is on the way to Sholgarah, a major city some 55 km south of Mazar. Between November 5 and 9, the forces made their way to Sholgarah and then reached a place called "the Gap" outside Mazar. In this period, Taliban suffered heavy losses, mostly from US air attacks, and ordered reinforcements to go to the frontlines south of Mazar.

Around December 6, the US Air Force spotted a large group of seventy fighters coming from the Takhar front to reinforce the Taliban positions at Mazar-e-Sharif. They started dropping bombs on them, and the attack killed Juma Namanjani, the commander of the Foreign Brigade, and a high-ranking Yemeni commander known as Abd al-Salam al-Hadrami, along with ten other Arabs and more than fifty other foreigners. Until now, it has been unclear exactly where and when Juma Namanjani was killed, but according to available sources, it turns out that the most correct version of the story was provided by the Pakistani journalist Hamid Mir and the Saudi jihadist web page *Markaz al-Dirasat*.[6] Hamid Mir wrote that Juma Namanjani had been killed on November 6 and that two days later, there was a memorial service in Kabul attended by Osama bin Laden and others.[7]

The intensification of the US air bombings in November 2001 had a massive and devastating psychological effect on the Taliban's forces. Taliban retreated from Mazar-e-Sharif in the evening of November 9, leaving the city without a fight. At this point Dostum and Atta's forces were on the outskirts of the city, expecting to arrive the next morning. The two warlords competed about who would reach the city first. Atta secured the strategically important airport to the east of Mazar, while Dostum took hold of his old headquarters from the pre-Taliban days—a nineteenth-century fortress named Qala-i-Jangi, 7 miles west of the city. The Taliban retreated east, toward the city of Pul-i-Khumri, the capital of Baghlan, which was still in Taliban-controlled territory.

Immediately after the fall of Mazar on November 10th, the United States intensified the air bombing of the Takhar frontline where the Foreign Brigade was stationed. Within a few hours, the frontline started collapsing and fighters fled to the west. In the evening of the 10th, Taliban division commander Mullah Fazl ordered all the fighters to regroup in Kunduz.[8] The retreat was rushed and chaotic, and physically challenging, as indicated by the autobiography of one Australian volunteer who had arrived just before the frontline fell.[9] The story contradicts stereotypical account of Arab fighters, which tend to emphasize that they stayed on the frontlines as others left and fought until death. The Arab sources reviewed for this book generally indicate that the majority of the Arab volunteers fought under Taliban command and withdrew as the Taliban withdrew.

Back in Kunduz, the Taliban's division commander Mullah Fazl held a meeting with the other Taliban commanders. The fleeing Taliban now found themselves squeezed between Northern Alliance forces in both the west and the east, and by the Tajik border, delineated by the mighty Amu Darya (or

Oxus) river, to the north. The main road south to Kabul, cutting through the 5,000-meter-high Hindu Kush mountains via the Salang tunnel, was blocked on the south side of the mountains by Massoud's forces. For Mullah Fazl, there was only one option left for escape. There was a lesser-known route south to Kabul through the Bamiyan province, where Taliban had destroyed a pair of giant Buddha statues just eight months before. Fazl ordered his commanders to take up positions along the road to protect the withdrawing Taliban forces.

The next day on November 11, word arrived that Bamiyan had fallen to the Northern Alliance. It thwarted Mullah Fazl's retreat plan. The enemy was also closing in on Pul-i-Khumri, the capital of Baghlan where a number of the Taliban forces coming from the west had assembled. The Taliban had no choice but to retreat to the city of Kunduz, the Taliban's last bastion in the north. Here, the Taliban who had been stationed in Mazar-e-Sharif met up with the Taliban and foreign fighters who had retreated from the eastern frontline. Mullah Fazl's division was now surrounded in a city of 250,000 civilians, while the US Air Force kept dropping bombs from the air. The Taliban started discussing what to do. Fight until the death? Or negotiate a surrender? There were no good options to choose from.[10]

The Fall of Kabul

On November 10th, while the Taliban's frontlines were collapsing in Northern Afghanistan, a car was making the 25-mile trip from Logar province to Kabul. Aboard it was an Arab commander, of whom we know little, except that years later, he appeared on Muslim online forums under the pen name "Qotoz." Perhaps he drew inspiration from the thirteenth-century Egyptian Mamluk Sultan, Sayf al-Din Qutuz. His detailed writings about the Arab community in Kabul under the Taliban, containing details that are not commonly known, suggest he was a trusted member of that community. Some details of his story, and his chosen nickname, further suggest he was from Egypt.[11]

On this particular night he was making a last trip to Kabul to stock up on weapons and ammunition. The Northern Alliance was expected to attack Kabul soon, and the Taliban were setting up a secondary line of defense in Logar province, along the road between Kabul and the southeastern city of Gardez. Some of the Arabs who lived in Afghanistan at the time of 9/11 had historical ties to mujahidin commanders in Logar who had fought the Soviets in the 1980s, and some of these commanders later joined or supported the Taliban.[12] This may explain the presence of Egyptian volunteers like Qutuz there in 2001. The defense line in Logar was presumably set up to protect the Taliban strongholds in the Loya Paktiya region in southeastern Afghanistan in the event that Kabul fell to the Northern Alliance.

As Qutuz was approaching Kabul, he spotted unusual movements of cars and fighters. He set his radio to the wavelength used by the Arabs in Kabul. But all he could hear was radio noise, and then chopped words: "*General mobilization … horizontal spread … the forward trenches …*" The car moved closer to Kabul and the words became clearer. He heard a man speaking in the dialect of the Gulf Arabs: "*Our dead bodies! They can only enter it over our dead bodies! This is the moment we have been waiting for. Come on guys, come to jihad!*" Qutuz told the driver to speed up and go to the Al-Jazeera office, the only working Arabic news station in Kabul. Hopefully they could find out what was going on.[13]

As Kabul was under an imminent threat of attack, Arabs were being mobilized to the frontline. The frontline at this point cut across the Shomali plains, a flat area some 30 miles long and 15 miles wide on the north of Kabul. To the north of the Shomali plains started the Hindu Kush mountains. Massoud's Army now controlled the northern section of the Shomali plains which included the strategically important entrance to the Salang pass, the road north to Mazar-e-Sharif. In the northeastern corner of the Shomali plains was the entrance to the Panjshir valley, where Massoud's forces had their headquarters.

The frontline on the Shomali plains had existed since the Taliban took power over Kabul in 1996. During the next five years, the frontline would move back and forth on the plains, but Massoud would never reach Kabul, and Taliban—like the Soviets before them—never conquered the Panjshir.[14] Panjshir was a narrow valley with natural fortifications and a Tajik-dominated population hostile to the Taliban. Right now, they were also allied with the Americans and were hosting the CIA's top commander in Afghanistan, Gary Bernsten.[15]

General Fahim Khan, the commander of Massoud's Army, was impatiently waiting for the American airplanes to start bombing the Taliban positions. He could not understand why the Americans had prioritized helping Dostum, a small-time guerrilla leader, when it was clearly him, Fahim, who commanded the largest and most professional army in the Northern Alliance. He had told the Americans, again and again, that taking Kabul was the key to conquering Northern Afghanistan, and not the other way around. But he sensed that the Americans were wary about who would enter Kabul first. It was a politically sensitive subject, and there was potential that the conquering soldiers would carry out atrocities, like what had happened too many times in the past. Fahim promised the Americans there would be no revenge killings.[16]

The day after the northern Takhar front fell, on November 12, US airplanes started bombing the Kabul front. The frontline fell as quickly as the frontlines in the north. In the evening on November 12, Taliban were leaving Kabul just as they had left Mazar three days before. The deputy of the Taliban's Foreign Brigade, the Iraqi commander Abd al-Hadi al-Iraqi, was present in Kabul at that time because he had been unable to travel back to Northern Afghanistan after Bamiyan fell. He claimed that he had telephone contact with the Arabs in the north from his headquarters in Kabul, but he could do little for them, except telling them they should follow the orders from the local Taliban chain of command.[17] He then fled Kabul with the rest of the Taliban and made his way south toward Gardez and the Afghanistan-Pakistan border.

The Al-Jazeera office was evacuated shortly before it was hit by two 500-pound bombs on November 12th, 2001. The circumstances were never resolved, and Al-Jazeera was furious because it was not the first time their offices had been bombed by the United States during a war. Al-Jazeera's journalist in Kabul, Tayseer Alouni, had recently made a scoop as the only journalist to interview bin Laden after 9/11.[18] The interview took place in Kabul on October 21, 2001, after the US attack on Afghanistan started and the United States had started an intense manhunt for bin Laden. Moreover, the Al-Jazeera office had recently been frequented by al-Qaida fighters like Qutuz, who in the chaos of war came there to seek information just like anybody else. After the bomb attack, one US source claimed that they had bombed a known al-Qaida facility, while another claimed it had been a mistake, and the truth will probably never be known. After Kabul fell, Tayseer Alouni was briefly captured by the Northern Alliance. In the end he made a dramatic escape and went east, toward Jalalabad.

Unlike in northern Afghanistan, few eyewitness accounts exist of the Arabs who fought on the frontline north of Kabul. The Kabul frontline went through a major re-organization in the spring of 2001, when many of the Arab fighting groups there were sent to the north. We know that some Arabs stayed at Bagram airbase, and they were probably part of the Taliban's Foreign Brigade. Other Arabs kept their rear base or supply area north of Kabul, which may also have been used as a training facility for new foreign volunteers after 9/11.[19] After the US attack on Afghanistan started, and especially during the general call to arms around November 10th, which we heard about in Qutuz' account, the Kabul frontline was filled with newly arrived volunteers. There was presumably a chaotic and spontaneous withdrawal, similar to what happened at the Takhar front.

The Egyptian journalist and veteran of the Afghan-Soviet war, Mustafa Hamid, was not present at Kabul, but he is one of the few insiders of the Afghan-Arab community who later wrote an account of the Kabul battle. He claimed that several hundred Arabs died during the attack on Kabul and in revenge attacks around the city after Massoud's forces had arrived.[20] Western journalists who accompanied Massoud's vehicles into Kabul recalled that the city's streets were lined with dead and mutilated bodies. They were said to be Arabs, who were killed by Tajik forces to avenge the assassination of their leader, Ahmed Shah Massoud, on September 9, 2001.[21] The total number of Arabs who fought at Kabul is hard to estimate, except that it was probably somewhere in the low hundreds.

Many of the Arabs who fought at the Kabul front managed to escape. They went either east toward Jalalabad, or south toward Gardez. These two areas were the two main assembly points of the Arabs fleeing from the US invasion of Afghanistan. They were also sites of two well-known mountain battles where Arabs participated. Jalalabad is close to Tora Bora where bin Laden built a guerrilla base in December 2001. Gardez is close to Shah-i-Kot, where the United States carried out Operation Anaconda in March 2002. The two battles appear similar on the surface, but their circumstances were very different. We shall return to these two battles, and the Arabs who fought there, later in this chapter.

Prison Uprising in the North

On November 16, a few days after the retreat from the Takhar frontline, a group of twenty-five rough-looking, haggard Arab fighters wandered into Kunduz city. They were led by a Yemeni nicknamed Gharib al-San'ani, who was now the most high-ranking Arab in the North after the Yemeni commander Abdul Salam al-Hadrami had been killed. Stories were created about the group of fighters. One popular account said they had stayed and fought heroically at the frontline, even as the rest of the Taliban had retreated.[22] Another story said that during their retreat, they had taken a wrong turn and had gotten lost in the desert. But they had survived and found their way, owing to God's miracles (*al-karamat*).[23] Both stories are typical examples of the standard narratives of jihadi propaganda literature, where facts are molded to fit certain genre conventions. What actually happened with the twenty-five Arabs in the three days between the frontline retreat and their arrival in Kunduz will probably never be known.

The outcome, in any case, was that there were now around 150 Arab fighters trapped in Kunduz along with hundreds of other Uzbeks and Pakistanis, in addition to Afghan Taliban fighters and commanders. The Foreign Brigade commander, Juma Namanjani, was dead, and his deputy Abd al-Hadi al-Iraqi was stuck on the other side of the Hindu Kush mountains. The most high-ranking Arab in the North was probably Gharib al-San'ani, the leader of the twenty-five desert wanderers. The Pakistanis and Uzbeks presumably selected their own leaders based on who was the most high-ranking commander alive. We shall see how these new command-and-control relationships played out when the foreign fighters were surrounded in Kunduz.

The Taliban force in Kunduz was in a dire situation. The city was surrendered from all sides, and ammunition and supplies were running low. General Dostum was eager to negotiate a surrender deal, because he wanted to get to Kunduz before his rivals in the Northern Alliance. So, he offered a deal to Mullah Fazl, the overall Taliban commander for the North. Surrender all your weapons, and we will guarantee you safe passage out of Kunduz.[24] The Taliban were divided. Some of them wanted to fight until death, while others favored a deal with the enemy. They all viewed General Dostum as a despicable man who could not be trusted, but for a majority of the Taliban, there was no tradition of fighting until death. Because the issue was so contentious, Mullah Fazl took the matter to the Taliban's highest decision-making body, the Ulama Council in Kandahar. The Ulama ruled that under the current circumstances, surrender was advisable.[25]

When Mullah Fazl announced the decision, one of the commanders, the flamboyant, one-legged veteran of the Afghan-Soviet war, Mullah Dadullah, stood up. "I will surrender to no one but God," he declared. He then asked for permission to leave before the deal was implemented. Leave granted, he jumped into a car with a few of his men, drove straight through enemy territory in Mazar-e-Sharif without being discovered, and escaped—or so the legend goes.[26] An alternative account says that Mullah Dadullah hid in a house in the Balkh province until the Northern Alliance stopped looking for him, and then he made his way to the south with the help of a human trafficker.[27] Mullah Dadullah later surfaced as one of the leading Taliban commanders in Southern Afghanistan. In 2007, Osama bin Laden and the other al-Qaida leaders were brooding over whether his death at the hands of British Special Forces had been caused by an internal Taliban betrayal (more on this in Chapter 5).

On November 21, Mullah Fazl came to Dostum's fortress at Qala-i-Jangi outside Mazar with a group of Taliban fighters. As both sides observed the local honor code, the Taliban were allowed to enter armed and to leave again without being taken prisoner. In the meeting, the Taliban commander agreed to surrendering the city of Kunduz in return for safe passage, and the agreement would be implemented four days later on November 25. A US Special Forces officer, Lt. Col. Max Bowers, was witness to the meeting. He recalled that the meeting had been deliberately vague about the fate of the foreign fighters in Kunduz. Dostum said he would deal with them later. "They are safe for now," he said uncommittedly. It was understood by all sides that the Arab, Uzbek, and Pakistani fighters would not be offered safe passage out of Kunduz.[28]

What happened next is subject to some debate, but most primary sources suggest that Taliban commanders in Kunduz designed a plan to try and save the foreign fighters from ending up in Dostum's custody.[29] On the night of November 23, one and a half day before Dostum had agreed with Mullah Fazl to enter Kunduz, a group of around 350 armed Uzbek, Pakistani, and Arab fighters were loaded into trucks along with some locals acting as guides.[30] The convoy of five trucks packed with armed men inched out of Kunduz. Somewhere along the way, a betrayal happened, probably among one of the shady Balkh commanders whom the convoy depended on as local guides. These commanders were local opportunists—neither fully with Dostum, nor fully with Taliban. Whatever the truth, the end result was that the convoy was halted by Dostum's men outside Mazar-e-Sharif in the morning of November 24. Dostum's men promised them safe passage if they first handed in their weapons. The foreigners did not trust Dostum to keep his word and refused. If they had no weapons, they had nothing. The negotiations came to a stalemate. The sun rose in the sky, and it was almost noon.[31]

The Taliban's senior commanders were brought into the negotiations. The Arabs finally gave in, but only after getting direct orders from Mullah Fazl via radio. The leader of the Arabs, the Yemeni Gharib al-San'ani, told his fighters to hand in their Kalashnikovs but to hide some smaller weapons, like knives and hand grenades, on their bodies. The Uzbeks and Pakistanis probably did the same. The hidden weapons were later used to start the prison uprising at Qala-i-Jangi. The five trucks with the Arabs and other foreigners drove through Mazar-e-Sharif on their way to the Qala-i-Jangi fortress west of the city. The civilians in Mazar were aware that something was brewing. The night before, the city had been tense, as there were rumors that the Taliban was coming. In the morning, people heard word of the surrender negotiations. Now they stood ready to mock the captives.

After the foreigners arrived at Qala-i-Jangi, they were unloaded from the trucks and taken prisoner by Dostum. The prisoners' hands were tied; they were placed in groups on the ground and interrogations started. Then, there was suddenly a hand grenade explosion in the courtyard, probably carried out by an Arab, which killed one or two high-ranking Northern Alliance commanders along with the bomber. Sensing that the situation was about to spin out of control, Dostum's guards locked the prisoners into the basement for the night.

The next day, November 25, they were taken out in small groups and interrogated in the courtyard. Most accounts suggest that the prison uprising started when there was a group of Uzbeks left in the basement. An Uzbek exploded a hand grenade on his way out of the basement. In the ensuing chaos, other prisoners overpowered their guards and took their weapons. They managed access the pile of weapons that Dostum's guards had confiscated from them the day before. It was during this initial phase that a group of prisoners overpowered the CIA officer Johnny "Mike" Spann and killed him. Later, the prisoners broke into the ammunitions and weapons depot in the fort and armed themselves. They managed to temporarily take control over a section of the fort and fortify themselves for several days.[32]

Mullah Abdul Baqi, who was probably among the most high-ranking Taliban commanders in the prison, did not intend to die there. On the night of the first day of the uprising, he and a group of about thirty others managed to escape the fort. For the next several months, he hid among Taliban sympathizers in the Balkh countryside. He eventually made it back to Kandahar.[33]

The foreigners still in the fort continued the battle for six more days. With the help of US airpower, Dostum managed to seize back control of the fort three days later, on November 28. There were still a group of prisoners who hid in a basement, and clearing it would take three more days. Dostum's forces tried various methods. They brought the Taliban commander Mullah Fazl to talk to them, but the stubborn prisoners stayed in the basement. Dostum's men tried to throw down hand grenades. They also tried gasoline, and lastly, they started filling the basement with water. The remaining group of about eighty fighters chose to surrender on November 31.

The prison uprising at Mazar-e-Sharif received much media attention, perhaps more than any other battle in the early phase of the War on Terror. This was undoubtedly because of the dramatic events that unfolded, but also because there happened to be a number of Western journalists present in Mazar-e-Sharif who could report directly from the events. The United States suffered its first casualty in the War on Terror when Mike Spann was killed during the prison uprising. Another event creating headlines was the discovery of a young, white man named John Walker Lindh from Marine County, California, among the captured Taliban soldiers. The prison uprising was thoroughly investigated, but the details of what actually happened remain disputed. We do not know for sure if the uprising was planned or spontaneous.[34]

There are some lesser-known Arab and Afghan eyewitness accounts of the battle, which I have quoted in this chapter. Some of these stories are embellished or changed to fit a certain propaganda narrative. For example, a popular story about Qala-i-Jangi, which is repeated in many of these accounts, is that the prison uprising started because the Americans were insulting the Quran. In reality, the uprising probably started because the foreigners, and especially the Uzbeks, were terrified of the prospect of being Dostum's prisoners. Dostum had a reputation of torturing and executing prisoners of war.

About thirty-five of the prisoners in Qala-i-Jangi were Arabs who were sent to the US prison facility at Guantánamo Bay, Cuba. Over the next decade, almost all of them were cleared for release. None of them were high-ranking al-Qaida members. As stated previously the prisoners at Qala-i-Jangi were from the Taliban's Foreign Brigade, not from al-Qaida's core organization. At this stage in late November 2001, al-Qaida's core organization was preparing to defend Kandahar. Other al-Qaida members could be found along the two main exit routes out of Afghanistan with their assembly points: Paktiya (Zurmat) and Nangarhar (Tora Bora). The Arabs who were trapped in Qala-i-Jangi were either newly arrived volunteers who had come to Afghanistan to participate in the war, or they were Arab fighters loyal to one of the Kabul frontline commanders—people like Abd al-Hadi al-Iraqi, Gharib al-San'ani, or Abd al-Salam al-Hadrami. These commanders may have had ties to al-Qaida, but they largely operated as individual commanders fighting for the Taliban.

A part of al-Qaida was now busy organizing the defenses of Kandahar city and airport, and another part was setting up defenses in Tora Bora on the ill-advised orders of Osama bin Laden. These events illustrate that al-Qaida was far from a unified military force. The group scrambled to do what best it could, in the chaos of the war, but military leaders such as Sayf al-Adl and Abu Hafs al-Masri, on the one hand, and bin Laden, on the other, had divergent views on strategy.

The Battle for Kandahar

After the fall of Kabul on November 12, 2001, the United States intensified the air campaign in and around Kandahar. The US strategy there was similar to the strategy in the North. The United States would provide air support to local Afghan militias who were fighting the Taliban on the ground. There were fewer anti-Taliban militias in southern Afghanistan than in the North. But the US forces had two candidates, who were now stationed around Kandahar city. The first was Hamid Karzai, who had recently been infiltrated into his home province Uruzgan, and who would attack Kandahar from the north. The second was Gul Agha Sherzai, based southeast of Kandahar city in a mountain range straddling the Afghanistan-Pakistan border. Gul Agha had the strongest militia, but Hamid Karzai was an important political figure. The Americans saw him as a potential presidential candidate for post-Taliban Afghanistan. The Arabs, who fought at Kandahar, mostly battled Gul Agha's forces southeast of the city.

According to Sayf al-Adl, who wrote a detailed account of the Kandahar battle, al-Qaida started planning the defense of Kandahar two weeks before the September 11 attacks, but "completely reformulated" the plans after 9/11.[35] He indicates that al-Qaida already before 9/11 was preparing to defend Kandahar against a ground invasion, but this is hard to verify, as his account is written with the benefit of hindsight in 2005. More likely, al-Qaida initially expected missile strikes to hit their training camps in Kandahar, similar to what had happened with the camps in Khost in 1998. That's why al-Qaida's immediate reaction after 9/11 was to evacuate the camps.

As the saying goes, no battle plan survives the first contact with the enemy, so whatever plan al-Qaida might have had before 9/11 became irrelevant as soon as the United States started attacking Afghanistan on October 7. Al-Qaida was probably as unprepared for the massive US bombing campaign as the Taliban, but managed to adapt. According to Sayf al-Adl, as they were preparing to defend Kandahar: "we did not form large military fronts, in order to prevent the Air Force from causing massive losses. We relied instead on highly capable small groups," and we strengthened each group with "a number of veteran jihadists who fought in many battles."[36] Among the veterans who fought at Kandahar were the Egyptian commanders Abu Abd al-Rahman "BM," Khaled Habib, and Amir al-Fath.[37] All of them survived the Kandahar battle and some of them would play prominent roles in al-Qaida's activities in Afghanistan and Pakistan after 2001.

As al-Qaida was preparing to defend Kandahar, the organization suffered its biggest loss so far in the war. Around November 16, 2001, a US bomb hit the safe house of al-Qaida's military chief Abu Hafs al-Masri in Kandahar, and killed him along with sixteen others.[38] Abu Hafs al-Masri, who is also known as Muhammed Atif and whose real name is Subhi Abd al-'Aziz 'Ali Sitta, was chief of al-Qaida's military committee and the second most powerful man in al-Qaida. He had been with bin Laden since 1987, when bin Laden established the first military base in Afghanistan to fight the Soviet occupation and was regarded as one of al-Qaida's three founding members.[39] Abu Hafs was one of only a handful of people in al-Qaida who knew all the details about the 9/11 attack planning, and he was directly involved in al-Qaida's much-exaggerated efforts to develop chemical and biological weapons in the early 2000s.[40] In January 2001, Abu Hafs' daughter married Osama bin Laden's son Abdullah, in an event that was videotaped and later used in al-Qaida propaganda.[41]

Only two Arabs survived the missile strike on Abu Hafs' house in Kandahar in November 2001 and managed to crawl out of the demolished building. One was Asadullah, one of the sons of the Egyptian "Blind Sheikh," Omar Abd al-Rahman. Asadullah fled to Pakistan, where he continued working for al-Qaida, but also took on the role as one of al-Qaida's internal critics of the 9/11 attacks. We shall hear from him later in this book.

A lesser-known fact is that Abu Hafs, at the time of his death, was said to be in poor health. During the last month of his life, he had to work from bed, and during the last week, he was unable to even move from his safe house in Kandahar.[42] In the end, it contributed to his death. Mustafa Hamid said that Abu Hafs had appointed a secretary to assist him in his work, which probably is a reference to a Kenyan al-Qaida member named Ahmed Salim Sweidan. In early 2001 Sweidan took over the secretary job from Fadil Harun, another al-Qaida member of African origin.[43] The two secretaries were members of al-Qaida's "East Africa network," who had been involved in the planning of al-Qaida's terrorist attacks against the US Embassies in Kenya and Tanzania in August 1998. They were trusted members of Abu Hafs' inner circle. Fadil Harun left Afghanistan and returned to East Africa in early 2001, while Sheikh Sweidan continued to work for Abu Hafs, but he was not present when Abu Hafs was killed. After the fall of the Taliban, he disappeared into the Tribal Areas of Pakistan, where he was killed in a drone attack in 2009.

Sayf al-Adl was in charge of al-Qaida's military forces at the Battle for Kandahar, a role that probably was a continuation of his past responsibilities as leader of al-Qaida's security committee. His duties included setting up security procedures for al-Qaida's training camps in Kandahar. Al-Qaida had two main installations close to Kandahar city: The first was located at Kandahar Airport, 20 km southeast of Kandahar city and was known simply as the Airport camp. The second was located around 5 km southwest of the airport in an area comprised of small Afghan villages and farms, and it was known as Tarnak Farms or the Abu Ubaydah camp. Initially, al-Qaida planned to defend these two locations against the US attack on Afghanistan, whatever form that might take.

However, after the start of the US bombing campaign, Sayf al-Adl claims he devised a more elaborate plan, which included three fighting forces: one force to defend the Airport and Tarnak Farms; one force that would form a security perimeter around Kandahar city; and a rapid reaction force called the "Martyrs Group," which could be sent to any area that needed reinforcements.[44] This account was partly corroborated by David Hicks, an Australian who was present at the start of the Battle for Kandahar and who later ended up at Guantánamo. He said that he came to Kandahar around October 1, 2001, and was given the choice of serving at three different locations: "City, mountain or airport."[45] Sayf al-Adl's account claims that a total of 800 Arabs were involved in defending Kandahar, which seems like an inflated number based on the total number of Arabs present in Afghanistan in 2001. It is true that many Arab volunteers arrived in Afghanistan after 9/11, and they may have contributed to swelling the ranks. But these volunteers typically went to Kabul, Jalalabad, or Northern Afghanistan, because most of them needed basic military training and al-Qaida closed the training camps in Kandahar after 9/11.

It is theoretically possible that fighters came to Kandahar after the other frontlines fell, but this appears to have been uncommon. As we have heard, the fighters on the Northern frontline mostly ended up surrounded in Kunduz, and from there, they were imprisoned by Dostum. Some of the foreign fighters in the North left the area before the fall of the Takhar frontline on November 11, and before the closure of the Bamiyan road. They include Abdul Hadi al-Iraqi, who was in Kabul when Takhar fell, and a group of Uzbek fighters who later appeared in the Battle for Shah-i-Kot in March 2002. They may have gone to Kabul for a number of reasons, including to attend the memorial service of the Uzbek Foreign Brigade commander, Juma Namanjani, on November 8, 2001. This apparently saved them from being trapped in the North. The fighters on the Kabul frontline went either south toward Loya Paktiya or east to Jalalabad, where some of them ended up in Tora Bora. In sum, there are few, if any, credible stories of Arabs who fled to Kandahar after fighting on one of the other frontlines. One possible exception is the group of Abu Musab al-Zarqawi in Herat, which fled to Kandahar because this made sense geographically speaking. According to Sayf al-Adl, at least one of the Arabs defending Kandahar had come from the Herat side.[46]

We do not have any other sources that can confirm Sayf al-Adl's description of an 800-man strong force of Arab fighters defending Kandahar city.[47] Even if an Arab force existed to defend the city, it had no apparent role in the actual battles that took place in late November and early December 2001. The ground fighting around Kandahar was mainly with two local Taliban opponents—the Afghan warlord Gul Agha's force in the southeast, and to a lesser extent, with a tribal force led by future Afghan president Hamid Karzai, in Uruzgan to the north of Kandahar.

Other parts of Sayf al-Adl's account are verified: we know that there was an Arab force at Kandahar Airport, who tried to prevent Gul Agha's forces from advancing toward Kandahar city.[48] They resisted Gul Agha's forces for five full days, from December 1–5, while US airplanes bombed their positions from the air. In addition, Arab sources refer to a mobile reaction force known as the "Martyrs Group" led by Hamza al-Zubayr, but we have no detailed information about what this group did during the battle.[49]

The Americans estimated there were around 400 Arabs at Kandahar Airport, and Sayf al-Adl's account indicates that they were around 500.[50] However, if we read Sayf al-Adl's description of what the Arabs actually did during the battle, they seem to have been fewer, maybe around 250 at most. Sayf al-Adl's account claims that thirteen group commanders were involved in the battle. Two of these commanders had a tank. One drove a pickup-truck with a mobile rocket launcher, and one manned a machine gun position. The remaining nine commanders had presumably only light weapons. Sayf al-Adl writes somewhere else that the Arabs were divided into small groups with ten men in each group. If we assume that Sayf al-Adl's memory is correct and that each of the thirteen Arab commanders had around ten fighters, it leaves us with only 130 Arabs defending the airport. However, even if he forgot to mention some commanders, or some of the groups were larger, it seems fair to assume that the number of Arabs defending Kandahar was 200 or 250 at most. He further says that only four Arab fighters died. Again, the number is hard to confirm, but it is probably not too far off the mark. Other sources say that the commanders of the two tanks survived, even if their vehicles were destroyed. One member of the rocket launcher crew died. The Arabs fought Gul Agha's forces by hiding in dried-out and partly covered irrigation channels, and were therefore a hard target to bomb from the air.[51] Finally, there is an eyewitness account saying that a large group of Arabs left Kandahar city in a convoy of vehicles in the morning of December 7.[52] The day before, the Taliban had made an agreement with Karzai and Gul Agha to surrender the city in return for free passage. Unlike in Kunduz, the deal allowed the Arabs to leave unhindered. In the North, the Northern Alliance commanders despised the foreigners fighting with the Taliban and insisted on arresting them. In the south, the negotiations for surrendering Kandahar were of a different character as all the negotiating parties were from different Pashtun tribes.

It is unclear how the Taliban forces in and around Kandahar were organized. Sayf al-Adl's account mentions sporadic cooperation with Taliban units: He says that Mullah Baradir was in charge of the Taliban groups fighting Karzai's militia, and that al-Qaida offered to send a group of 100 men to help him. He says that the Arab groups who operated inside Kandahar city arrested spies and handed them over to the Taliban. Finally, he says that a Taliban unit fought with the Arabs at the airport, operating two mobile rocket launchers. However, they were bombed and their vehicles destroyed on the second day of the battle, i.e., on December 2. "They were the last Taliban group to fight with us," he lamented.[53] This suggests that the Arabs fought independently for three days after that, and were the main force standing between Gul Agha's forces and Kandahar city.

We do not know how much it mattered in the end. It seems clear that the Taliban were preparing to negotiate a surrender of Kandahar, just as they had done in other large cities in Afghanistan. The talks with the enemy started already in the last half of November.[54] The US side speculated that the Taliban were dragging out the negotiations while they were waiting for the situation in Northern Afghanistan to be resolved. If the Taliban forces in the north were given free passage out of Kunduz, they could perhaps reinforce the Taliban ranks around Kandahar. However, on November 25, when Dostum entered Kunduz he imprisoned Mullah Fazl and two other high-ranking Taliban commanders, and in the end handed them over to the Americans. It is unclear if any Taliban forces from the north reached Kandahar in time to fight the opposing forces, and it is unknown if it would have mattered. Both the Arab and the US accounts of the Kandahar battle lack references to Taliban forces actively fighting at Kandahar, with the exception of local Taliban in Uruzgan who were fighting Karzai.

As soon as the Taliban decided they would surrender Kandahar, all the Arabs evacuated the area as well. According to the memoirs of the Taliban official Abdul Hai Mutma'in, Taliban at this stage conveyed a message to the Arabs at Kandahar Airport, requesting them to evacuate their positions.[55] He claimed that a few Arabs stayed behind to fight until death, but it is unclear if this is true. A group of wounded Arabs in the Mirwais Hospital in Kandahar stayed behind when the other Arabs left the city, but it seems likely that they were either forgotten in the chaos of war, or were simply too wounded to move. Some of them later armed themselves in order to not fall into captivity.[56]

The Arab convoy left Kandahar in the early morning hours of December 7, 2001, and arrived in Zurmat, Paktiya, the same day.[57] That morning, two CIA guys were seated on a nearby ridgeline, watching the Arab convoy leave. They said there were no airplanes available to bomb them, because all the US airpower was used in Tora Bora where the United States thought bin Laden might be.[58] There was indeed intensive bombing in Tora Bora at this time, starting on

December 3 and until a temporary ceasefire on December 12, which is probably when bin Laden managed to escape.[59] An alternative interpretation is that the Arabs were part of a civilian refugee stream out of the city, which was a protected target according to the US rules of engagement at that time.[60]

Once in Zurmat, the Arabs met Qutuz, the Egyptian who had formed part of the defense line in Logar, and the other Arabs who had withdrawn from the Kabul area three weeks before. That group had first gone to Gardez to hide from the US bombings. On November 16, the US Air Force bombed a house belonging to Haqqani in Gardez, and killed Mohammed Salah and two other senior members of Ayman al-Zawahiri's group, the Egyptian Islamic Jihad (EIJ), along with their families. The attack also killed the wife, son, and daughter of Ayman al-Zawahiri who were accompanying the three other families.[61] Al-Zawahiri later described his loss in a letter he wrote to the leader of al-Qaida in Iraq, Abu Musab al-Zarqawi, in 2005. "[I have] tasted the bitterness of American brutality," he wrote, and went on to describe the scene of his dying family members under the collapsed concrete structure in Gardez. In the next paragraph he is back to business, telling Zarqawi that despite the Americans' brutality, he needs to stop issuing videos showing decapitation of hostages, because "we are in a media battle in a race for the hearts and minds of our Umma."[62] Zawahiri's correspondence with al-Zarqawi in Iraq is further discussed in Chapter 4.

Qutuz and the rest of the Arab group in Gardez decided to leave the area shortly after the bombing of Haqqani's house. He says that this was because of rumors that the "Americans were coming" from the direction of Miran Shah, Pakistan.[63] Other, or additional, reasons why they left Gardez may have been that there was not sufficient accommodation in the town or that the people did not want to host the Arabs owing to the risk of US air strikes. The Arabs then continued southwest on a small road leading to the Zurmat District, which is known as "Little Kandahar" because many Taliban leaders are from there.[64] Zurmat is the home of the "Mansur network," which is a network of a group of commanders and leaders who supported the Taliban since 1995, but who maintained their independence on the local level. Zurmat village is around 20 km away from the mountain range known as Shah-i-Kot, which in March 2002 became the site of a major battle where many Uzbek and Arabs participated. The Arabs later referred to the battle as The Battle for Shah-i-Kot, while US forces called it Operation Anaconda. The battle was initiated and led by a local commander called Sayf al-Rahman Mansour, who had previously worked for the Taliban and who was the son of Nasrullah Mansour, a famed mujahidin leader from Zurmat and the founder of the "Mansur network." We shall return to the battle of Shah-i-Kot in Chapter 2.

In the period from late November 2001 until March 2002, Arabs and their families who had fled the US-led invasion of Afghanistan seem to have lived in hiding in Zurmat, and in a district 80 km to the south called Barmal. Barmal is the home of the Pashtun Wazir tribe. The Wazir tribe straddles both sides of the Afghanistan-Pakistan border, which is an important factor explaining how the Arabs eventually ended up in South Waziristan, Pakistan. Several Wazir tribesmen, whether from the Afghan or Pakistani side of the border, served in the Taliban government in Afghanistan in 1996–2001.[65] A young man from Wana, Pakistan, named Nek Muhammed Wazir specifically served in the Taliban military in the Qargha division in Kabul, and probably worked directly with Arabs. He was also a close friend of Sayf al-Rahman Mansour, the previously mentioned commander from Zurmat who would lead the Shah-i-Kot battle.[66]

The Battle for Tora Bora

The Tora Bora battle is best known in the West for being the battle where the US failed to kill Osama bin Laden. We know today that bin Laden was present in Tora Bora in the beginning of December 2001, but that he probably escaped on the night between December 12 and 13, when the Arabs had negotiated a ceasefire with one of the local Afghan commanders. From Tora Bora, he did not go directly to Pakistan as many believed. He went instead northeast, to Kunar, where he was sheltered by an old-time Hizb-e-Islami commander for a few months.[67]

Osama bin Laden later described the Tora Bora battle as a battle involving 300 Arab fighters, and this number has often been repeated later.[68] But the reason why bin Laden referred to 300 fighters probably had more to do with propaganda than reality. The Battle of Tora Bora coincided in time with the Battle of Badr, a famous battle in Islamic history, where the Prophet Muhammed won an epic battle against an army of the Quraysh tribe with only 300 fighters. Using the symbolism of dates and numbers, bin Laden wanted Tora Bora to go down in history as another epic battle against the contemporary enemy of the Muslims—the Americans. The reality was a bit different.

After 9/11, Osama bin Laden started talking about building a guerrilla base in Tora Bora.[69] The only source to this information is the Egyptian journalist and veteran of the Afghan-Soviet war, Mustafa Hamid, but the story seems plausible. Bin Laden's security team had already determined the year before that Tora Bora was the most suitable place to go into hiding, should an emergency happen.[70] According to Mustafa Hamid, after 9/11 bin Laden planned to make a guerrilla base in Tora Bora and to fight the Americans from there. He wanted to assemble a force of 500 men, and to store food for six months. He thought that the Americans would start with an air assault, followed up with ground forces, but he also thought the United States was weak and would not be able to stay in the fight for long.

If this is correct, bin Laden's assessment was rather naïve, much like the military assessments he had made during the Afghan-Soviet war, and everyone told him so. Afghan commanders who had fought in Tora Bora in the 1980s told bin Laden the plan would not work—that the Arab force would simply come under siege, be bombed from the air, and forced to surrender. A high-ranking Taliban member, Mullah Abdul Kabir, also sent a message to bin Laden, advising him to pick a different spot than Tora Bora.[71] According to Mustafa Hamid, even Abu Hafs al-Masri, bin Laden's military chief, was against the plan, like he had been in 1987 when bin Laden wanted to establish a military base in Afghanistan to fight the Soviets. Back then, Abu Hafs had nevertheless helped bin Laden carry out the plan. This time, Abu Hafs was in too bad health to move, so all he could do was to send bin Laden an advisory letter from his sick bed.[72]

It is often assumed that the Arabs who fought at Tora Bora were "hardcore" al-Qaida members. This is most likely untrue. The Arabs who assembled in Tora Bora were an eclectic group of fighters and refugees. Some of them were probably bin Laden's followers, who went there to carry out bin Laden's vision of an epic battle with the Americans. They may have gone to Tora Bora prior to the fall of Kabul, to start preparing the mountain base that bin Laden envisioned, but there is no concrete evidence for this. According to various US sources, the United States mainly became aware of the Arab presence at Tora Bora in the latter half of November, i.e., after the fall of Kabul on November 13. After this, bin Laden went to the eastern city of Jalalabad, which had not yet fallen into the hands of the Northern Alliance. The city remained under the control of a Shura led by the old bin Laden ally, Sheikh Yunus Khalis.[73] From here, bin Laden incited Arabs to go to Tora Bora and fight, and at some point in late November or early December, he went to Tora Bora himself.[74] In this context it is relevant to mention that bin Laden built a house in Tora Bora back in the fall of 1996, and had some sort of agreement with local landowners or tribal leaders to use the area as his residence.[75]

Arab and other sources confirm that the bulk of Arabs who assembled at Tora Bora came after the fall of Kabul. At this point, they could have had various motivations for going there. All Arabs in Afghanistan were now in a perilous situation owing to the bounty that the United States put on suspected al-Qaida members, and all the official border crossings with Pakistan were closed. We must assume that some of those who went to Tora Bora after the fall of Kabul went there because they were already in the region and saw Tora Bora as their best option for survival—either as a place to hide over the winter, or as an unofficial escape route out of Pakistan. Finally, in the chaos of war, there were most certainly people with mixed or unclear motivations. Some may have gone there because that's where their friends went, out of a quest for adventure, or because of a vague admiration for bin Laden. Many were new arrivals to Afghanistan with little or no military experience, and with no knowledge of the local language or geography.[76]

It is hard to know exactly who was at Tora Bora, because of a lack of detailed, first-hand accounts of the battle. A large percentage of those who were later captured fleeing Tora Bora were young Yemeni men. US military analysts labeled them "bin Laden bodyguards," but we do not know their full stories, and most of them were later released or transferred to the custody of other countries.[77] Some of them may at one point have served as bin Laden's bodyguards, which sometimes was a real job and other times, a pretext for bin Laden to surround himself with admirers from his ancestral home country.[78] However, it is telling that none of al-Qaida's well-known senior military leaders—the likes of the Egyptian commanders Abu Jihad, Khalid Habib, and Amir al-Fath—who had been in the organization since the 1980s and early 1990s—fought at Tora Bora. These veterans stayed behind in Kandahar to fight under the command of Sayf al-Adl. This might have been a matter of old battle comrades sticking together, and also a matter of using heavy weapons resources where they belong. Khalid Habib and Amir al-Fath were both tank drivers, and the plains around Kandahar were presumably more suitable for tanks, than the rugged terrain of Tora Bora.

If we assume that most of the Arabs who fought at Tora Bora assembled there after the fall of Kabul on November 12, 2001, they had about two weeks to get organized before the US bombing started on December 3, 2001.[79] In this period, it seems likely that bin Laden was in the area and that he visited the fighters' positions. Various sources say that bin Laden left Tora Bora for good sometime between December 6 and 12.[80] One of the more credible theories is that he left on the night between December 12 and 13. On December 12 there were negotiations between the Arabs and the US-backed Afghan militias, which led to a brief ceasefire that night. This is probably the time where bin Laden slipped out of Tora Bora.[81] The next day, bin Laden ordered the Arabs to evacuate the frontlines and by December 14, most of the Arabs had left on foot toward Pakistan.[82] Out of an estimated group of 200–300 Arabs at Tora Bora, at least thirty-seven were killed according to an internal al-Qaida document, but the number could be higher.[83]

There are many unanswered questions about Tora Bora. There seems to be a mismatch between the United States and media narratives about the battle, and what can actually be documented and be proven true after the event. As mentioned, no veteran military leaders of al-Qaida appear to have been present during the battle.[84] Bin Laden left Sayf al-Adl and the other experienced Egyptian military leaders in Kandahar shortly before 9/11, and probably had a limited opportunity to communicate with them after this. This is not to say that there was a split in al-Qaida between Sayf al-Adl on the one hand, and bin Laden on the other. More likely there was a division of responsibilities, where the core of al-Qaida would stay in Kandahar to defend their headquarters, while the two political leaders, bin Laden and Zawahiri, would go underground and hide, then escape if the Taliban regime collapsed. Bin Laden probably did not start planning the Tora Bora battle until after leaving Kandahar. At this stage he received advise from several individuals including high-ranking Taliban officials, local commanders in Nangarhar, and possibly his own military chief, Abu Hafs al-Masri, to not carry out his plans. He ignored all of them. Al-Qaida insiders later testified that once bin Laden had made up his mind, he did not listen to others but preferred instead to surround himself with yes-men.[85] Overall, one could say that the Tora Bora battle reflected the need to improvise in the chaos of war, combined with bin Laden's own stubbornness and ambition to wage a "private war against the Americans," as Mustafa Hamid later put it.[86]

The Tora Bora battle was a great personal failure for bin Laden, but it is unclear if he himself interpreted it that way. According to radio communications that were picked up at the time, bin Laden left the battle defeated after ten days of intense bombings. He ordered a complete withdrawal, and he asked the Arabs to go back home to their home countries.[87] The next day, from a safe house somewhere in Eastern Afghanistan, he sat down to write his last will. He told his children that he was sorry for not spending more time with them and advised them to not work with al-Qaida.[88] However—if these sources are genuine—bin Laden's defeated mood did not last very long. During 2002, he returned to preaching and organizing war against the Americans in Afghanistan and elsewhere, and, with the help of a core group of surviving al-Qaida members, slowly started re-building his organization from Pakistan. We will hear more about these activities in Chapters 2 and 3.

Exit from Afghanistan

The Arabs who had fled from Kabul in mid-November first gathered in Gardez and then in the Zurmat district in Paktiya province. The Arabs fleeing from Kandahar went east toward Zurmat as well, although some individuals including bin Laden's spiritual adviser, Abu Hafs al-Mauritani, split off from this group before reaching Zurmat and went south, crossing into the Baluchistan province in Pakistan and then on to Quetta.[89] From Zurmat, there is a direct road to Barmal, where there is an official border crossing with Pakistan called Angor Adda. The Arab families fleeing from Kabul and Kandahar most likely went this direction.[90]

There were meetings and discussions in Zurmat about what to do next. Some Arabs wanted to stay in Afghanistan and fight the American-led invasion, but the majority wanted to withdraw to Pakistan. A small group of Arab fighters, along with a larger group of Uzbeks and other Central Asians, stayed with the Taliban commander Saif al-Rahman Mansour in Zurmat and later fought in the Battle of Shah-i-Kot in March 2002. The rest probably withdrew southwest to a district called Barmal. Over the next few months these Arabs moved from Barmal into South Waziristan, and from there, some went to hide in Pakistani cities while others stayed in the tribal areas.

Before the Arab groups separated in Zurmat, there were a series of meetings, or *Shuras*, about what to do next. These were not al-Qaida meetings, but meetings of Arabs who had gathered together in a dire situation. Al-Qaida members such as Sayf al-Adl were present, but so were independent figures, like Abu Layth al-Libi, Abu Musab al-Suri, and the Canadian-Egyptian cleric, Abdul Rahman al-Kanadi. There were ideological questions to be discussed. Where does the jihadi movement go from here? Should we stay and fight in Afghanistan, or go somewhere else? There were also practical challenges to solve, such as what to do with the hundreds of women and children who were accompanying the men.[91]

Many years later in 2007, one of the Arabs who ended up imprisoned in Iran recalled the discussions that were held in those meetings.[92] He was in Kandahar when it fell, and was in the group of al-Qaida members who withdrew to Zurmat on December 7, 2001. In a letter addressed to bin Laden he described the Shura meetings in Zurmat in detail. He said that various options were put on the table.

They included out-of-the-box thinking such as going to Hezbollah in Lebanon, or to Saddam Hussein's Iraq. Abu Mus'ab al-Suri allegedly suggested the Iraqi solution because he had previously worked with Saddam regime officials during the civil war in Syria in 1979–82. However, the majority of Arabs rejected these proposals. Instead, the Shura decided that most of the Arabs, including the families, should withdraw to Pakistan and from there, whoever was able to go home, should go home. The rest needed to hide as best they could. The Arabs should also keep a small presence in Afghanistan, to remain and fight the Americans.[93]

The withdrawal began shortly after this discussion took place. The first step was probably withdrawing to the Barmal district in Paktiya. Some sources indicate that prior to the battle of Shah-i-Kot in March 2002, there were still a number of Arabs gathered in Barmal.[94] Sometime during 2002, the Arabs moved into South Waziristan. A smaller group of fighters, which included about a hundred Uzbeks led by Tahir Yuldashev and a handful of Arabs led by Abu al-Layth al-Libi, among others, stayed with Sayf ul-Rahman Mansour in Zurmat to help him prepare a guerrilla base there. Sayf ul-Rahman believed—correctly—that the Americans were coming to attack his valley, like the Soviets had done in the 1980s. So like his father, the famed Afghan resistance leader Nasrullah Mansour, he would fight back from the mountains of Shah-i-Kot.

The letter from 2007 gives an accurate description of what the Arabs in the Afghanistan-Pakistan borderlands did over the next three years. Most of them went to Pakistan, while a small group initially stayed behind to fight a guerrilla war in Shah-i-Kot. US sources describe the Shah-i-Kot battle as the final phase in the US invasion of Afghanistan—a last battle to clear out remaining al-Qaida elements. From a US perspective this may be an accurate description. After Operation Anaconda, the US Army started preparing for going to Iraq. From an Arab perspective, however, Shah-i-Kot was not the end, but the beginning of guerrilla war in Afghanistan. As we shall see in the next chapter, this war was not initiated by al-Qaida, but by local Afghan guerrillas, supported by remnants of the Taliban's Foreign Brigade.

Concluding Remarks

The quote at the start of this chapter sums up what the US attack on Afghanistan in 2001 meant for al-Qaida: A "rapid collapse, dispersion, confusion, and complete chaos." The letter confirms that al-Qaida was taken aback by the fierce

US military response to 9/11. The author of the letter remembers that some people in al-Qaida expected the United States to respond to 9/11 with a few dozen missile strikes, like they had done after the 1998 East African Embassy bombings. Others expected the United States to fight but to give up easily and ask for a truce. The latter observation seems to corroborate Mustafa Hamid's account of how bin Laden planned to defeat the United States at Tora Bora. Bin Laden believed that the US forces would give up after no more than six months of war. What we now know is that it was the Arabs who had to give up after only ten days, and the United States stayed in Afghanistan to fight a counterinsurgency war for twenty more years. There has seldom been a greater mismatch in perception and reality. But this was rather typical of Osama bin Laden, who was a visionary and a charismatic leader, but also a believer in conspiracy theories and preferred to surround himself with yes-men rather than listening to well-informed military advice.

As we have seen in this chapter, the consequences of 9/11 were detrimental for al-Qaida. In the chaos of war, everyone scrambled to do the best they could. A few of al-Qaida's members fought within the framework of the Taliban's Foreign Brigade in Northern Afghanistan and north of Kabul, until these frontlines fell in mid-November 2001. Another part of al-Qaida, led by Sayf al-Adl, worked with the Taliban in Kandahar to defend the city, and al-Qaida's own installations at Kandahar airport, against the expected US attack. A third contingent were the followers of bin Laden, mostly young men from the Arabian Peninsula, who heeded bin Laden's call to fight in Tora Bora. The battle was neither called for nor approved by the Taliban. However, it reflected the fact that after 9/11, the Taliban needed to claim ignorance about bin Laden's whereabouts. The easiest and least controversial solution was to have him "disappear" from Kandahar, like had happened in the past when international pressure mounted on the Taliban. After that, most sources indicate that bin Laden did his own thing, in cooperation with local supporters, and that there was little communication with al-Qaida headquarters in Kandahar.

In retrospect, while al-Qaida was severely damaged by the US invasion of Afghanistan, some things worked to al-Qaida's favor. After 9/11, and especially after the fall of Kabul in mid-November, the United States was mostly focused on finding and killing bin Laden. And the US intelligence at the time said that bin Laden had gone East, far away from the Taliban and al-Qaida headquarters in Southern Afghanistan. Meanwhile, most of al-Qaida's military wing fought in the Battle for Kandahar, and on November 7, after a truce agreement between the Taliban and the Pashtun politician Hamid Karzai, the Arabs were allowed to leave the city unharmed. We lack inside sources from the truce negotiations at Kandahar, and we do not know if the Arabs at Kandahar Airport were even a topic for discussion between the parties, who were all representatives of different Southern Pashtun tribes. The dynamics were obviously different than in the North, with its stark ethnic divisions and history of warlordism, and where General Dostum had an obvious self-interest in taking foreign prisoners and handing them over to the Americans for handsome rewards, through much fanfare and international media attention. The different outcomes in the North and at Kandahar reflect the US policy at the time to only provide close air support to battles, and to otherwise let local Afghan militias handle the local politics.

It is often argued that the greatest failure of the US invasion of Afghanistan was bin Laden's escape at Tora Bora. In retrospect, the combined escape of bin Laden and Zawahiri from Tora Bora was probably the most essential, singular event that ensured al-Qaida's survival as an organization. Another crucial event was the escape of a critical mass of experienced al-Qaida members from Kandahar in December. They included senior administrative personnel such as bin Laden's accountant, the Egyptian Mustafa Abu al-Yazid (aka Sheikh Saeed), and military veterans such as the Egyptian tank commander Khalid Habib, whom we will meet later in Chapter 2. But al-Qaida's fortunes were not due to any cunning plan of al-Qaida's leadership. If there was a plan, it was probably that bin Laden should go underground after 9/11 in order to give the Taliban plausible deniability about his whereabouts. Another plan was to fight with the Taliban to defend Afghanistan. When the Taliban withdrew, so did the Arabs. The Taliban policy of leaving cities in return for free passage, and the geography of the Afghanistan-Pakistan borderlands, ensured the Arabs had time and ways to escape from both Kabul and Kandahar. Bin Laden's escape from Tora Bora was important, but it was only one piece of the puzzle of what al-Qaida became after 2001.

The most detrimental consequence of the US-led invasion, for al-Qaida, was the loss of its base in Afghanistan and the geographical dispersion of its members. On a micro-level, al-Qaida's greatest loss by far was the death of the military chief and founding member of al-Qaida, Abu Hafs al-Masri, on November 16, 2001. We shall see in the next chapters how al-Qaida dealt with the new challenge of being a dispersed organization on the run in a partially hostile environment. In this context it is useful to repeat the main message of this chapter, which is that al-Qaida did not operate in Afghanistan in a vacuum, and did not escape in a vacuum. A number of other Arabs and other foreigners escaped as well. Many of them had fought in the Taliban's Foreign Brigade. Some of them were affiliated with independent commanders or were affiliated with other militant groups than al-Qaida. Some were international in their outlook, while a majority were affiliated with groups rooted in national Islamist struggles. Prior to the fall of the Taliban, there was a constant struggle for influence and control among the various groups. The tensions continued to exist after they escaped to Pakistan, and continued to shape their relationships with the local militant scene.

2

The Start of the Afghan War

Here's another suggestion: I think that we should send all the brothers to Iraq.[1]
—Khalid Habib (Al-Qaida commander in Afghanistan)
to bin Laden, fall 2004

After al-Qaida's chaotic exit from Afghanistan, the group had to gather and decide what to do next. This process started slowly during 2002–3, when Osama bin Laden reconnected with al-Qaida members in the tribal areas of Pakistan. In addition to staging follow-up attacks to 9/11, bin Laden's first instinct and priority were to start a jihad against the United States in Afghanistan. Many of the others who had fled Afghanistan with al-Qaida had the same idea. Afghanistan thus became a frontline in several meanings of the word. It was a frontline for an Afghan jihad against foreign occupation, a frontline for the Taliban's war to restore the Islamic Emirate, and a frontline in al-Qaida's global war against the United States. Over time, the Afghan frontline became dominated by the Taliban, who sought to bring back Taliban to power in Afghanistan.

In this chapter I discuss how al-Qaida navigated between these different understandings of the Afghan frontline and how bin Laden tried, but ultimately failed, to shape it into a frontline for his global jihad. This chapter covers the initial years of the war from 2002 to 2005, when al-Qaida's role in the Afghan jihad was most visible. Initially in 2002–3, insurgent violence was driven by several actors including bin Laden, who started financing local Afghan commanders in eastern Afghanistan. At this early stage, bin Laden prioritized activities that would ensure that the jihad started as soon as possible, including high-profile suicide attacks that would grab media attention. He financed the Hizb-e-Islami leader Gulbuddin Hekmatyar, as well as local insurgents in Nangarhar and Southeastern Afghanistan. Early on, bin Laden believed it was essential to have an "Afghan face" on the jihad, which relied in part on describing Mullah Omar as the overall Emir, because this was already the dominant propaganda narrative among Arab jihadists. In reality, there was probably no contact between Mullah Omar and bin Laden at this stage.[2]

By late 2002, bin Laden had reconnected with al-Qaida members in Waziristan and started supporting a cluster of Arab and Afghan commanders fighting under old Taliban command structures. Around 2003, the Taliban's senior leadership started getting organized again and at some point, al-Qaida went from supporting a variety of actors to only supporting the Taliban. In other words, al-Qaida went from waging an insurgency that was symbolically staged in the name of Mullah Omar, to operating within the formal and informal structures connected to the Taliban's senior political leadership, known as the Quetta Shura.[3]

I start this chapter by outlining how al-Qaida propaganda promoted the US invasion of Afghanistan and start of the Afghan insurgency in 2001–2, before describing some of the major, early battles such as the Battle for Shah-i-Kot ("Operation Anaconda") in March 2002, and then describing how al-Qaida gradually re-organized and became involved in the insurgency in 2003–5.

The Arab Narrative of the Afghan War in 2001–2

The war in Afghanistan coincided with the emergence of the phenomenon of "jihadism online." The early webpages that were set up by al-Qaida, Taliban, and others were thus dominated by battlefield news from Afghanistan—including stories of the Mazar-e-Sharif prison uprising and the nascent insurgent operations that were carried out from 2002 onwards. I was able to study these sources directly, through an extensive archive of online jihadist sources gathered by colleagues at the Norwegian Defence Research Establishment.

The story of these early webpages provides an important backdrop for understanding how al-Qaida's narrative was shaped in the years immediately following 9/11. There is much to the story that will not fit in this book, including the online reactions to the 9/11 attacks, but here I will concentrate on how the jihadist online community helped shape and define the battle that al-Qaida entered in Afghanistan in late 2001. Al-Qaida itself was a direct part of the online effort because—as transpired much later—some of the early webpages were run by individuals connected with Yusuf al-Ayeri, later Emir of al-Qaida in Saudi Arabia, and with Abu Yahya al-Libi, a member of the Libyan Islamic Fighting Group (LIFG) who later joined al-Qaida and became head of al-Qaida's Sharia committee.[4]

The story starts with an online interview with a famous Libyan commander using the *nom de guerre* Abu al-Layth al-Libi, who fought on the Taliban's frontline north of Kabul in late 2001.[5] He was not part of al-Qaida at that time but represented a breakaway faction of the LIFG, one of many Arab groups active in Afghanistan and fighting for the Taliban. Abu al-Layth was one of the first and most visible Arabs who fought in the Afghan insurgency from 2002, and he was probably the main Arab commander in the Battle for Shah-i-Kot, which we will return to below.

Abu al-Layth said in the online interview in 2002 that there were two "trusted" webpages that carried news about the jihad in Afghanistan, namely *al-Neda* (the Call) and *al-Emarah* (the Emirate).[6] Al-Neda was a Saudi-based propaganda operation set up in 2000 by individuals associated with a 26-year-old Saudi activist named Yusuf al-Ayeri. Al-Ayeri had gone to Afghanistan in 2000 to meet with bin Laden and had subsequently been appointed by bin Laden to lead the revolutionary organization that was launched in 2003 as al-Qaida on the Arabian Peninsula (QAP).[7] Al-Neda was al-Qaida's first and primary "homepage" in the early 2000s, and carried exclusive news and statements from al-Qaida leaders in addition to publishing a high number of battlefield reports from Afghanistan.

The other webpage was al-Emarah, which appeared to be a homepage representing the Taliban, carrying news in Arabic and other languages. Internet records show that Al-Emarah was set up in August 2000 by the same person that created the homepage of the Libyan Islamic Fighting Group (LIFG).[8] According to the American professor and al-Qaida expert Jarret Brachmann, the person running these webpages was the LIFG member Abu Yahya al-Libi, who was based in Karachi until he was arrested by the Pakistani police in May 2002.[9] Parts of the LIFG had moved to Taliban-controlled Afghanistan in 2000, while the group was in a transitionary stage. After failing to stage revolution against the Gaddafi regime in Libya, and after several years on the run, the LIFG in 2000 declared a temporary halt to operations inside Libya. Some of their members, like the commander Abu al-Layth, subsequently became involved in fighting on the Taliban's frontline.[10]

The Al-Emarah webpage had exclusive rights to interviews and battlefield reports from Abu al-Layth, who commanded a group of fighters at the Shah-i-Kot battle. This makes sense given that the page in fact appears to have been a LIFG-run propaganda operation. Al-Neda, on the other hand, was associated with the Saudi Yusuf al-Ayeri, who was a personal acquaintance of Osama bin Laden.[11] This webpage was in contact with Khalid Sheikh Mohammed among others, giving them the exclusive right to publishing statements from Osama bin Laden and the al-Qaida spokesman Sulayman Abu Ghayth. These two webpages played an important role in presenting a narrative of the Afghan war to an Arab audience.

One of the consistent themes in their narrative was that the Arabs in Afghanistan operated under the command of the Taliban and that Mullah Omar was the leader of the insurgency.[12] In reality, Mullah Omar appeared to have gone into hiding after December 2001, and the senior Taliban leadership did not get organized until about March 2003, when they established the senior leadership council known as the Quetta Shura.[13] It took more time, until about 2005, until the Taliban was actually running a functional insurgent organization. However, Taliban and Arab propaganda narratives mirrored each other in 2002–3, in their claims that the Taliban had only conducted a "tactical retreat" from Afghanistan in late 2001, and that they had re-grouped and started an insurgency.[14] The difference between official propaganda narratives and realities on the ground is important to keep in mind when interpreting primary sources from this period.

The Battle for Shah-i-Kot

By the end of December 2002, the US-led coalition had won a series of successful battles against the Taliban, and had succeeded in installing a US-friendly government in Kabul. The US focus was now to destroy any remaining al-Qaida resistance in the country. So, in January 2002, when the United States started gathering intelligence on foreign fighters in Shah-i-Kot, they did not see a brewing local insurgency, but rather a large gathering of "Al Qaeda fighters" that had to be destroyed.[15] The US forces initially believed there were about 150–200 enemy fighters in the area, but later, the estimates were inflated to 800–1,000 fighters.[16] In reality, the lower and earlier estimates were probably closer to the truth.

As the United States believed they were facing a large al-Qaida force, they started planning for a large ground operation involving thousands of US and local Afghan troops. The operation was named "Operation Anaconda," after the giant non-venomous snake known for suffocating its prey. It was the first operation in Afghanistan that involved a large number of US ground forces. The US plan was probably influenced by the criticism the US administration got after the Tora Bora battle.[17] The narrative at the time—and for many years after—was that the absence of US ground forces in the Tora Bora battle had allowed Osama bin Laden to escape.

From the perspective of the Arabs in Afghanistan, the battle for Shah-i-Kot did not mark the end of a phase, but a beginning. The battle was carried out in response to a general call to jihad, prompted by what was seen as a US invasion of Afghanistan.[18] Regardless of what had prompted the invasion, and the broad international support it enjoyed, from an Islamic legal perspective the US presence in Afghanistan was no different than the Soviet invasion in the 1980s, or the British invasions in the late nineteenth century. The Afghans who first took up arms against the United States were typically the veterans, or the sons of the veterans, of the mujahidin fighting in the Afghan-Soviet war. Some of them wanted the Taliban back in power while others simply rose up to defend their villages. The Battle for Shah-i-Kot thus marked the beginning of the anti-US insurgency in Afghanistan, which culminated almost twenty years later with the Taliban taking power in Kabul.

The Shah-i-Kot battle was initiated in Zurmat by a local commander named Sayf al-Rahman Mansur, who was the son of the famed mujahidin leader Mawlawi Nasrullah Mansur. Nasrullah Mansur had served as the deputy leader of Harakat al-Inqilab al-Islami during the Afghan-Soviet war, but at some point, he left the party and established his own, independent group. He briefly served as governor of Paktiya province during the mujahidin government, before being assassinated by political rivals in 1992.[19] In 1995, Nasrullah Mansur's relatives started supporting the Taliban in Paktiya. During the Taliban government, Nasrullah's son Sayf al-Rahman served on the Taliban's front lines as a tank commander, but left active duty after sustaining severe battle injuries to his hands.[20]

According to the legends, Nasrullah Mansur fought the Soviets in the Shah-i-Kot mountains in the 1980s, and his son Sayf al-Rahman followed in his father's footsteps when he took up arms against the Americans in 2002. It is unclear if Sayf al-Rahman took direct part in the Shah-i-Kot battle due to his disability, but most sources close to the events describe him as a well-respected and charismatic leader who played a pioneering role in starting the guerrilla war against the US-led invasion of Afghanistan in early 2002.

The fighters at Shah-i-Kot were a mixture of Afghans and foreign volunteers, many of whom had previously been part of the Taliban's Foreign Brigade. They include a group of Uzbeks led by Tahir Yuldashev, and a group of Arab volunteers from various groups, the most prominent of which was the Libyan LIFG member Abu al-Layth al-Libi. Al-Libi, who used the online name "Sheikh Abd al-Azim," noted later, in a propaganda piece he wrote for the Al-*Emarah* home page, that the force comprised some 50 Afghans, 120 Uzbeks [from the Islamic Movement of Uzbekistan], and 30 Arabs.[21] The estimated total of 200 fighters is consistent with the earliest number estimates that were given by US forces at the start of Operation Anaconda. The numbers also make sense if we compare them with the number of fighters who fled from Kabul and Kandahar, coupled with other sources saying that most of the Uzbeks got trapped in the North, and most of the Arabs left for Pakistan.[22]

In the winter of 2001–2, Tahir Yuldashev and Abu al-Layth al-Libi initiated discussions with Sayf ul-Rahman Mansur about setting up guerrilla bases in the mountains above the Shah-i-Kot valley.[23] This was in line with the decisions made in a series of Shuras (consultations) among the Arabs in Zurmat in December 2001, which were detailed in Chapter 1.[24] Senior al-Qaida leaders such as Sayf al-Adl—who was present in the December 2001 meetings—may have endorsed the plan to initiate a guerrilla war against the Americans from Shah-i-Kot. But save for a handful of individual volunteers, al-Qaida played no large part in the actual battle. According to jihadist sources, the Uzbeks were the main fighting force, and they were involved in the most famous incident of the battle—the downing of a US helicopter and killing of eight US servicemen.[25]

Among the thirty Arabs who fought at Shah-i-Kot, there was one individual who, with relative certainty, can be identified as an al-Qaida member. This was the Egyptian Mustafa Muhammad Fadhil (aka Abd al-Wakil al-Masri, Abu Jihad al-Nubi), who was indicted for his role in the 1998 East African Embassy bombings.[26] He had participated in the Battle for Jalalabad in 1989 and had been member of al-Qaida since at least the early 1990s and went with bin Laden to Sudan in 1992. He became part of al-Qaida's training mission in Somalia, supervised by al-Qaida's military chief Abu Hafs al-Masri. It is unclear if he returned to Afghanistan in 1996, but it is said that he married a Kenyan woman, and it is therefore quite possible that he stayed on in East Africa after al-Qaida left Sudan. In the spring of 1998, he became part of the operational team that prepared the bombing of the US Embassy in Dar-es-Salam, Tanzania.[27] He assisted the team in buying a safe house, and in constructing the suicide truck bomb that was detonated by another Egyptian, Hamden Khalif Allah Awad (aka Ahmed al-Almani). He fled the country on August 2, 1998, five days before the attack, and subsequently went to Afghanistan.[28]

By November 2000, Abd al-Wakil had become a commander on the Taliban's frontline north of Kabul. It is unclear what happened with the frontline organization of Arabs in this period. The few documents that exist suggest that the frontline organization was in disarray and there were internal discussions among the Arabs about how to improve it.[29] There was not much actual fighting going on in this period, because the conflict with Massoud had entered a stalemate. It was probably in this period that al-Qaida suggested to establish an umbrella organization for Arab fighters, named the "Ansar Brigade," in the hope that it would reduce tension among the many independent groups present on the Taliban's frontlines in Afghanistan.[30]

Then, to the surprise of al-Qaida, in the spring of 2001 Mullah Omar announced the creation of *Liwa al-Mujahidin*, or the Foreign Brigade, under the leadership of the Uzbek commander Juma Namanjani. Abd al-Hadi al-Iraqi, who had previously served as a commander on the Kabul frontline, was appointed as his deputy. The Brigade was tasked with fighting on a section of the frontline in Takhar, Northern Afghanistan, under the overall command of Mullah Fazl, Taliban's commander for all of Northern Afghanistan. In the spring of 2001, Abd al-Hadi took some trusted veterans with him to Northern Afghanistan to establish a fighting unit there, while Abd al-Wakil al-Masri stayed on the Kabul frontline with a group of Arabs to man some of the Taliban's defensive positions. After the fall of Kabul, both Abd al-Wakil and Abd al-Hadi went to Zurmat and then further on to Barmal.

At some point in the winter of 2001–2, the Arabs who had stayed behind in Zurmat issued a call for volunteers to come help them fight in the upcoming battle for Shah-i-Kot. The call reached the Arabs in Barmal, and several of them went back to Shah-i-Kot, including Abd al-Wakil "who became their leader" according to a hagiography published many years later.[31] At least five other Arabs went with him, including two who had fought in the Kandahar battle, and three who had fought under Abd al-Wakil at the Kabul front.[32] They were affiliated with various groups and commanders. One had trained in Abu Musab al-Suri's camp and another with LIFG. Some might also have been al-Qaida members although it cannot be verified with available sources.[33] As for Abd al-Hadi al-Iraqi, he probably went to Pakistan and did not participate directly in the battle.[34]

The battle of Shah-i-Kot has been chronicled in detail elsewhere.[35] Put simply, the US strategy was to encircle and destroy the enemy in the Shah-i-Kot valley and the surrounding mountains. The operation started on March 2 and went badly from the beginning. The most well-known events happened on March 3–4. It started with an air insertion of a reconnaissance team, but in the landing zone, the helicopter came under fire and a Navy SEAL fell out. The rescue teams that were sent for him also came under fire, leading in the end to one crashed helicopter and eight dead US servicemen. This battle took place at the Takur Ghar mountain which peaks at 3,700 meters.[36]

US forces worked together with other NATO forces and with Afghan allies, numbering thousands of troops in total. The Afghan force that supported the United States was initially only 200 men strong, and the United States asked for reinforcements from Kabul, which arrived on March 10. The villages in the Shah-i-Kot valley were cleared on March 12 by a large Afghan force. Clearance operations in the mountains continued from March 13 to 19, but by now most enemy fighters had fled.

Abu al-Layth al-Libi's eyewitness account of the battle, which was published online in 2002, has relatively few similarities with the US accounts. But he describes an event where a group of Uzbek mujahidin downed a US helicopter at a peak they called Abdul-Malik, which is probably the mountain referred to as Takur Ghar in US accounts. Like other Taliban and Arab propaganda, his account is rather vague about the day-to-day developments in the battle. It concentrates instead on telling anecdotes about massive US air bombings, the cowardice of the Western Coalition forces, and the bravery of the Arab and local guerrillas. He does say, however, that he agreed with Sayf ul-Rahman Mansour and Tahir Jan to withdraw from the villages in the valley about a week after the battle started, which is around March 9, one day before the Afghan reinforcements arrived.[37] The main Afghan commander in the battle, a man named Maulawi Jawad, was killed on this day, which probably contributed to the decision to withdraw.[38] This detail corresponds with US Army accounts of the battle saying that the villages the US forces entered on March 12 were empty. The account reinforces the impression that it was the Uzbek leader Tahir Yuldashev, the Libyan commander Abu al-Layth, and the local Taliban commander Sayf ul-Rahman who were the top three officials in charge of the battle.[39]

While al-Qaida did not play a leading role in the Battle for Shah-i-Kot, the group undoubtedly benefited from the propaganda that were spread on jihadist webpages after the event. The death of eight US servicemen on top of the Takur Ghar mountain was a huge propaganda victory for the nascent jihad movement against the US-led invasion of Afghanistan, a cause which Osama bin Laden was actively supporting from 2002.

Al-Qaida's Senior Leadership in 2002

In 2002, al-Qaida was more or less dysfunctional as an organization, but Osama bin Laden continued to promote al-Qaida's political agenda from his various hiding places first in Afghanistan, then in Pakistan. After leaving Tora Bora on

December 13, 2001, bin Laden and Zawahiri went to the Shigal district of Kunar where they were protected by associates of Gulbuddin Hekmatyar. From here, the two leaders parted ways and went to different parts of the northwestern Frontier Province of Pakistan. Zawahiri probably went to the Bajaur or Mohmand tribal agency, while bin Laden went to Peshawar. In mid-2002, bin Laden was reunited with one of his wives and moved with her to the Swat valley. Around mid-2003, they moved to Haripur, a city between Islamabad and Abbottabad, and in 2005 they moved to Abbottabad.[40] This means that after leaving Afghanistan in spring or summer 2002, bin Laden hid in various parts of northwestern Pakistan, in the province known as Khyber-Pakhtunkhwa, which shares a border with Afghanistan.

Until March 2002, most of al-Qaida's remaining leadership stayed on the Afghanistan-Pakistan border or in Karachi. From March, most of the senior leadership, including Sayf al-Adl, left Pakistan and went to Iran, but Khalid Sheikh Mohammed (KSM), who is of Pakistani Baluchi origin, stayed behind in Pakistan. From here, he was running most of al-Qaida's affairs from safe houses in large cities, including Karachi and later Rawalpindi, where he was arrested in March 2003.[41] There are indications that KSM communicated directly with bin Laden during this time, but if any of these communications still exist, they have not been released to the public.[42]

KSM was acting as al-Qaida's operational chief in this period, and was involved in organizing attacks in Pakistan and internationally. In addition, he was in direct contact with the administrator of the al-Neda home page, and used al-Neda to publish communiqués from al-Qaida.[43] He might also have been involved in financing operations inside Afghanistan.[44] KSM himself later confessed to being involved in a long list of planned and executed attacks by al-Qaida in 2002, but relying on these confessions is problematic owing to the extensive use of waterboarding and other forms of torture by KSM's interrogators.[45]

In the following, I will discuss how al-Qaida operated in Pakistan in this period by relying on the few internal communications that exist from this period. Three internal letters have been recovered: a letter from Sayf al-Adl to KSM dated June 13, 2002; a letter from "Asad" (probably Asadullah Abd al-Rahman, the son of the Egyptian "Blind Sheikh" Omar Abd al-Rahman) to bin Laden in September 2002; and a letter from Abu Sa'd (likely a pseudonym for bin Laden) to Abu Faraj al-Libi and Abd al-Hadi al-Iraqi, dated November 19, 2002.[46] The three letters give insights into the internal dynamics of al-Qaida's senior leadership after the group lost its sanctuary in Afghanistan.

The letters support the impression that KSM acted as an all-powerful al-Qaida executive in Pakistan after the fall of the Taliban. The fact that he ended up in this role makes sense given that he was the main planner of the 9/11 attacks and a close confidant of Osama bin Laden. His view on how to fight the Jewish-Crusader alliance was similar to bin Laden's, and this made him one of the "yes-men" that bin Laden trusted and liked to surrender himself with.[47] Another reason that made KSM immensely powerful in al-Qaida after 2001 was his extensive contact network in Pakistan, which the rest of al-Qaida had to rely on to hide and survive. Bin Laden thus entrusted KSM with making sure of the safety of his family members, who were later smuggled to Iran and ended up in Iranian custody. Throughout 2002, KSM was probably the only person with a direct line of communication with bin Laden, while all other communications to bin Laden had to first go through KSM.

KSM's sidelining of Sayf al-Adl throughout 2002 led to tension between the two, which is apparent in a letter from al-Adl to KSM dated June 13, 2002.[48] At this time, al-Adl had probably crossed the border into Iran, but had not yet been taken into Iranian custody.[49] This increases the likelihood that the content of his letter is genuine. In the letter, Sayf al-Adl is harshly critical of KSM's conduct, accusing him of a number of failures over the last six months which were caused by his "rushing into action." Sayf al-Adl suspects that bin Laden is pressuring KSM into acting quickly, which has led to a series of badly planned operations that have been detected by security services, leading al-Qaida to be the "laughingstock of the world," as he puts it. He wants KSM to "stop all external operations" for now, until things have been properly assessed and evaluated. Furthermore, he wants KSM to hand over administrative responsibilities to someone named Abu Musab who is with Sayf al-Adl in Iran, and he wants KSM to hand over operations in Pakistan and in Southern Afghanistan to Abu Faraj al-Libi. In the handwritten original, the word "Southern" is added with an arrow pointing to the word Afghanistan, to better line up with the next sentence which states that "Northern Afghanistan is with brother Abd al-Hadi."[50]

The last statement may appear somewhat puzzling. "Northern Afghanistan" generally refers to the part north of the Hindu Kush mountains, and in 2002, the region was firmly in the hands of the Northern Alliance. The Arabs who had fled Afghanistan were based along the southeastern border with Pakistan, and it was neither practical nor feasible for al-Qaida to carry out guerrilla attacks in the north of the country. Sayf al-Adl's statement about Abd al-Hadi being in charge of Northern Afghanistan in 2002 is therefore not a statement about the current operational realities of al-Qaida. It is rather a historical reference to the command-and-control relationships that existed prior to the fall of the Taliban, when Abd al-Hadi had been appointed by Mullah Omar to be the deputy of the Foreign Brigade, which was stationed on the Takhar frontline, and which in practice made Abd al-Hadi the highest-ranking Arab commander in Northern Afghanistan. After Taliban fell and Mullah Omar disappeared, the Taliban's command-and-control relationships became unclear, but it did not stop some Taliban and al-Qaida members from declaring the start of an insurgency in the name of Mullah Omar. For the Arabs in Waziristan, this raised a principal question, which would be the topic of contention throughout 2003 and 2004. If Mullah Omar was still the Emir of the Taliban, did that also mean that Abd al-Hadi was still the Emir of the Arabs fighting for the Taliban? Mullah Omar was not available for comment, and the question was up for interpretation. Bin Laden wrote a letter in late 2002 in which he supported Abd al-Hadi, but as we shall see, his order was not heeded by a number of individual al-Qaida members who in principle had never acknowledged al-Qaida's subordination to the Taliban.

The Arabs who had fled Afghanistan, and who were eager to participate in the insurgency, had various opinions. Some, like Abu al-Layth al-Libi, seem to have preferred to work independently and directly with local Afghan commanders. Others, especially the various parts of al-Qaida, believed that there should be an overall Emir to ensure unity of rank, and prevent unhealthy internal competition, but also to better plan and coordinate the insurgency. However, there was disagreement on how to select the Emir. Some of the Arabs believed that Mullah Omar's previous appointment of Abd al-Hadi as Emir for all Arabs in Afghanistan was still valid, while others preferred to only work directly under bin Laden. There were various other options too, including an election by a Shura council of Arab commanders active in the insurgency. Sayf al-Adl, who by now was far removed from the battlefield in Iran, seemed to take a middle position, suggesting that Abd al-Hadi should keep the position that was given to him by Mullah Omar (i.e., to be in charge of foreign fighters in "Northern Afghanistan"), and suggesting Abu Faraj as an al-Qaida-appointed leader of Arabs fighting in parts of Afghanistan that were not previously associated with Abd al-Hadi.

Returning to the tension between Sayf al-Adl and KSM in mid-2002, it is clear from Al-Adl's letter that he is seeking to marginalize KSM's role in al-Qaida. He seeks to remove KSM from much of al-Qaida's administrative and operational affairs, and to leave him in charge of media and propaganda only. KSM did not heed Sayf al-Adl's advice. Throughout 2002 he continued planning operations in Pakistan and internationally, probably in cooperation directly with Osama bin Laden, whom he managed to visit in the Swat valley on several occasions, including in February 2003.[51] KSM published statements on the al-Neda webpage praising several international terrorist attacks, including the attack on the French oil tanker MV Limburg outside the coast of Yemen on October 6, 2002: an attack on US Marines in Faylaka, Kuwait on 8 October 8, 2002, and the twin attack on an Israeli-owned hotel and an Israeli charter plane in Mombasa, Kenya on November 28, 2002.[52] These attacks were most likely planned by operatives who had left Afghanistan before the 9/11 attacks. KSM may also have been involved in financing the Bali bombings on December 22, 2002, and other operations carried out by the al-Qaida-affiliated Jamaah Islamiyya in Indonesia, as well as a number of other terrorist conspiracies around the world.[53]

As for Afghanistan operations, we do not know how much KSM was involved to begin with or if his involvement changed during 2002. What we do know is that in the fall of 2002 the Arabs in Waziristan took steps to resolve the Emir question. Sometime in probably October, a meeting was held in South Waziristan in which Abd al-Hadi al-Iraqi was appointed Emir of all Arabs fighting for the Taliban.[54] Battlefield participation for Arabs in Afghanistan was coordinated through an umbrella organization called *Shura al-Dakhil* ("The Shura for the interior").[55] Around the same time, a Libyan al-Qaida veteran nicknamed Abu Faraj al-Libi started working as Abd al-Hadi's deputy and assistant. After these changes were made, Osama bin Laden became directly involved in financing and advising the Arabs working under Abd al-Hadi.[56]

Bin Laden's involvement is documented in a letter to Abu Faraj and Abd al-Hadi dated November 19, 2002.[57] The letter was later found in bin Laden's Abbottabad compound. It is addressed to "Abu Faraj, the deputy Emir" and to "Abd al-Hadi al-Iraqi, the Emir of al-Ansar Brigade." In the letter, bin Laden refers to previous correspondence from Abd al-Hadi dated October 22, 2001, in which Abd al-Hadi said that he had been appointed to be Emir of all foreign fighters in Afghanistan, replacing Juma Namanjani who was appointed by Mullah Omar in that position, and who was killed during the US-led invasion in November 2001. Bin Laden expressed his support for this arrangement, which is apparent from the opening paragraphs of his letter:

> This means that the Ansar Brigade (*Liwa' al-Ansar*), which was set up by the Emir of the Believers, continues working in the country, and continues to be the official cover (*ghita'*) authorized by the Islamic Emirate. This is intended to be known to all Ansar brothers in and outside the country. It is the core and point of reference for every move made by the Arabs, Pakistanis, and everyone else from the Ansar brothers.[58]

Bin Laden's immediate support for the Ansar Brigade lines up with what we otherwise know about his philosophy and history with Taliban and Mullah Omar. Bin Laden certainly had differences with Mullah Omar when it came to their views on international terrorism and fighting the Americans. But in matters concerning the war inside Afghanistan, bin Laden was generally supportive of the Taliban and eager to be at Mullah Omar's service. This is apparent from the memoirs of Mustafa Hamid, who remembered the first time Mullah Omar asked bin Laden for help on the Kabul frontline in 1997. Bin Laden saw it as a "historical opportunity" and sought to support it, although in practice, there were a number of practical challenges in working with the Taliban on the frontline.[59] Al-Qaida was one of the groups that systematically supported frontline fighting for the Taliban between 1997 and 2001. When Mullah Omar declared the formation of a Foreign Brigade in early 2001, led by the Uzbek IMU commander Juma Namanjani, bin Laden supported it too, although others interpreted the event as a sidelining of al-Qaida in favor of the IMU.[60] In light of this previous history, it makes sense that bin Laden would support Abd al-Hadi's appointment as leader of the Arabs in 2002 and the continuation of the Foreign Brigade.

Bin Laden had previously, in August 2002, issued a propaganda statement supporting the insurgency in Afghanistan.[61] There were initially some doubts as to the letter's authenticity, but we can conclude today that the letter was most likely authentic, because it was very similar to another set of handwritten pages from 2002, that were later found in Abbottabad. These and other writings suggest bin Laden was personally invested in supporting jihad in Afghanistan. His letter to Abu Faraj and Abd al-Hadi in November 2002 gives a glance into how bin Laden sought to contribute in practice.

Apart from supporting the idea that all activity of foreign fighters in Afghanistan should be organized under Abd al-Hadi, bin Laden's main contribution was money. The letter contains a list of cash amounts be distributed to various individuals and projects in Waziristan and the Loya Paktiya region. Based on this and later correspondence, it appears that Abu Faraj al-Libi had access to one or more money sources belonging to bin Laden, and that he was directly responsible for accessing the money and distributing it.[62] The letter does not say what currency is used, but based on other correspondence from 2002 and 2004, we can assume it is USD.[63] In any case, when we look at their relative values, there is no doubt that "military work" is the main expense, with funds distributed to Abd al-Hadi, the Emir of the Arabs, and to a certain Mullah Rajab, whom bin Laden sees as the overall Taliban commander in "his area" (most likely Khost) and Paktika. Another, large expense is charity for families of foreign fighters, including the families of the Uzbeks, who currently live in South Waziristan. A third expense is a charitable work in the border region carried out by an old bin Laden acquaintance, Sheikh Muhammad Yasir. Bin Laden wanted Yasir to form a charitable committee of local Pashtuns, who would be involved in proselytizing (*da'wa*) work like buying and handing out Qur'ans and schoolbooks, and in addition, construction work like digging wells, and building and repairing mosques and madrassas. He specified that religious books should follow the Hanafi theology, which is the law school adhered to by most Afghans. The philosophy of following local religious customs, rather than trying to import a strict Salafi or Wahhabi interpretation of Islam in Afghanistan, was supported by both bin Laden and his former ideological mentor, the Palestinian Sheikh Abdullah Azzam, who is regarded as the founder of the international jihadist movement.[64]

Bin Laden's financial support to Muhammad Yasir was meant to further the military aims of al-Qaida. Similar to Western armies who carry out construction projects to win "hearts and minds" of Afghan villagers, bin Laden also wanted to use charitable work as a way to support the Pashtun border region, "which will be our back belt for operations inside Afghanistan."[65] But unlike ISAF soldiers who carry out charitable work, bin Laden specifically did not want an al-Qaida, or Arab face on the charity. He asked Sheikh Yasir to only employ Afghans on the project. He did not want to promote a group, but rather, religion itself, thinking that strengthening Islam in the region would make people more inclined toward supporting the jihad against the Americans.

Overall, bin Laden provided a fair amount of money for the war: Abd al-Hadi was given 100,000 (presumably USD) to spend on military work as he sees fit. Mullah Rajab was given two one-time amounts of 25,000 USD and a monthly stipend of 10,000 USD. These types of money handouts were not unusual in a Taliban context, at least if we believe the autobiography of Abdul Hai Mutma'in. He recalled a meeting among Taliban leaders in late 2001, during which Mullah Omar handed out cash to a number of commanders to finance their jihad: "A few received USD 100,000, others received USD 50,000," he recalled.[66] We shall see in the next section what type of military operations were carried out in Loya Paktiya in 2003, presumably aided by the money from bin Laden.

Bin Laden's letter to Abu Faraj and Abd al-Hadi in November 2002 shows that bin Laden had not disappeared from al-Qaida after fleeing from Tora Bora. He was actively involved in restarting the insurgency in Afghanistan. To carry out this task he communicated directly with Abu Faraj al-Libi, who after the arrest of KSM in March 2003 remained bin Laden's communications officer, financial officer, and right-hand man until his arrest in Pakistan in May 2005. As for Abd al-Hadi, it appears that his relationship with bin Laden continued the same way it had been before 2001, as a relationship of mutual benefit. Bin Laden was dependent on Abd al-Hadi to restart the insurgency and gather the ranks fighting in the name of Mullah Omar, while Abd al-Hadi benefited from bin Laden's financial contributions to cover the day-to-day expenses of the Arabs in South Waziristan.

Another fact to be gleaned from bin Laden's letter is that the Afghan insurgency started out as a local uprising that was not led by senior members of the Taliban, in spite of being portrayed as such in Taliban propaganda. As far as we know, none of the senior Taliban leaders were in touch with al-Qaida in 2002 and bin Laden had no way to communicate with Mullah Omar. In Afghanistan, bin Laden chose to work through "Mullah Rajab," a provincial-level leader, and Sheikh Muhammad Yasir from Logar province, who was a senior cleric affiliated with the Taliban movement, but who was never part of the core Kandahari Taliban. In the letter, bin Laden also handed out some money to a certain "Kabir," who appears to operate out of South Waziristan. This could be Mullah Abdul Kabir, a senior Taliban member who had worked with al-Qaida in Afghanistan prior to 9/11 and who later served on the Taliban's Quetta Shura, but it is hard to confirm because "Kabir" (meaning "big" in Arabic) is a common nickname.

The Taliban insurgency that bin Laden sought to restart was led by individual commanders such as Mullah Rajab, who worked mainly in Khost and possibly in neighboring Paktiya. Mullah Rajab was supported by a coalition of foreign fighters known as the Shura al-Dakhil, which was endorsed by bin Laden. Other individuals ran insurgent operations in Khost too, such as Abu al-Layth al-Libi, who had his own sources of income to finance his troops.[67] In the November 2002 letter, bin Laden tried to dissuade Abu al-Layth from working independently and from paying local commanders directly, preferring all operations on Khost to be organized through Mullah Rajab. As far as we know, Abu al-Layth did not heed bin Laden's advice, but continued maintaining his financial independence. In 2004, after Abd al-Hadi quit as Emir of the frontline in Afghanistan and the Egyptian veteran Khalid Habib took over, Abu al-Layth agreed to giving a "limited bay'a" to bin Laden for carrying out operations in Afghanistan and Pakistan, but the bay'a did not include giving up control over finances.[68] The fact that he swore bay'a in 2004, and not before, could simply reflect the fact that the bay'a process was institutionalized by Khalid Habib, while it previously had not been a requirement under Abd al-Hadi's leadership. In addition, the departure of Abd al-Hadi may have made the bay'a more acceptable to some Salafis, because it now allowed them to swear a bay'a to Osama bin Laden rather than to Mullah Omar.[69]

In early 2003, KSM visited bin Laden in the Swat valley. On March 1, 2003, KSM was arrested in Rawalpindi and a few months after this, bin Laden moved to Haripur. In the Abbottabad collection, there is a gap in bin Laden communications for all of 2003 and until late 2004. There are references to communications in 2004, and also to an incident in mid-2004 where a batch of letters got lost and had to be resent in December the same year. Some of these problems probably had to do with KSM's arrest in March 2003, and bin Laden's subsequent move to Haripur in mid-2003. Other dramatic events happened during this time too. In October 2003, the Pakistani military raided one of the safehouses in the Shakai valley used by Shura al-Dakhil members, and killed the senior member Ahmed Said Khadr.[70] Around January 2004, Abu Faraj left the Shakai valley and thus probably became less directly involved in Shura al-Dakhil activities; and in July 2004, al-Qaida's Documents office in Pakistan was busted and a number of people associated with al-Qaida's External Operations department (the cell responsible for international terrorist planning) were arrested.[71]

As there is no communication from bin Laden during this time, we do not know how involved he was in al-Qaida activities in 2003 and 2004. We know for sure that there was no outgoing communication from bin Laden between the "lost letters" incident in mid-2004, and until December 2004, when bin Laden was able to resend these letters as well as answers to other letters he received in October 2004. There was ingoing communication from Abu Faraj to bin Laden at least once in the first half of 2004 (which bin Laden attempted, but failed to reply to in mid-2004), and in October 2004 (which bin Laden replied to in December 2004). As for the period after KSM's arrest on March 1, 2003, we do not have any certain indications of whether there was communication with bin Laden or not.[72] What we do know is that bin Laden was able to deliver a number of audio messages to the media during both 2003 and 2004. There were seven audio messages published in 2003, and six messages in 2004.[73] The longest gap without any published messages from bin Laden was between May 6, 2004, and October 29, 2004, which supports the observation that there were no in- or outgoing letters in the Abbottabad documents collection between mid-2004 and October 18, 2004. As we shall discuss later, the lack of communication in the fall of 2004 caused bin Laden to miss a crucial event in al-Qaida's history, namely, the decision to establish an al-Qaida branch in Iraq led by Abu Musab al-Zarqawi.

We shall hear in later chapters how this process was run in bin Laden's absence. But first, let us look at what happened with the insurgency in Afghanistan from 2003 onwards.

Insurgent Activities in Waziristan and Loya Paktika

Many of the Arabs who participated in the early stages of the Taliban insurgency were organized under Shura al-Dakhil, based in the Shakai valley in South Waziristan. The Shura al-Dakhil mainly operated in the southeastern province of Paktika, and from mid-2003, in the Afghan capital Kabul. From 2004, there was activity in Zabul and Nangarhar. In addition to Shura al-Dakhil, there were groups led by independent Arab commanders, the most prominent of which was Abu al-Layth al-Libi.[74]

The main Arabic-language source to document the early years of the Afghan insurgency is a collection of so-called "martyr biographies" issued by Islamist websites in 2006, and entitled "Martyrs in the Time of Alienation."[75] The book purportedly contains the biographies of a number of foreign fighters who were killed in Afghanistan and Pakistan during 2002–6. They include stories of Shura al-Dakhil members, such as Ahmed Said Khadr, al-Qaida members such as Hamza al-Rabia, and various other Arabs, Pakistanis, and Central Asians including Hassan Mahsum, the leader of the East Turkistan Islamic Movement (ETIM). Another type of source which sheds light on the activities of Arabs in Afghanistan in this period is US court documents connected to the Guantánamo prisoners Abd al-Hadi al-Iraqi, and two of Ahmed Said Khadr's sons, Omar and Abdurrahman Khadr.[76]

The first attacks that US intelligence sources connect to Shura al-Dakhil took place in December 2002, when there was a series of rocket attacks on a small US base at Lwara, Paktika. The small outpost in Lwara was abandoned after the attacks, and footage from the attack was later featured in an al-Sahab propaganda video known as *War of the Oppressed*, which was released in 2005.[77]

Around the same time in December 2002, there were attacks in Barmal district of Paktika, in a place called Shkin, which is probably near a US base called FOB Checho, close to the Pakistani border crossing at Angor Adda. Shkin continued to be attacked by Shura al-Dakhil forces several times throughout 2003. In April 2003 and September 2003, there were attacks in which three US soldiers were killed.[78] Footage from the September 2003 attack, later known as the "medevac scene," also made its way into the al-Qaida propaganda video *War of the Oppressed*.

On October 25, 2003, there was an ambush in the neighboring district of Gomal with disastrous results for the Arabs. A group of Arabs was taken in an ambush by US forces and killed. The number of fatalities varies from eleven to twenty-two Arabs killed. They included experienced fighters, such as the Egyptian al-Qaida member Abu Ayman al-Masri.[79] These attacks along the eastern border of Paktika with Pakistan may have been overseen by the Egyptian Khalid Habib, who was a local commander at the time and who became the overall Emir of the frontline after Abd al-Hadi resigned in mid-2004.[80] All the attacks took place in areas only a few kilometers away from the Pakistani border, and the attackers probably infiltrated from south and north Waziristan. According to Khalid Habib, in 2004 attacks in these areas became more difficult to execute because of lack of support from local people—likely a result also of Pakistani Army operations, which began in South Waziristan in 2004.[81] These operations were in part provoked by a series of assassination attempts on high-ranking military officials in Pakistan, including General Musharraf, carried out by some Pakistani networks with apparent links to groups in the Shakai valley. These activities were later tied to al-Qaida's cell for external operations, led at the time by Hamza Rabia, and will be further discussed in Chapter 3.

Court documents associated with the Khadr family cases give some additional information about Shura al-Dakhil activities in 2003. The documents say that Abdullah Khadr was involved in purchasing weapons on behalf of Shura al-Dakhil. More specifically, in the spring of 2003, Ahmed Said Khadr gave his son, Abdullah Khadr, at least 20,000 USD to buy ammunitions and explosives precursors for manufacturing Improvised Explosive Devices (IEDs) for use in the insurgency in Afghanistan. After purchasing the items in Pakistan, he delivered the procurements to a "third party" who was a high-ranking al-Qaida member. After his arrest in Pakistan, Abdullah Khadr told the FBI that the IEDs were going to be used in Barmal.[82] This overlaps with the types of operations that Shura al-Dakhil were involved in, suggesting that Shura al-Dakhil was a joint effort by Arabs and others, which probably received financing from various individuals including bin Laden and other senior ideologues such as Ahmed Said Khadr. Khadr was a Canadian of Egyptian origin who lived in Afghanistan with his family prior to 9/11, and as far as is known, he was not a member of al-Qaida, but he was involved in the larger community of Arabs living in Afghanistan during the Taliban regime.

In addition to Shura al-Dakhil, there was another group that pioneered the insurgency in Afghanistan in 2002. The group was led by Abu al-Layth al-Libi, who mainly carried out operations in Khost province, and who seemed to have his own sources of financing. In November 2002, bin Laden complained to Abu Faraj that Abu al-Layth was paying local commanders in Khost directly. Bin Laden thought all money should be distributed through the overall Taliban leader for the area, whom he called Mullah Rajab, and wanted to "encourage" Abu al-Layth to do the same.[83] The call was not heeded by Abu al-Layth. He continued to run his own, independent insurgent operation.

Abu al-Layth's group pioneered the use of internet and video propaganda in Afghanistan. His group made some of the first battle videos from Afghanistan, which were generally made to generate sympathy for the cause as well as fundraising and recruitment. Some of the most famous battles that Abu al-Layth participated in were the "Dabqay Operation" on May 22, 2003, the "First Shinkay Operation" in *c.* mid-2003, and the "Second Shinkay Operation" sometime in 2004.[84] All these battles were turned into propaganda videos, similar to those videos that jihadists by now were making from the Iraq war. In contrast, al-Qaida's al-Sahab media agency did not publish a battlefield video from Afghanistan until 2005. This video, called *War of the Oppressed*, incorporated footage from as early as late 2002, but the production and editing process were long and slow, in part because al-Qaida in this period had difficulty communicating with Osama bin Laden. Based on the Abbottabad documents, it appears that bin Laden's input finally reached al-Sahab in late 2004, and the video itself was distributed to news agencies and released online in the fall of 2005.[85]

The Suicide Bombing Campaign

There is another, significant operational activity in 2003 which was marginally connected to Shura al-Dakhil, namely the start of a suicide bombing campaign against the International Security Assistance Force (ISAF) in Kabul. On June 7, 2003, a suicide bomber attacked a bus carrying German soldiers in Kabul, which killed four Germans. It was the first confirmed suicide attack in Afghanistan since the US-led invasion started, and the second suicide attack in the country's history—the first one was the al-Qaida attack that killed Ahmed Shah Massoud on September 9, 2001. In 2004, there were at least four more attacks against ISAF targets in Kabul—three suicide bombs, and one RPG attack, which were most likely carried out by the same network.[86]

The exact motivation and perpetrators of this early suicide bombing campaign in Kabul will probably never be fully known. The standard narrative is that al-Qaida was behind the campaign, but the reality is more complex. Osama bin Laden supported the campaign ideologically, by issuing a speech calling for suicide attacks in Afghanistan in the spring of 2003. We also have indications that Osama bin Laden financed the campaign, and that the three first suicide bombers were two Arabs and a Chinese Uighur who had been recruited from among the foreign fighters who had fled to Waziristan after 2001. Abd al-Hadi al-Iraqi, who was Emir of the Arabs fighting in Afghanistan in 2003 and until mid-2004, admitted many years later that he had passed on bin Laden's money and the volunteer suicide operatives to a local commander named "Layaqat," who would plan and execute the suicide attacks.[87]

"Layaqat's" identity is unknown, but an unconfirmed US intelligence report identifies him as "Commander Zadran," a veteran of Gulbuddin Hekmatyar's Hizb-e-Islami. The same source claims that there was a meeting between al-Qaida, Hizb-e-Islami, and Taliban representatives in Peshawar in February 2002, where they discussed how to cooperate in the Afghan insurgency.[88] The information is indirectly backed up by other sources, which claim that both Abd al-Hadi and Khalid Sheikh Mohammed were in Peshawar in early 2002. More significantly, a letter to bin Laden written about 2004 confirms that bin Laden paid Hekmatyar 50,000 USD per month to contribute to the insurgency in Afghanistan, and that the money stopped sometime in 2004.[89] An ISAF officer who served in Kabul in 2004 said it was common knowledge that the attacks on ISAF in Kabul were carried out by Hizb-e-Islami Gulbuddin, which the military refers to with the acronym HIG.

The greatest clue to "Layaqat's" identity is the fact that he operated a suicide attack network around Kabul in 2003, which only a few insurgent actors at the time had the capability of doing. The Taliban were not very organized at that time, the Haqqani network had not yet started to operate around Kabul, the Pakistani Inter-Services Intelligence (ISI) was likewise not systematically involved at this early stage.[90] But Hizb-e-Islami had the manpower, skill, and presence in the Kabul area to pull off a relatively complex operation like this, and as the Abbottabad documents now indicate, they had financing from Osama bin Laden. Another letter written to bin Laden around 2007, from an Arab associated with Hekmatyar, points in the same direction. The author expresses dismay that bin Laden has switched to only supporting the Taliban, and reminds bin Laden that it was Hekmatyar's group, Hizb-e-Islami Gulbuddin (HIG), that provided most of the logistical support for the suicide attacks in Kabul.[91]

The first suicide bomb attack in 2003, on the bus of German ISAF soldiers, was carried out by a Saudi volunteer named 'Abd al-Ilah al-Musa (aka Abd al-Rahman al-Najdi) from Riyadh, Saudi Arabia, who had come to Afghanistan together with a friend, to train in al-Qaida's camps sometime prior to 9/11. He fought the US invasion, fled to the tribal areas, and signed up as a volunteer for suicide operations. When his turn came, he was told to travel to Kabul and to wait for a phone call. Early in the morning on June 7, 2003, he sat down in the driver's seat of a yellow-and-white Kabul taxi (typically a Lada station wagon) filled with at least 150 kg explosives, with a local guide in the passenger seat. They drove around until the spotting team called them on the radio, saying they had a target: a military bus, exiting from an ISAF base in eastern Kabul known as Camp Warehouse. It carried German soldiers, who were on their way to Kabul International Airport for their leave. The Saudi bomber let the guide out of the taxi, then drove up on the side of the military bus, and pushed the button. The explosion hurled the bus into a nearby farm field. Four German soldiers were left dead and many more damaged for life.[92] The next year, 2004, there were at least three more suicide attacks in Afghanistan carried out by the same network. After 2004, the tactic spread like wildfire. In 2006, more than eighty suicide attacks were carried out by various insurgent networks all over Afghanistan.[93]

Based on the above sources, there seems to be some support for the hypothesis that it was al-Qaida that started the suicide bombing campaign in Afghanistan, supported by the Hizb-e-Islami of Gulbuddin Hekmatyar. But there is still much we do not know. We do not know who built the bombs, or where they were built. The infamous al-Qaida bomb maker, Abu Abd al-Rahman al-Masri, was based in Waziristan from 2002 and built bombs used in suicide attacks in Pakistan—such as the attack on the US consulate in Karachi in 2006.[94] But we do not know if he built any of the suicide bombs for Afghanistan. In at least one of the cases the suicide bomb was primitive—it was made of one or several Russian 82 mm artillery shells, tied to the attacker's body. This was a type of bomb that could have been constructed by a number of individuals trained in making improvised IEDs.

Another unknown is the identity of the people who initiated and executed the suicide bombing campaign. It was probably financed at least in part by Osama bin Laden. He personally recorded an audiotape in the spring of 2003, in which he called for suicide attacks to take place in Afghanistan.[95] Bin Laden supported the insurgency by giving money to Shura al-Dakhil, which he saw as the most legitimate umbrella organization for Arabs fighting for the Taliban, but he generally did not dictate how the Shura leaders should spend the money. The Shura had a system in place for recruiting suicide bombers. Three of the four first suicide bombers were recruited from among the foreign fighters who fled to Waziristan in 2002, but not exclusively from al-Qaida: one was a Saudi, one Egyptian, and one Chinese Uighur. The Saudi and Egyptian came to Afghanistan shortly before, or after 9/11 and fought the US invasion before fleeing to Waziristan. The Uighur was a member of ETIM led by Hassan Mahsum.[96] The fourth suicide bomber was identified in US intelligence as being from the "Afghan Taliban," which could indicate that he was either Afghan or Pakistani. We know little of the layers in between—that is, the attack organizers on the ground. As mentioned, the prime suspects are militants associated with Hizb-e-Islami of Gulbuddin Hekmatyar, who had a strong network around Kabul and historical connections to al-Qaida.

In hindsight, these early attacks pioneered the use of suicide bombing in Afghanistan but in terms of strategic significance, they soon paled in comparison to tactics used at later stages in the insurgency by the Haqqani network and others, including complex "Mumbai-style" attacks where teams of gunmen attacked and laid siege to high-profile buildings in Kabul.[97]

The Impact of the Iraq War

The year 2004 marked a turning point for the Arabs operating out of Waziristan. The activities of the Shura al-Dakhil dropped significantly that year, which was probably related to various security operations in the region carried out by the Pakistani Army. The first US drone attack was carried out in June 2004, and it killed a local Waziri commander named Nek Muhammad, who had helped host al-Qaida and other groups in and around Wana, South Waziristan.[98] Over the next year, Arabs who belonged to al-Qaida and other groups would relocate to areas further north, and by 2006, most of them had ended up in North Waziristan.

The mood among the Arabs in Waziristan in the fall of 2004 is well described by two letters sent to bin Laden this time, one from the Saudi commander Abu Hassan al-Sa'idi, and the other from the Egyptian Khalid Habib.[99] Both these individuals were veterans of the Battle for Jalalabad in 1989 and al-Qaida's training mission in Somalia in 1993. Their letters seem to be prompted by internal rumors in al-Qaida that Abd al-Hadi al-Iraqi was going to leave Waziristan and go back to Iraq to participate in the insurgency there. This prompted an internal discussion in al-Qaida about what Abd al-Hadi's role in Iraq should be, and also, more generally about al-Qaida's future ambitions in Iraq. Around this same time, direct negotiations were taking place between the Iraq-based Jordanian militant Abu Musab al-Zarqawi and bin Laden's representative in Pakistan,

Abu al-Faraj al-Libi, for Zarqawi to formally join al-Qaida. This process will be further discussed in Chapter 4. Here, I will briefly discuss how the Iraq War affected al-Qaida's operations in Afghanistan.

The start of the war in Iraq coincided with a period of great difficulty for the Arabs operating out of Waziristan. In 2004 in particular, the Arabs suffered some devastating losses on the battlefield inside Afghanistan, and the Pakistani Army started putting pressure on the population in Waziristan to not cooperate with Arabs. At the same time, there was an active insurgency raging in Iraq, and Abu Musab al-Zarqawi had entered the scene in the spring of 2004 with a highly visible propaganda campaign that attracted massive media attention. During 2004, Abbottabad documents confirm that several of the Arab commanders in Waziristan started contemplating going to Iraq, which seemed a more attractive battlefield than Afghanistan.[100] In this context Abd al-Hadi al-Iraqi, a native Iraqi from Mosul, also announced that he would leave Waziristan and go home to Iraq. It is not clear what his intentions were at the time, but it is known that the move was welcomed by Osama bin Laden, who asked Abd al-Hadi to report back on the situation in the country.[101] Needless to say, bin Laden was in need of information about the Iraqi battlefield and the various groups operating there, in order to exploit the opportunity that had been created by the US invasion to promote al-Qaida's global jihadist agenda. However, Abd al-Hadi's announced move sparked an internal discussion in al-Qaida, which illustrates that al-Qaida was far from having a unified strategy for Iraq at this time.

This is the background for why two veteran al-Qaida commanders, Abu al-Hassan and Khalid Habib, in the fall of 2004 sent letters to bin Laden. The main theme in their letters is to express worry that Abd al-Hadi might be a divisive commander in Iraq, that he needs to have a clearly defined role, and above all, that he should not be sent there to take over as Emir of the insurgency, as this might "ruin everything Zarqawi has built up."[102] We do not know if these observations are based on rumors and perceptions, or actual facts, and in any case one must presume that letters are colored by ideological, personal, and cultural differences between individuals within al-Qaida, who can be roughly divided into pragmatics and hardliners. The discussion was, however, taken seriously by bin Laden, who in December 2004 recommended that Abd al-Hadi should "delay his travel for now."[103]

What is more interesting in the context of this chapter is that Khalid Habib's letter to bin Laden paints a grim picture of al-Qaida's involvement in the Afghan war. His opinion is summed up in the quote that was introduced at the start of this chapter, where he says, "I think that we should send all the brothers to Iraq." He claims that al-Qaida has only been able to conduct a few operations, and that Pakistani Army has made it extremely difficult to operate in Waziristan. He also complains about the Afghans, saying they are involved in infighting and that it is difficult to find operations to participate in. In sum, he suggests to bin Laden that al-Qaida should contemplate moving most of their activities to Iraq, and to only leave a skeleton staff in Afghanistan.[104] From other Abbottabad communications, we know that Hamza Rabia, al-Qaida's chief of External Operations, in 2004 suggested moving al-Qaida's international terrorist planning to Iraq.[105]

On the other hand, the picture is not fully pessimistic. Abu al-Hassan's letter in September 2004 suggests that al-Qaida operations are still active and expanding in Afghanistan, and he indicates that after Abd al-Hadi al-Iraqi resigned in 2004, "we now have a Shura led by al-Qari [Sheikh Saeed]."[106] This is the first indication that Sheikh Saeed, a veteran of al-Qaida who is best known as bin Laden's accountant, had started taking over a broader set of administrative responsibilities for al-Qaida in Waziristan. While it is hard to get to the bottom of the organizational dynamics of al-Qaida in this period, one can read between the lines that Abd al-Hadi's departure as Emir of the foreign fighters in Waziristan had led to a temporary gathering of the ranks of the Arabs under a more Egyptian and Salafi-dominated leadership, drawing together some of the Egyptian, Libyan, and Saudi commanders who had reservations about Abd al-Hadi's leadership role and close affiliation with the Taliban. It is unclear if this had much impact in the long run, as Abbottabad documents in 2009–10 indicate that the Arabs in Waziristan were far from ideologically or organizationally united. If anything, it might have contributed to forging closer ties, and in the end formal unity, between al-Qaida and the Libyan Islamic Fighting Group (LIFG).

In any case, the Iraq war had a profound impact on al-Qaida as a global organization, which will be discussed in detail toward the end of this book. As for Afghanistan, al-Qaida continued to contribute to guerrilla attacks on a local level. As the Taliban's senior leadership became more organized and expanded the insurgency, al-Qaida and other Arab fighters were able to expand as well, but their tactical contributions remained small. As for the political relationship between al-Qaida and the Taliban, it seems that it became more active from 2007, when al-Qaida started getting drawn into internal powers struggles in the Taliban movement. We will return to these in more detail in Chapter 5.

Summary

When the anti-US insurgency started in Afghanistan in 2002, bin Laden was one of several individuals who took a direct interest in supporting it. Both al-Qaida and the Taliban were in disarray at this time, and there was no clear command-and-control. But there was a general religious edict, or *fatwa*, calling for jihad against the foreign invasion of Afghanistan. Various local commanders answered to the call for jihad, such as local Taliban commanders and others who had been mujahidin in the past. They took local initiatives to fight the US invaders. Some of them, like Sayf al-Rahman al-Mansur in Zurmat, had support from Arabs and Uzbeks whom they had previously worked with in Kabul during the Taliban regime. The Arabs and Uzbeks who volunteered to fight later established a Shura to coordinate their efforts with the Taliban. Al-Qaida documents referred to this organization as Shura al-Dakhil—the shura for the interior (i.e., Afghanistan). Bin Laden supported the Shura's work financially from late 2002, and may have played a direct role in sponsoring the first suicide attacks against ISAF forces in Kabul in 2003–4. But overall, al-Qaida's contributions to the insurgency were small. Al-Qaida started gathering their ranks in mid-2004, when an Egyptian al-Qaida veteran named Khalid Habib took over leadership of the "Arab frontline" in Afghanistan on behalf of al-Qaida. At the same time, the Pakistani Army put increasing pressure on the Arabs in Waziristan, pushing many al-Qaida members to look to Iraq as a more promising battlefield. The next chapter about al-Qaida's "External Operations cell" looks at how al-Qaida in part brought this pressure on themselves, because they actively supported groups that promoted a violent anti-Pakistan agenda.

External Operations 2002–6

*After a couple of days of the [9/11] attack ... people in the [Iqra] bookshop,
even myself, would believe that it was a Jewish conspiracy against Muslims.*[1]
—Waheed Ali, arrested but later acquitted in the 7/7 bombings case

Al-Qaida's 9/11 attacks were designed to incite Muslims to fight the United States. Yet, in Europe, the attacks got a mixed reception. Some individuals, such as the above-quoted Waheed Ali, preferred to believe the attacks were part of a sinister Jewish conspiracy. Others, like the 7/7 bomber Mohammed Siddique Khan, accepted the attacks after "a few months."[2] The turning point for many UK radicals was not the 9/11 attacks themselves, but the retaliatory US attack on Afghanistan and security crackdowns on Islamists in the UK. In this chapter, I discuss how al-Qaida sought to exploit the anti-US sentiment in Europe after 2001 to stage new international terrorist attacks.

The story of how al-Qaida in the mid-2000s turned their focus to attacking Europe has been covered in many academic studies.[3] However, al-Qaida's exact role in these attacks remains subject to debate. While there is generally a consensus that the London bombings in 2005 were connected to al-Qaida leaders in Pakistan, researchers disagree on whether al-Qaida was connected to the Madrid attack in 2004.[4] There has also been a debate on whether al-Qaida had "strategies" for how to fight the United States and their allies after 2001 and to what extent al-Qaida were able to implement them.[5]

The reason why it has been so hard to determine al-Qaida's exact role can be ascribed to two factors. First, that the information about al-Qaida's involvement in terrorist attacks in Europe belongs to intelligence and security agencies and is therefore often classified. When such information is leaked to the press, it is often provided without context, which makes it challenging for academic researchers to independently assess how credible the information is.

The best type of information in this respect is original documents and other materials used as evidence in terrorist trials, such as the internal al-Qaida documents found on a German terrorist suspect in 2011 which appeared to contain lessons-learned reports by Rashid Rauf, one of the organizers of 7/7 bombings.[6]

The other challenge is that al-Qaida in Pakistan also practiced a high degree of operational security. The Abbottabad documents contain hints of this operational security, for example, when bin Laden in 2004 ordered his External Operations chief Hamza Rabia to restrict his movements and only conduct activities through middlemen.[7] When Western security services investigated terrorist plots and their ties to Waziristan, the information often ended at such "middlemen," who used anonymous nicknames and who could not be further identified except as being "from al-Qaida," whatever that means. This is one reason why there in the 2000s has been some confusion in Western media about the identity of al-Qaida's External Operations chief.

The Abbottabad documents released by the CIA in 2017 contain several new pieces of information about al-Qaida's external operations in the decade after 9/11, which I will discuss in the following chapter. But they do not tell the whole story, because in the Abbottabad archive there are large gaps in bin Laden's communications between 2002 and 2006. We do not know the reasons for this, but a likely scenario is that bin Laden himself may have destroyed or lost the information while he was moving between safe houses in Pakistan in 2002, 2003, and 2005.[8] Other, possible explanation is that the Navy SEALs might have missed it when they raided the Abbottabad compound, or the documents are in CIA custody but remain classified.

One of the overall research questions in this book is to investigate how al-Qaida sought to implement the ideology of global jihadism after 2001, while operating within the restrictions and opportunities brought about by the US-led War on Terror. The aim in this section is not to tell a detailed story of each terrorist plot against the West, and how they were linked to al-Qaida in Pakistan. Instead, I look for broader clusters of plots that reflect particular operationalizations of the ideology of global jihadism. Next, I look at how al-Qaida's leadership interacted with these plot clusters, and what this says more broadly about how al-Qaida operationalized ideology after 2001.

For al-Qaida's external operations in 2002–6, the pattern that emerges is as follows: In 2002–3, Khalid Sheikh Mohammed (KSM) led the activity, and the main goal was to continue the war against the "Jewish-Crusader alliance" that was declared by bin Laden in 1996–8, and that was intensified with the 9/11 attacks and the invasions of Afghanistan and Iraq. After KSM's capture, the activity continued with a reduced capacity, and was led by Egyptians who appear to have been part of Zawahiri's Egyptian Islamic Jihad, including Hamza Rabia and Abu Ubaydah al-Masri. The main international terrorist attack to emerge from this activity was the 7/7 London bombings in 2005, which was driven by a semi-independent network of al-Qaida sympathizers who formerly lived in Europe, including Abu Ubaydah al-Masri and a British-Pakistani citizen named Rashid Rauf, who fled the UK in 2002 after he was sought by UK police in connection with his uncle's murder. In addition to fulfilling the general, strategic goals of al-Qaida, their plots appear motivated by Rauf's personal hatred for the UK.

Besides the 7/7 bombings, the largest terrorist attack on European soil in this period was the Madrid train bombings in 2004. The Abbottabad documents can neither confirm nor deny that al-Qaida played a role in the attacks, because there is a gap in the archive from 2003 until mid-2004, when the bombings were planned and executed. In general, I lean toward the interpretation that the Madrid cell was largely self-radicalized and self-driven, and if there was a link to al-Qaida it appears to have been tenuous at best. Because of the information gap, I chose to not speculate further on this but instead, concentrate on another, relevant story that emerges from the Abbottabad documents, namely the story of how Osama bin Laden reacted to the Madrid attacks and sought to adapt al-Qaida's external operations strategy as a result. In mid-2004, bin Laden ordered his external operations chief, Hamza Rabia, to attack the weakest links in the US-led coalition in Iraq in order to weaken, and hopefully break apart the coalition. At the same time, he maintained that attacks on the United States and economically damaging targets, such as aviation, should receive the highest priority.

We never saw the fruit of bin Laden's ideas, because around the same time as he sent his strategic advice to Hamza Rabia, in mid-2004, Pakistani security forces carried out a major crackdown on al-Qaida's external operations network in Pakistan. Al-Qaida itself can be partly blamed for this fallout, because the group had started assisting Pakistani militants who were plotting to kill President Musharraf and other high-ranking members of Pakistan's military establishment. The 7/7 bombings in London which happened a year later were carried out by a different network within al-Qaida, and succeeded because this cell was compartmentalized from al-Qaida's other activities.

External Operations under Hamza Rabia

The role and activities of Khalid Sheikh Mohammed (KSM) in Pakistan were discussed in Chapter 2. In 2002 and until his arrest on March 1, 2003, KSM tried to stage a number of follow-up attacks to 9/11, and some of them succeeded. The deadliest attack in this period was the Bali nightclubs bombings in December 2002, carried out by the Indonesian al-Qaida affiliate Jemaah Islamiyah. I also discussed previously how there were disagreements between Sayf al-Adl and KSM regarding al-Qaida's terrorist strategy. But Sayf al-Adl was in Iran, and only had limited influence on events in Pakistan.

The story in this chapter starts with Hamza Rabia, who took over al-Qaida's External Operations office (*qism al-ʿamal al-khariji*) after KSM's arrest. Unfortunately, we do not have many primary sources that can shed light on Hamza Rabia's activities, but we have some: they include the US Senate's report on the CIA's detention and interrogation program from 2014, which contains a section on Hamza Rabia's activities in 2003, and a personal letter from Osama bin Laden to Hamza Rabia written a few months after the Madrid bombings.[9]

Hamza Rabia's promotion to chief of External Operations sometime between March and October 2003 coincided with the US-led invasion of Iraq, which started on March 20, 2003. It is generally acknowledged that the invasion of Iraq led al-Qaida to widen its list of enemies to include the countries that supported the US-led coalition in Iraq. This was expressed most clearly by Osama bin Laden in a speech published in October 2003, where he singled out the "UK, Spain, Australia, Poland, Japan and Italy" as enemies, alongside Arab countries that directly assisted the US war effort, such as Kuwait.[10] Another question is whether there was any connection between this propaganda statement, and al-Qaida's operational plans and abilities, and whether al-Qaida thought about using international terrorism as a strategic tool to weaken the US-led coalition in Iraq. The Abbottabad documents give some partial answers.

We know that Hamza Rabia wrote bin Laden one or several letters after he took over as External Operations chief in 2003, which bin Laden received.[11] Bin Laden seems to have not been able to reply until about mid-2004, when he wrote a letter back to Rabia which outlined a new strategy for External Operations inspired by the Madrid bombings in April 2004. This letter never reached Rabia, but was lost or got destroyed on the way. We therefore do not have the full version of the letter. However, in December 2004 bin Laden copied and pasted parts of the letter into a new document, and sent it to Rabia with a note that "we wrote this letter many months ago."[12] We must assume that some paragraphs were deleted, and others added, since the first version was written.[13] The new letter is written in a different context, namely, to assist Hamza Rabia in moving al-Qaida's External Operations activities to Iraq, and thus it is perhaps more relevant to read it as a collection of bin Laden's brainstormed thoughts about how to conduct external operations work. This might be a good reason why the final version of the letter does not actually mention the Madrid attacks, in spite of originally being written at a time when bin Laden was concerned with the political fallout from Madrid and he himself decided to pursue a strategy of attacking the weakest link, in order to possibly replicate the political fallout of the Madrid bombings.

The Abbottabad documents suggest that Hamza Rabia seemed to work in External Operations already prior to the capture of KSM in March 2003. We know this only indirectly, by reading bin Laden's instructions to Hamza Rabia in mid-2004 which are styled as an answer to the previous letter sent by Hamza Rabia to bin Laden. From bin Laden's answer, we gather that Rabia reported to bin Laden on the activities of al-Qaida affiliates and cells in East and South Africa, Indonesia, and the Philippines. He displayed the most intimate knowledge about al-Qaida cells in East and South Africa that were part of al-Qaida's and Egyptian Islamic Jihad's old networks there going back to al-Qaida's revolutionary activities in Sudan and Somalia in the early 1990s. If we look at a biography of Hamza Rabia published in 2006, we find that he fought in Afghanistan in the 1989 Battle of Jalalabad, and that he was a member of Ayman al-Zawahiri's Egyptian Islamic Jihad (EIJ) from the late 1980s and a close associate of Zawahiri, being responsible for his personal security. He spent time in Yemen in the early 1990s, like many EIJ members at that time, and moved to Afghanistan sometime after Taliban came to power, where he continued to work for Zawahiri.[14]

In the letter Rabia sent to bin Laden in 2003 or early 2004, he wrote a detailed report about the activities of al-Qaida's African network, run by two individuals nicknamed "Zul" and "Dosari," who were active on the African East Coast including in Sudan and Kenya. Rabia reported that they had carried out a twin terrorist attack in Mombasa on November 28, 2002: A car bomb against the Israeli-owned Paradise Hotel, killing thirteen including three Israelis, and a failed attack with surface-to-air missiles on an Israeli charter plane taking off from Mombasa airport. Rabia's intimate familiarity with these attacks suggests he was running the operation in cooperation with KSM before the latter's capture. In addition, we gather from bin Laden's reply that Rabia in 2003–4 was in communication with the Indonesian group Jemaah Islamiyah, and with the Abu Sayyaf guerrilla in the Philippines, groups that were previously part of KSM's "portfolio." So, while there is not much evidence linking Hamza Rabia directly (and physically) to working with KSM in Pakistan prior to KSM's arrest, one can assume, as a minimum, that Rabia from 2002 was the main link between Pakistan and al-Qaida's East Africa network, and that he and KSM had shared associates in al-Qaida. KSM was closer to bin Laden, while Rabia was presumably closer to Zawahiri owing to their historical relationship.

After KSM's arrest, we can assume that Rabia sought to rebuild al-Qaida's external operations capacity by relying to a greater extent on his EIJ-affiliated personal networks.[15] The Abbottabad documents suggest that Rabia in 2004 was at some point physically co-located with Ahmed Khalfan Ghailani who ran al-Qaida's document forgery office in Gujrat, Punjab in 2004; and with Abd al-Rahman al-Muhajir, al-Qaida's explosives expert, who was probably based in South Waziristan.[16] Both of these individuals were part of al-Qaida's East Africa network, and had played roles in the 1998 East African Embassy bombings.

Regarding Rabia's activities in Pakistan, we know from a US Senate Intelligence Committee report from 2014 that Rabia in the fall of 2003 set up a safe house in the Shkai valley in South Waziristan.[17] Hassan Ghul, a courier who was in the valley in the fall of 2003, stated that there was an "electronics course" at the house that fall, and he believed they were involved in planning an assassination attempt on Musharraf. This probably refers to an attempt that was executed in December 2003 by a Pakistani group named Jundallah, which was associated with students at Karachi University.[18]

In the winter of 2003–4, Rabia's group was associated with training anti-US Pakistani militants, and with the first known al-Qaida plot to specifically target the UK, involving an old associate of KSM, the Indian-born British Muslim, Dhiren Barot. According to the US Senate Intelligence Committee, Barot "met with al-Qaida leaders in Pakistan in early 2004 to discuss potential terrorist attacks against targets in the United Kingdom."[19] Specifically, he met with the al-Qaida explosives expert, al-Muhajir, in February and March 2004 to discuss bombs made out of gas tanks. These plans differed from the template of the 7/7 bombers and associated plots in 2005–6, which were based on the homemade explosive tri-acetone triperoxide (TATP). This is one of several indications that the London bombers came from a different network, as I will explain in more detail below.

This means that in the winter of 2003–4, Rabia and al-Qaida's office for External Operations started researching options for targeting Europe, and specifically the UK. This is not surprising, because the UK was regarded by bin Laden as an integrated part of the "Jewish-Crusader alliance," especially after

9/11, when the UK became the first ally to the United States in the War on Terror. On the other hand, the Dhiren Barot plot seems somewhat opportunistic. Barot was already part of the network around KSM, and it was likely he who took the initiative to propose an attack on the UK. Plots to target the UK did not really gain traction until mid-2004, when Rabia seems to have outsourced the activity to two young individuals with European backgrounds, Abu Ubaydah al-Masri and Rashid Rauf. But before that the Madrid train bombings happened.

The Madrid Attacks and al-Qaida's Reactions

While Hamza Rabia was rebuilding al-Qaida's external operations capacity in the fall of 2003, a group of militants in Spain had started planning an attack inside Spain.[20] This attack manifested as the Madrid train bombings on March 11, 2004. As many as 193 people were killed and more than 2,000 were injured when a series of bombs exploded almost simultaneously on four commuter trains going to Madrid between 7:37 and 7:40 am in the morning. Thirteen rucksack bombs were placed on the trains, of which ten exploded. The attacks took place three days before the general elections in Spain, and the Spanish authorities' incompetent handling of the event—when Spanish President Aznar's party insisted that the Basque separatist group *Euskadi Ta Askatasuna* (ETA) was responsible for the bombing—ultimately led them to lose the election. The Spanish Socialist Workers' Party (PSOE) came to power and announced they would deliver on their election promise to withdraw Spanish forces from the US-led coalition in Iraq. The event gathered enormous attention—besides being a devastating terrorist attack, it attracted interest among academics within terrorism studies, because the Madrid attack appeared to be a case of terrorism that "worked" to instantly achieve the terrorists' political goals.

Over the next few years, the debate became more nuanced. The investigations and subsequent court case against surviving Madrid cell members suggested that the attacks were a result of a local radicalization process with only vague ties to Pakistan. None of the attackers had traveled to Pakistan for training prior to the attack, and there were no traceable money transfers from al-Qaida to the attackers. The Madrid cell made their own bomb devices, based on an industrial explosive bought on the black market inside Spain. The bombers made their own statements and sent them to Spanish media. There was no coordination with al-Qaida's official media agency, al-Sahab. Unlike in the 7/7 case, al-Sahab did not publish any videotaped "testaments" by the attackers. All these factors make it hard to determine what, if any, role al-Qaida leaders in Pakistan had played in the attack. The attacks were carried out by a group of disaffected Muslims living in Spain, who by the time of fall 2003 had a number of independent reasons to carry out a terrorist attack against Spanish targets. If al-Qaida was involved it appears to have been in the capacity as "indirect inspirator" or at most, as "approving authority" for the plot rather than the main organizer and driver.

The Abbottabad documents do neither confirm nor deny that al-Qaida had a role in the attacks, but they contain hints about how Osama bin Laden reacted afterwards. Specifically, they confirm that bin Laden after Madrid ordered his external operations chief, Hamza Rabia, to pursue a strategy of hitting the weakest links of the US-led Iraq coalition in order to break apart the coalition. What the documents do not reveal is whether bin Laden had thought of this strategy before Madrid, or whether he was simply inspired by the chain of political events in Spain. There was certainly online literature published in 2003 talking about strategies for how the mujahidin should win the war in Iraq, including a document called "Jihadi Iraq ... Hopes and Risks" published in December 2003. This document specifically proposed a strategy to target Spain to break apart the US-led coalition in Iraq.[21] But as I shall argue, bin Laden's private communications to Hamza Rabia after the Madrid attacks suggest that he was an opportunist, rather than a strategic thinker with intimate knowledge of European politics. Most likely, bin Laden became directly inspired by the way the attacks had affected the election results in Spain. This caused him to put together a hurried strategy to try and replicate this result elsewhere, while at the same time retaining his focus on hitting the United States and attacking aviation and other economically damaging targets.

Bin Laden reacted to the Madrid attacks on two levels. In public, he offered a "truce" to European countries on April 15, 2004, a month after the attacks, giving them a three-month deadline to pull out of Iraq.[22] In private, bin Laden wrote a letter to Hamza Rabia, suggesting that Rabia should target countries with large popular resistance against the Iraq war, such as "Japan, Italy, Poland, and Australia." The reason is that such attacks "... will push the electing masses to oust the sitting regimes, and to elect new regimes that will pull their forces out from Iraq."[23] Later in the letter, he repeated this point and explicitly stated that " ... our goal is to weaken and to tear apart the international alliance occupying our countries," adding South Korea and Thailand to the list of countries that should be attacked. It is worth noting that bin Laden's discussion in this letter is not as strategically sophisticated as the "Jihadi Iraq ... Hopes and Risks" document. He lists a number of countries he believes has strong popular resistance against the Iraq war, but he does not differ or prioritize between them, unlike the author of "Iraqi jihad."[24]

Further outlining the new strategy, he tells Hamza Rabia that "… it is important to send positive messages to the countries that do not participate in the occupation, and the ones that started withdrawing its forces, by releasing the citizens of these countries, and by killing the citizens of the occupying countries." In a section on hijacking airplanes, he specifies to attack airplanes "inside America, or an American airplane going to America from a country which is part of the occupation in Iraq, and in clearer words, you should avoid hijacking a plane from France or Germany."[25]

He does not suggest targeting Spain at this stage, but he encourages attacks on less important coalition partners such as South Korea and Japan. It seems plausible that the letter was written around the time of, or in preparation for, the expiration of his "truce offer" with Europe on July 15, 2004.[26] He states in the letter that he would like Rabia to try and carry out attacks in connection with elections, and specifically mentions the upcoming elections in the UK in May [2005]. All in all, this suggests that the Madrid bombings in March 2004 served as a direct, inspirational event for how bin Laden thought about international terrorism in the spring of 2004. His "strategy" is fairly simple, as it rests on prioritizing the most important enemies and neutralizing or harassing less important enemies, for example, by entering into truce agreements with them. The topic of whether al-Qaida should enter into truces with less important enemies becomes a prominent topic in later Abbottabad correspondence from 2009–10, which will be further discussed in Chapter 7.

The letter makes clear that bin Laden's top priority remains the United States and attacks on aviation, as he states, "The reason why we are so concerned with the topic of planes, is that the attack on New York left a big scar in the mentality of the Western peoples in general, and also in their economy."[27] He goes on to list a number of suggestions for how to attack airplanes in the post-9/11 security environment, and also adds a section on how to attack railways in the United States. It thus appears as if bin Laden's strategic thinking is still the same as in 2001, and that his main priority is to stage follow-up attacks to 9/11. The attacks on the weak links of the US-led coalition in Iraq are treated as an additional activity, seemingly motivated by the fact that such attacks are perceived as easy to execute and yet, they can have a large political impact.

To expand on the above discussion, the Madrid attacks can be used as an example to illustrate how al-Qaida leaders interacted with the rather murky world of "online jihadism," which I discussed in Chapter 2 as a sprawling new enterprise in the early 2000s driven forward in part by al-Qaida's Saudi branch and its leader, Yusuf al-Ayeri. After 2001 there was a need to set a course for the jihadist movement's way forward, which included various online discussions about what enemies to prioritize. Some of these discussions were pasted into Word documents and transmitted to bin Laden, although we cannot be sure that he read them in real time or were influenced by them to any significant degree.

One of the topics in this debate was how to deal with secondary enemies of al-Qaida from the US-led coalition in Iraq. The Madrid bombings fed directly into this debate because it represented an attack on a secondary enemy as opposed to the primary enemy, the United States, the UK, and Israel. Based on his public and private statements in 2002–4, bin Laden was inclined to differ between various enemies, and to prioritize the most dangerous ones. This became especially clear in his reaction to the Madrid attacks, as I have outlined above. To capitalize on the fallout from Madrid, but without being side-tracked from the real battle, bin Laden designed a low-cost campaign that would harass less important members of the US-led Iraq coalition, while al-Qaida would still retain focus on the United States.

The same type of prioritization was also promoted by individuals from the Arabian Peninsula, such as the online persona "Hazim al-Madani," whose strategic writings from 2002 were found in bin Laden's house in Abbottabad.[28] In 2002, Hazim al-Madani wrote about who to target: "Concentrating on the enemy who is working against us (the triangle of global distress) and neutralizing the lackeys." Al-Madani's writings were sometimes re-posted and quoted by the official media channels of al-Qaida in Saudi Arabia, which suggests he was a trusted source. Some journalists have suggested that Hazim al-Madani is Sayf al-Adl, but this is hard to verify.[29]

There were more sophisticated "strategic studies" posted on jihadist forums online, including the above-mentioned document "Jihadi Iraq … Hopes and Risks," published by affiliates of al-Qaida in Saudi Arabia in December 2003.[30] The document talked about strategies for fighting the US invasion of Iraq, and it specifically recommended targeting Spain before the Spanish elections in order to influence the election result.[31] However, this strategy document seems less relevant for understanding the al-Qaida leadership's attitudes toward Europe. For bin Laden and other al-Qaida leaders, the debate was about whether to pragmatically offer "truce" to European countries versus the more principled attitude that all infidels should be attacked. This debate was repeated within al-Qaida in other settings, such as in the late 2000s when al-Qaida and its various "branches" in Yemen, Algeria, and elsewhere debated whether al-Qaida could enter temporary truces with local regimes in order to avoid opening too many "frontlines" in their war at the same time (more on this in Chapter 7).

Bin Laden's truce offer to Europe on April 15, 2004, can be seen as a natural outcome of his deeply held belief that al-Qaida must wage war on the real enemy of the Muslims, the United States, and Israel. However, the truce strategy was also promoted explicitly online, in the statements of responsibility issued by a shady, online entity called the "Abu Hafs al-Masri Brigades" on March 11 and 13, 2004, respectively. These statements were issued a whole month before bin Laden's official truce offer to Europe. The identity of the Abu Hafs al-Masri Brigades has never been confirmed. While posing as an official mouthpiece for al-Qaida, its writing style and manner of dissemination did not match al-Qaida's official publications, and it was therefore met with suspicion. According to the Spanish professor Fernando Reinares, some of the Abu Hafs al-Masri Brigades' statements originated from Iran, but this does not say much because Iran was host to a large and diverse cast of militants at the time, working within and without Iranian oversight. While one might speculate that the Brigade was a state-run intelligence operation, or the creation of Iran-based al-Qaida leaders such as Sayf al-Adl, it seems equally likely that it was a private initiative by al-Qaida-supporters or -associates in the Middle East who simply wanted to create attention and amplify al-Qaida's message.[32]

A collection of documents found in Abbottabad and attributed to the above-mentioned Hazim al-Madani allude to this possibility. They contain specific discussions, probably around 2002, about how to conduct online "psychological warfare" against the West, and suggest in particular a campaign to spread false messages online to exhaust the enemy's intelligence services.[33] This brainstorming is not so far off what the Abu Hafs al-Masri Brigades actually did in 2003–4, when they claimed real al-Qaida attacks alongside a number of false ones—including a massive power outage on the East Coast of the United States in 2003. There is not enough similarity to link the particular discussion about "psychological warfare" to the formation of the Abu Hafs al-Masri brigades, but the documents show that there were individuals in the online jihadist community who certainly were thinking along those lines.

As for al-Qaida's leaders, they did not seem to mind that the Abu Hafs al-Masri Brigades existed and claimed to be al-Qaida—after all, the Brigades' statements stayed in line with an overall al-Qaida narrative and served to amplify it. The Madrid attackers saw it differently. After the Abu Hafs al-Masri Brigades claimed responsibility for the Madrid bombings and offered a ceasefire in Europe, the Madrid bombers themselves—who were hiding in an apartment in Léganes immediately after the bombings—issued their own statement in which they annulled the ceasefire proposal and announced that their attacks against Spain would continue. We do not know if bin Laden was aware of this public exchange at the time. But a month later, bin Laden announced a detailed offer for a truce with Europe, which lined up with the Abu Hafs al-Masri Brigades' initial truce offer. In return, the Abu Hafs al-Masri Brigades issued a series of statements in June-July 2004, when the truce offer was about to expire, designed to amplify bin Laden's message.[34]

This exchange illustrates how there was an interplay between al-Qaida leaders and various online entities which served to amplify al-Qaida's message. The Abu Hafs al-Masri Brigades sought to create attention-grabbing messages and to increase the impact of bin Laden's statements, while bin Laden, in return, occasionally lined up with the Abu Hafs al-Masri Brigades' statements. This did not happen very often, so it might have been a coincidence.[35] In any case, the suspicions that the Abu Hafs al-Masri Brigades might be an impostor probably did not matter in this context as long as both served to amplify al-Qaida's common policy goals.

The End of Hamza Rabia's Period (2004–5)

To continue the story of Hamza Rabia and al-Qaida's external operations, the next major thing that happened after the Madrid attacks was that there was a serious crackdown in mid-2004 by Pakistani authorities on al-Qaida's activities in Pakistan. The most likely reason for this was that Rabia's activities were associated with training of Pakistani militants, including the "Jundullah" group which staged assassinations on high-ranking Pakistani leaders, including two assassination attempts on President Musharraf in December 2003, and an attempt on a high-ranking general in Karachi in early June 2004. In mid-2004, Pakistani authorities carried out a large crackdown on these networks, including an army operation against militants in South Waziristan, during which a militant leader, Nek Muhammad Wazir, was killed in a (presumably US) drone strike. This was actually the first drone strike on Pakistani soil to kill a high-ranking militant, and it is no coincidence that it was Nek Muhammad, as he was tied to supporting and hosting anti-Pakistan militants committed to fighting the United States and—more importantly as far as Pakistani authorities were concerned—assassinating the Pakistani president.[36]

From June to August 2004, Pakistani security forces also carried out a number of raids on al-Qaida-associated safe houses in Karachi, Gujrat, and other cities. One key arrest was that of a Pakistani individual named "Abu Talha al-Pakistani" aka "Sulayman," who, according to some sources, also had in his possession the "paperwork" for the Dhiren Barot plot in the UK.[37] His arrest led to a large crackdown on al-Qaida members in Pakistan over the following two months.[38] On July 24, 2004, Pakistani security forces raided al-Qaida's document forgery office in Gujrat, Punjab, and they arrested Ahmad Khalfan Ghailani, while Hamza Rabia narrowly escaped. On August 3, 2004, they arrested Dhiren Barot in the UK.

The importance of these arrests to al-Qaida was later confirmed by Abu Faraj in a letter to bin Laden in October 2004. He says that the arrested individuals included Musab Al-Balochi, a nephew of KSM, "Abu Talha al-Pakistani" and "Haytham," aka Ahmed Khalfan Ghailani.[39] Abu Faraj confirmed that Rabia only barely escaped from the Gujrat safe house prior to the raid and that after the raid on the Documents office, many secrets were discovered and "his work half-stopped." In the same letter, Abu Faraj proposed to move al-Qaida's external operations office to Iraq, and on December 7, 2004, bin Laden approved the request, but asked Rabia to coordinate the move with Abu Mus'ab al-Zarqawi, who had recently joined al-Qaida.[40] We do not have any further trace of this communication, but one can assume that in practice, the move was made difficult by the security situation in Iraq, including the Second Battle for Fallujah in November 2004, which led to a dispersal of al-Qaida in Iraq. We know for sure that Hamza Rabia never made it to Iraq, but continued to be based in Waziristan where his family also lived, and at the start of December 2005, Rabia was killed in a drone strike in a village in North Waziristan. The other senior member of Rabia's team, the explosives expert al-Muhajir (real name Muhsin Musa Matwalli Atwah b. 1964) was killed in North Waziristan about four months after that, in April 2006. Al-Muhajir's passing marked a generational shift in al-Qaida's External Operations branch, because he was the last of the members who had been directly involved in al-Qaida's East African operation in 1998.

External Operations Led by "Haji" and Rashid Rauf (mid-2004–6)

At the time of Rabia's and al-Muhajir's death, another team has already taken over part of the External Operations activities. The Abbottabad documents in 2009 confirm the existence of this team, referred to as "the team of Abdul Hameed," and they also confirm that Abdul Hameed is an alias for Abu Ubaydah al-Masri. This team started working around mid-2004, at the same time as Hamza Rabia's activities were severely disrupted by Pakistani counterterrorism operations. We can only guess how they started, but one hypothesis is that when Rabia was facing pressure in South Waziristan and in the Pakistani cities, he might have outsourced some activity to militants active in a different tribal region—the Bajaur are in NWFP, home to a number of Egyptian and other Arab militants, probably including Ayman al-Zawahiri himself. One Abbottabad letter states that "Abu Ubaydah" is a field commander for al-Qaida in this region in 2004, which might be the same as "Abu Ubaydah al-Masri," who took over External Operations later. Furthermore, in December 2004, bin Laden instructed Abu Faraj to take the oath of allegiance from Abu Ubaydah, "if he hasn't done so already." Another hint can be found in the bin Laden letter to Hamza Rabia, which was sent around the same time, where he states (in a paragraph that seems to be added between July and December 2004):

> I confirm what you mentioned in your letter, that those who work together with us, from other groups, in special operations, should cut their ties with their organizations, as a minimum until the agreed work (with us) has ended.[41]

The term 'special operations (*'amal khass*)' is used by al-Qaida to refer to international terrorist attacks abroad. Together, the sources suggest that Rabia in mid-2004 outsourced some "special work" to Abu Ubaydah, and that bin Laden, in return, wanted to make sure that Abu Ubaydah had sworn an oath of allegiance to al-Qaida.

This interpretation makes sense when we consider the after-action reports written by Rashid Rauf in 2008 and smuggled to Germany with some al-Qaida recruits in 2010 who were subsequently arrested.[42] In these reports, Rauf describes the planning of three terrorist plots in the UK in 2005 and 2006, namely the 7/7 London bombings, the 21/7 failed London bombings, and the so-called "Transatlantic plot" to target commercial airliners over the Atlantic, which was thwarted in August 2006. He describes the plots as organized by himself and "Haji," with Haji being a senior al-Qaida member based in a tribal area of Pakistan. These reports describe Haji as "an Egyptian who lived most of his life in Europe," and who was involved with planning plots against the UK from mid-2004 until Rauf's arrest in August 2006. It is likely that "Haji" and Abu Ubaydah al-Masri are the same person.

According to Rauf's description, his and Haji's plotting against the UK were not visibly affected by the many afflictions that harmed al-Qaida's external operations office in the 2004–6 period. Rauf said that Haji started training the first UK operative in mid-2004, at the same time as the major Pakistani security crackdown in June-August 2004 on KSM's Pakistani network in Karachi and al-Qaida's documents office in Gujrat, Pakistan, where Rabia narrowly escaped and had to go into hiding. Rauf's account made no mention of, and was seemingly unaffected by, the killing of Hamza Rabia on December 1, 2004. Rauf's account was also unaffected by the killing of al-Muhajir in April 2006, which seems to confirm there was no overlap between al-Muhajir and the "liquid bombs plot" in 2006. According to Rauf, he and Haji started developing the liquid bombs after April 1, 2006, and they continued until May 22, when one of the transatlantic plotters returned to Pakistan and they could train him on the bomb. In other words, their research on liquid bombs ran independently of al-Muhajir, who was killed on April 13, 2006.

Rashid Rauf was a British-Pakistani citizen who went to Pakistan in 2002 and joined Harakat ul-Mujahidin (HuM). HuM was originally a Pakistani militant group fighting in Kashmir, but after the US-led invasion of Afghanistan, the group was split into several factions. A majority of the group wanted to continue fighting India in Kashmir, an effort supported by the Pakistani state. However, some splinter factions wanted to fight jihad against the United States in Afghanistan, and/or fight against the Pakistani regime who had supported the US-led invasion of Afghanistan. Rashid Rauf was said to have joined one such splinter faction, called Khuddam al-Furqan, and from here he came into contact with Haji and al-Qaida. It is not clear where Haji and Rauf were geographically located, but there are some indications that they were tied to Bajaur, a staging area for militants fighting in Kunar, Afghanistan. Bajaur was also where Ayman al-Zawahiri was probably located for most of the decade following his escape from Afghanistan in 2001.

Another al-Qaida connection, in case of the London bombings, was that Rauf videotaped two "martyr's testaments" by two of the bombers before they left Pakistan, and these clips were later included in two Al-Sahab propaganda videos. Thus, one gets the impression that the three above-mentioned plots were coordinated with al-Qaida, but compartmentalized from al-Qaida's other external operations activities.

The story of the 7/7 and 21/7 bombings is now well-known, after Rauf's after-action report was found in Germany. What is worth adding here is that the planning of the 7/7 bombings started independently of bin Laden's communications with Hamza Rabia about attacking the "weakest links" in the US-led coalition in Iraq. Two of the 7/7 bombers, Siddique Khan and Tanweer, arrived in Pakistan around November 20, 2004. They wanted to fight in Afghanistan, but "Haji" convinced them to attack in the UK, and this whole discussion was said by Rauf to have happened before bin Laden's letter to Hamza Rabia was sent around December 9, 2004. The 7/7 bombers received bomb training by an unknown individual named "Marwan al-Suri" who mastered a signature bomb-making method that appeared in several al-Qaida plots in Europe, namely, making homemade explosives using TATP as the main charge (rather than as detonator). A separate group, the 21/7 bombers, received training by another individual in a separate location a bit later, as Marwan al-Suri was not available at that time, but they were trained to make the same type of device.[43]

The Attempt to Move al-Qaida's External Operations to Iraq (2004)

To sum up the above discussion, after the death of Hamza Rabia in December 2005, there were two different activities in al-Qaida related to international terrorism. The first was an ongoing and separate activity to train operatives to attack the UK, primarily with home-made bombs made of TATP. This activity was run by Haji and Rauf. We can assume Haji is Abu Ubaydah al-Masri, as suggested by some Western intelligence agencies as well as by the Abbottabad documents. In 2009, Abu Ubaydah al-Masri was described in internal communications to bin Laden as "an Egyptian who lived most of his life in Europe," which was the same phrase used by Rashid Rauf to describe Haji.[44] Rauf's report, which is written between December 2007 and August 2008, also makes it clear that Haji had died by the time he wrote his report, which corresponds roughly to information saying Abu Ubaydah died of hepatitis in December 2007 or January 2008.[45]

The second activity was that associated with Hamza Rabia in late 2004, which was to move al-Qaida's external operations activities to Iraq. After the death of Rabia in December 2005, this activity was partly continued by a Libyan al-Qaida member named Atiyah Abd al-Rahman (aka Atiyatullah al-Libi). But due to a deteriorating security situation, in early 2006 Atiyah suggested that instead of trying to send al-Qaida personnel to Iraq, al-Qaida instead should "consult" Zarqawi on how to carry out international terrorist attacks with his own resources.[46] Developments inside Iraq may have contributed to the decision. We know that Zarqawi by now had started carrying out international terrorist operations on his own, most infamously the Amman hotel bombings in Jordan on November 9, 2005, killing fifty-seven people. A majority of the victims were Muslims, including a number of Palestinians attending a wedding reception. Al-Qaida leaders were annoyed at this attack, which created negative publicity for al-Qaida. In December 2005, Atiyah sent Zarqawi a letter asking him to stop carrying out international terrorist attacks without first consulting al-Qaida's senior leadership:

> Concerning foreign activities, my brother, that is to say, outside of the Iraq arena, I would advise you not to expand that way until you have reviewed it with the brothers, and their collusion in such a thing. This is the opinion of the brothers here. They have some ideas and conceptions that they want to convey to you about this topic. They want to make arrangements with you regarding it. If only you could do your utmost to forge quick lines of communication with them to coordinate on it. Strive, may God bless you, to avoid repeating the mistake of lack of precision in execution, like what happened in Jordan.[47]

In January 2006, bin Laden and Atiyah corresponded further about this topic, and Atiyah said to bin Laden, "there is still nothing, as you are well aware," but asked UBL to write down ideas that he could transfer to Zarqawi.[48] Atiyah's words that there is still "nothing" from Zarqawi may refer to the fact that Zarqawi had not yet sent a delegation to al-Qaida in Pakistan to coordinate (and possibly get training on) external operations work. Al-Qaida attempted later to transfer external operations work to other "affiliates" abroad (more on this in Chapter 6), so their discussions with Zarqawi starting in the second half of 2004 were not unique; they were simply a result of al-Qaida External Operations branch being under severe pressure inside Pakistan.

The End of Abu Ubaydah and Rashid Rauf's Activities (2006–7)

While al-Qaida's effort to transfer external operations to Iraq came to nothing, the second effort by al-Qaida—to target the UK—came somewhat closer to staging a spectacular follow-up attack to the 7/7 London bombings, which was also in line with bin Laden's expressed wish in 2004 to target aviation. Throughout the fall of 2005, Abu Ubaydah and Rashid Rauf had continued their efforts to target the UK with homemade peroxide-based explosives, but the effort was slow-going. In spring 2006, the plots became more ambitious and innovative, which appears to have been a result of adaptation to increased security measures in the UK.

We do not know if there were any specific orders from the al-Qaida leadership at this stage. Bin Laden wrote much later, in 2009, that he had avoided getting directly involved in external operations for many years owing to operational security concerns.

Abu Ubayda and Rauf had already met some of the transatlantic plotters back in the winter of 2004–5, and may already have talked to them about an attack in the UK.[49] However, the plot was not very specific until about early 2006, when the plotters, back in the UK, started discussing targets and conducting research on how to buy explosives precursors. In the spring of 2006, Haji and Rashid Rauf managed to design an explosive that could be smuggled onboard planes, and the plot was now changed to target transatlantic airliners. They designed the "liquid explosive" device during April-May 2006, and the leader of the transatlantic plot, Ali, returned to Pakistan in mid-May 2006 to receive training on the new device.[50] This plot was stopped in August 2006, when Rashid Rauf was arrested in Pakistan, probably as a result of a tip-off from US intelligence.

After Rauf was arrested, Abu Ubaydah al-Masri seems to have continued his activity as a mid-level al-Qaida commander in Pakistan, but as far as we know, he did not manage to stage any more international terrorist attacks against the West. There are few references to Abu Ubaydah al-Masri in Abbottabad documents in 2006–7. The only reference is in letters from Atiyah, where he asks Abu Ubaydah to assist him in communicating with groups in the Levant and with Zarqawi in Iraq.[51]

Based on limited sources, it seems there was very low activity in al-Qaida's external operations branch in 2007, which may have had several reasons: Al-Qaida's main focus in its external work in this period was not international terrorism per se, but to try and control an escalating crisis in the jihadist movement in Iraq, where al-Qaida was directly involved through its Iraqi branch, which was increasingly becoming ostracized by the rest of the jihadi world. Atiyah was traveling (perhaps waiting in Iran or Baluchistan), trying to reach Iraq at this stage, and was busy solving the Iraq crisis. Furthermore, Abu Ubaydah's health might have started to deteriorate in 2007, as he is said to have died of hepatitis in late 2007 or early 2008. But even if he was healthy, Abu Ubaydah probably could not have recruited UK operatives on his own. For this, he needed someone who could move about Pakistan seamlessly and who knew the UK-based networks well—in other words, someone like the UK-Pakistani citizen Rashid Rauf. Finally, the crackdown on the "transatlantic plotters" in August 2006 was probably in itself a disruptive activity, forcing the remaining network into hiding in Pakistan, like the Pakistani security forces' crackdown on Rabia's network in mid-2004. Thus, several conflating factors led to a lull in external operations activities in 2007, and the activity did not pick up again until early 2008, when Rauf was back in the tribal areas after escaping from a Pakistani jail. This next stage of al-Qaida's External Operations will be examined further in Chapter 6.

Summary

In this chapter, I argued that bin Laden drew inspiration from the Madrid attacks in 2004 by adopting a strategy of low-cost attacks against weak links of the Iraq coalition, while retaining focus on the "heads of disbelief," the United States and Israel. But this initiative failed before it had been implemented, because al-Qaida's external operations office in Pakistan took a major hit right around the same time, in the summer of 2004, by Pakistani security services, and never truly recovered. As a direct consequence of this hit, al-Qaida started thinking about moving external operations activities to Iraq.

This means that al-Qaida tried to move external operations activity to its branches abroad many years before al-Qaida on the Arabian Peninsula (AQAP) started targeting the United States in 2009. In other words, al-Qaida's decision to move this activity abroad was not a direct result of the intensified drone campaign against al-Qaida from 2008, but rather a result of Pakistani counter-terrorism operations against al-Qaida in mid-2004. Pakistan had a history of carrying out security crackdowns on unwanted Arabs on their territory. The country had done the same in the early 1990s, in the aftermath of the Afghan-Soviet war, so this was not a new thing. Al-Qaida could have been more careful in the way they operated inside Pakistan, but the group was perhaps not strong or coherent enough to design a thoughtful strategy at this stage. Ultimately, al-Qaida itself was partly to blame for its own predicament because the group had started cooperating with anti-Pakistan terrorist groups, which was a red line for Pakistani military establishment.

The external operations activity that led to the most visible results for al-Qaida was the London bombings in 2005, which were tied to the effort by Rashid Rauf and "Haji" to attack the UK. While we cannot know for sure, there are indications that these plots were sanctioned at the highest level in al-Qaida, maybe not by bin Laden personally, but probably by Zawahiri, who had equal authority within al-Qaida as bin Laden. At the same time, the central role of Rauf in these plots suggests that they were equally driven by a hatred by the UK and opportunities created by access to a large pool of British-Pakistan recruits, who came to Pakistan primarily to fight in the jihad in Afghanistan.

Assuming that these plots were compartmentalized and independently driven, it opens up for several interpretations of what exactly "drove" al-Qaida to attack Europe at this stage. The plots against the UK were in line with bin Laden and KSM's intentions after 9/11, which was to carry out as many international terrorist attacks against the "Jewish-Crusader alliance" as possible. Both bin Laden and KSM generally included the UK in their definition of the Jewish-Crusader alliance after 9/11, because the UK was the first and most important ally of the United States in the War on Terror. But the UK-based plots were also driven by the radical Islamist networks within the UK, in combination with exiled UK radicals such as Rashid Rauf in Pakistan, who had access to resources needed to organize terrorist attacks at home. Al-Qaida had not yet adopted a fully de-centralized method of attacking Europe. This only happened in 2008–9 when al-Qaida lacked resources to carry out top-down organized terrorist attacks, as will be further discussed in Chapter 6. In 2004, it seems clear that al-Qaida had no unified strategy for what targets to prioritize, which in the end led to the demise of al-Qaida's "old generation" of external operations operatives. This was because the same individuals that were responsible for international terrorist attacks were also involved in supporting Pakistani networks that wanted to assassinate high-ranking Pakistani generals including President Musharraf.

4

Al-Qaida in Iraq

... we must strive to transfer the battlefield to the heart of the Islamic world ... And in this regard, these two steadfast fortresses [in Afghanistan and Chechnya] may not help us much, due to many circumstances, enormous pressure, and apparent weakness.[1]

—Ayman al-Zawahiri, July 2001

In July 2001, Ayman al-Zawahiri finalized the first draft of his 173-page autobiography, *Knights under the Prophet's banner.* At the end of the book, in a section musing about the future for the jihadist movement, he wrote presciently about the role of Afghanistan and Chechnya. While praising them as "fortresses of Islam," he also pointed out their weakness and said al-Qaida must transfer the battlefield to the Middle East, to avoid "exposing them to pressure and strikes."[2] In October 2001, Zawahiri's worst-case scenario came true when the United States invaded Afghanistan and toppled the Taliban.

While the War on Terror was initially devastating for al-Qaida in Afghanistan, the US-led invasion of Iraq in 2003 offered Zawahiri a golden opportunity to fulfill his vision of a battlefield "in the heart of the Islamic world." Zawahiri elaborated elsewhere in his autobiography what he meant: "The plan (*al-khitta*) of the jihadist movement must be based on controlling a spot of land in the heart of the Muslim world, where it can establish an Islamic state, and be able to protect it, and from where it can wage its battle to restore the Rightly-Guided Caliphate on the path of the Prophet."[3] His words again seemed prescient when al-Qaida's Iraqi affiliate in 2006 declared the establishment of "The Islamic State in Iraq" in 2006, and eight years later, after conquering large parts of Iraq and Syria, they upgraded it to a "caliphate." But by then, the group had broken all ties with Zawahiri and answered only to their own leader, the self-declared Caliph Abu Bakr al-Baghdadi.

The above quotes illustrate that parts of al-Qaida wanted to establish an Islamic state in the Muslim world which could be used as a "fortress" from which to "spread Islam." It is not surprising that al-Qaida's senior leaders in 2004–8 were preoccupied with the Iraqi battlefield and sought to exploit it to achieve al-Qaida's own goals. But somewhere along the way, al-Qaida lost control of their local affiliate, which morphed into a powerful competitor that ultimately surpassed al-Qaida as leader of the global jihadist movement. This chapter tells the story of how al-Qaida sought to influence the Iraqi battlefield and how they ultimately failed, which in 2010 set the stage for a "new phase of correction and development" in al-Qaida, which will be further discussed in Chapter 7.[4] As we shall see, the main motivation for this new phase was to not repeat the mistakes of the al-Qaida branch in Iraq.

Overall, I argue that the Iraq war was a much more challenging conflict for al-Qaida to exploit than the war in Afghanistan. For one thing, the geographic distance from Pakistan to Iraq was much greater than from Pakistan to Afghanistan. Secondly, US signals intelligence capabilities were improving rapidly, making communications and travel between Pakistan and Iraq increasingly challenging. The other complicating factor was the many powerful actors involved, including state sponsors such as Iran and Saudi Arabia and local stakeholders such as former Iraqi Ba'athists, who all sought to impose their visions of order in Iraq in direct competition with al-Qaida's global jihadist agenda.[5] As a result of distance and lack of resources, al-Qaida's leaders in Pakistan were mostly relegated to playing a secondary role in the dramatic events that unfolded inside Iraq.

The main instigator of events in 2004–6 was the Jordanian leader Abu Musab al-Zarqawi, who in early 2004 offered to join his group, *al-Tawhid wal-Jihad*, to al-Qaida. Al-Qaida accepted Zarqawi's pledge of allegiance (*bay'a*) in October 2004 and in retrospect, one can say that this move changed al-Qaida forever, because as I shall argue in Chapter 7, it brought about al-Qaida's transformation from a hierarchical organization to a network of regional affiliates.[6] But this transformation was not the result of a conscious strategy on part of al-Qaida— it was rather an effect of the spectacular military and media campaign of Zarqawi's group in Iraq, which other jihadist groups in Algeria, Yemen, and Somalia later sought to emulate. In 2009, senior al-Qaida leaders had given up on trying to control events in Iraq and turned their attention to other pressing issues.

The Story of How al-Zarqawi Joined al-Qaida

The historical ties between the Jordanian militant, Ahmad Fadil Nazal al-Khalayla (aka Abu Musab al-Zarqawi), and the al-Qaida leadership are relatively well known, and go back to the Afghan-Soviet jihad of the 1980s and meetings in Kandahar, Afghanistan in 2000.[7] After the fall of the Taliban regime in late 2001, Zarqawi went first to Iran and then to Iraqi Kurdistan, where he was supported by the Kurdish group Ansar al-Islam.[8] From there, he joined the anti-US insurgency in Iraq, initially in cooperation with Ansar al-Islam. In April 2004, Zarqawi announced the formation of his own group, Monotheism and Jihad (*al-Tawhid wal-Jihad*).

After the US-led invasion of Iraq in March 2003, Zarqawi's first contact with the al-Qaida leadership in Pakistan may have started as early as mid-2003. Initially, this contact seemed to only include discussions about the exchange of weapons and other resources between the two conflict areas.[9] The first indication that discussion had moved from material cooperation, to forming an alliance based on the *bay'a* (Islamic oath of allegiance), is from early 2004. At this stage, Kurdish authorities arrested a courier named Hassan Ghul while he was on his way back to Waziristan after meeting with Zarqawi in Iraq. Ghul carried a letter from Zarqawi to al-Qaida which was later published by US authorities.[10] In the letter, Zarqawi reported on the current situation in Iraq and described his future "work plan," which included a controversial strategy to drag the Iraqi Shia Muslims into a sectarian conflict. He ended the letter with a direct request to join al-Qaida:

> If you agree with us on [this work plan], if you adopt it as a program and road, and if you are convinced of the idea of fighting the sects of apostasy, we will be your readied soldiers, working under your banner, complying with your orders, and indeed swearing allegiance to you publicly and in the news media …[11]

Zarqawi's initiative in mid-February 2004 came at a time when his group had started to assert itself as a powerful actor in the Iraqi insurgency. Although the group had not yet announced its presence and intentions in Iraq, it had carried out large high-profile terrorist attacks, such as the bombing of the UN Headquarters in Baghdad on August 19, 2003, which killed twenty-three including the UN's Special Representative, Sergio Vieira de Mello. The group was also accused of being behind the August 29, 2003, bombing of the Imam Ali Mosque in Baghdad, which killed the Shia Ayatollah Muhammad Bakir al-Hakim and more than eighty others.[12]

The question of whether Zarqawi from the start had a strategy of inciting a Shia-Sunni conflict in Iraq has received much attention and has been subject to some controversy.[13] The February 2004 letter from Zarqawi to al-Qaida suggests that Zarqawi indeed had such a strategy, and he signaled that he intended to continue this strategy after joining al-Qaida. Internal al-Qaida communications from bin Laden's Abbottabad compound supports this interpretation. They confirm that Zarqawi at the time of joining al-Qaida in October 2004 insisted on the need to attack Shias, and he specifically admitted to al-Qaida's leadership (via an envoy he sent to Pakistan in October 2004) that he was behind the attack on the Imam Ali mosque in Baghdad, in addition to other controversial attacks such as the "Ashura massacre," a series of suicide bombings killing over a hundred civilians in Shia neighborhoods in Karbala and Baghdad on March 2, 2004. Zarqawi defended these attacks to al-Qaida by insisting they were necessary to counter Iranian influence in Iraq and to "protect" Sunni Muslim civilians from arbitrary violence by the Shia-dominated Iraqi government. Zarqawi's envoy mentioned that the terrorist campaign against Shias was necessary to stop the oppression of the Iran-sponsored Badr Brigades in Iraq. Thus, the anti-Shia violence appears to have had both an ideological dimension and a political (anti-Iran) dimension from the start. It has been frequently alleged that Zarqawi's group was cooperating with former Saddam regime officials, and "former Ba'athists" were often blamed for these early attacks against Shias in Iraq.[14] While the question is too complex to be investigated here, it needs mention in order to illustrate the multifaceted, local context in which Zarqawi's group in Iraq operated.

Al-Qaida's leaders voiced some concerns about Zarqawi's expressed intentions to attack Shias in Iraq, but nevertheless allowed Zarqawi to join al-Qaida. The formal relationship was made public on October 17, 2004, with Zarqawi's group announcing their pledge of allegiance to Osama bin Laden:

> We bring good news of the *bay'a* of the Emir and soldiers of The Monotheism and Jihad Group to the Sheikh of the mujahidin, Osama bin Laden, to listen and obey, in hardship and ease, to jihad for the sake of God until there is no more *fitna* [civil strife] and the religion is for God alone.[15]

Further details about how the affiliate relationship was established can be found in internal documents from al-Qaida from October and December 2004. The documents describe how the bay'a process took place and bin Laden's private reactions to the bay'a in December 2004, two months after it had been announced. Bin Laden happened to be cut off from communications with the rest of al-Qaida around the time the bay'a was announced, so the process itself was handled by two other senior leaders, Abu Faraj (bin Laden's communications officer) and Ayman al-Zawahiri. The Abbottabad sources highlight the informal and improvised nature of the relationship between al-Qaida and Zarqawi's group.

On October 18, 2004, a day after Zarqawi's group announced they had joined al-Qaida, bin Laden's communications officer Abu Faraj wrote to bin Laden describing how the joining process had been coordinated and approved by Ayman al-Zawahiri, who was bin Laden's deputy and who had the authority to make decisions in bin Laden's absence. However, Abu Faraj admitted that he had bypassed parts of Zawahiri's directions and that he had made independent decisions when approving Zarqawi's pledge of allegiance. According to Abu Faraj,

> I sent Zarqawi's message [requesting to join al-Qaida] to the Doctor [Zawahiri], and he answered the following: 1) The bay'a should not be in the name of a person, but in the name of a group of mujahidin in Iraq. 2) That the *murtaddin* [the Iraqi government] should be fought at a later stage. 3) To avoid opening a front with the Shia at this stage. I discussed it with some of the brothers around me, like Hamza Rabia, and Abd al-Rahman al-Maghribi, and we disagree to point 1) and 3). I sent Abu Musab the answer. (…) Abu Mus'ab answered that he is happy with the answer, and he will announce the bay'a within 48 hours.[16]

In the final version of the bay'a, Zarqawi decided to announce the bay'a in the name of "the emir and the soldiers of Tawhid wal-Jihad" rather than in the name of Abu Musab al-Zarqawi, which seemed to at least partly take Zawahiri's advice into account, although in practice the event was framed in al-Qaida's propaganda as Zarqawi [personally] pledging allegiance to bin Laden.[17] More importantly, one can read between the lines in Abu Faraj's letter that Zarqawi at this stage received at least a tacit permission to target Shia Muslims in Iraq, if the local context of the war made such tactics necessary. One can also discern from this and other Abbottabad letters that al-Qaida's senior leaders were divided in their views on the necessity of attacking the Shia, but that al-Qaida at this time did not practice a system of strict command-and-control, preferring instead to style their instructions to Zarqawi as "advise." In other words, al-Qaida at this stage had not established formal procedures for how to deal with affiliated groups such as Zarqawi's, especially not how to sanction them should they become disobedient. There was also no consensus in al-Qaida on how a bay'a should be formulated and interpreted. This ambiguity later became an issue when al-Qaida publicly disowned al-Qaida in Iraq (now called the Islamic State, or ISIS) in 2014.

While Zarqawi was negotiating to join al-Qaida in 2004, the Iranians reached out to al-Qaida with a secret proposal for dialogue. This proposal is documented in the Abbottabad letters, in a handwritten note from someone named "Hafiz" to Abu al-Faraj.[18] Based on other Abbottabad correspondence, it appears that "Hafiz" is an al-Qaida intermediary from probably Karachi, who was contacted by an intermediary from the Iranian authorities.[19] Hafiz reports [my interpretation of code words in brackets]:

> Also, the Iranians are very interested in working with someone from the chief [bin Laden]'s side, not just on the subject of the sick people [al-Qaida members imprisoned in Iran]. The Iranians' first priority is the situation in Iraq. Thus, they believe the brothers there, specifically al-Azraq [al-Zarqawi] and his group have a hand in the attacks on the Shi'a holy sites. Therefore, they want to meet with a delegate from the chief [bin Laden]'s side to discuss this matter openly; there is also the potential for cooperation.[20]

"Hafiz" continues by saying that the Iranians would like to receive a signed statement from bin Laden, "assuring them that the Shi'a holy sites will not be targeted by the brothers ... The letter should also say that what had happened was a result of planning over there, and the chief [bin Laden] and his associates are not pleased and had not agreed to targeting those sites."[21] It is unclear what the Iranians were willing to offer al-Qaida in return, but the intermediary assumed it to be "material support."

The letter indicates that the Iranians wanted to use bin Laden's authoritative status within the jihadist movement to influence Zarqawi's military operations on the ground in Iraq, and more specifically, to stop Zarqawi's attacks on Shia shrines. It can be noted that the letter was written before Zarqawi officially joined al-Qaida in October 2004. The announcement of Zarqawi's pledge of allegiance to al-Qaida received overall little attention, probably because most observers, in the West and in the Middle East, already took for granted that al-Zarqawi was part of al-Qaida.[22] The Iranians' outreach effort is unsurprising, given that Iran, and in particular its Revolutionary Guard, had styled itself as a protector of Shia shrines and had previously invested large sums in restoring the Shi'ite holy sites around Iraq.[23]

Osama bin Laden was lukewarm to the offer, as might be expected. Bin Laden's answer was that to start negotiations, the Iranians had to first release Abu Muhammad al-Masri, or Abu al-Khayr al-Masri, who were the two most high-ranking al-Qaida leaders in Iranian custody. This "should be a condition for starting a dialogue that should not be abandoned," he instructed to Abu al-Faraj.[24] The Abbottabad documents do not contain any indications that the dialogue with Iran moved forward in any significant way after that, and there are several reasons to believe that it stalled, owing to the arrest of two important intermediaries—"Hafiz" in 2004 and Abu al-Faraj in May 2005. The dialogue between al-Qaida and Iran picked up again in 2007, and achieved somewhat of a breakthrough in 2010–11, when Iran finally decided to release many of bin Laden's family members.[25]

Existing literature on the al-Qaida-Iran relationship has emphasized bin Laden's deep distrust of the Iranian regime and also argued convincingly that there was no direct cooperation between the two countries on the operational level, although there was some level of indirect communication—as the above-quoted letter illustrates.[26] This is also my impression from reading the Abbottabad documents, noting that the documents only cover the period until April 2011. I would perhaps add here that prior to bin Laden's death, the al-Qaida leaders in Pakistan were far from united in their views on how al-Qaida should relate to Iran. This is exemplified in Chapter 6, when there was an internal discussion in al-Qaida about moving part of al-Qaida's External Operations cell to Iran—a move which bin Laden was categorically against, but which several of the other al-Qaida leaders supported.

Al-Qaida's Criticism of Zarqawi

In 2005, there were several disruptions in the communications between Zarqawi and al-Qaida's senior leadership in Pakistan. Part of the disruption was presumably caused by the arrest by Pakistani authorities of Abu al-Faraj, bin Laden's communications officer, in May 2005. Additionally, US authorities managed to intercept a letter from Zawahiri to Zarqawi, dated July 9, 2005, before the letter reached Zarqawi.[27] There were some doubts regarding this letter's authenticity, but a senior al-Qaida leader later confirmed in private communications to Zarqawi that the letter was authentic.[28]

The Zawahiri letter is the first publicly known criticism of Zarqawi coming from al-Qaida's senior leadership, after the former re-named his group "Al-Qaida in the Land of the Two Rivers" (hereafter al-Qaida in Iraq, or AQI) in October 2004. In the letter, Zawahiri stressed the importance of having a long-term plan for Iraq, which requires that Zarqawi must connect with the Iraqi masses. Zawahiri's letter includes the following advice: First, he says, we must set up an organization that can rule Iraq after the Americans leave.

This organization must represent the people of Iraq. "We must not repeat the mistake of the Taliban," who only represented Kandahar. Second, "we must strive for the unity of the mujahidin." Zawahiri asks Zarqawi to inform him of the details of other groups in order to better understand the militant landscape in Iraq. Third, he advises Zarqawi to not criticize Iraqi Ulama, but rather to include them and benefit from them, "... even if they are Ash'ari or Maturidi ... We must not repeat the mistakes of Jamil al-Rahman," who "neglected realities on the ground," he wrote. Jamil al-Rahman was a Salafi militant who declared an Islamic Emirate in the Kunar province of Afghanistan in the 1990s, but the "Emirate" was soon crushed by a local militant faction belonging to Gulbuddin Hekmatyar, and Jamil al-Rahman was assassinated.[29] Fourth, he tells Zarqawi to avoid attacks on the Shia, especially their mosques, because it will cause al-Qaida to lose popular support. Fifth, he tells Zarqawi to avoid "scenes of slaughter" in his propaganda, referring to a series of brutal propaganda videos showing beheadings of hostages issued by Zarqawi's group in 2004. Sixth, he asks an open question about whether the Iraqi jihad can be led by a non-Iraqi (Zarqawi is a Jordanian national).

Around the same time as Zawahiri's letter to Zarqawi was intercepted, another al-Qaida member, the Libyan Jamal Ibrahim Ashtiwi al-Misrati (aka Atiyah Abd al-Rahman, Atiyat Allah), managed to establish contact with Zarqawi's group. Initially, the contact was established via jihadi internet forums. Atiyah rose to fame on these forums in mid-2005, when Zarqawi publicly commented on a post Atiyah had written. Atiyah had written a critical response to an al-Qaida in Iraq (AQI) communiqué commenting on the withdrawal of Italian forces from Iraq, announced on March 15, 2005.[30] Atiyah's criticism apparently angered some AQI supporters on the jihadi forums. However, seemingly to calm down matters, Zarqawi himself issued a response to Atiyah's post, entitled "leave it to Atiyat Allah, because he knows what he is talking about." In the post, Zarqawi praised "my big brother" Atiyah and lauded his scholarly credentials.[31]

The next thing we know happened is that Atiyah went on a trip to Waziristan to have meetings with al-Qaida members there in early December 2005. He met with a group of Egyptians and Libyans who included Abu al-Layth al-Libi, Abu Sahl al-Libi, [Khalid] Habib, and [Abd al-Rahman] al-Muhajir,[32] and after consulting with them, he wrote a letter of advice to Zarqawi.

One can assume, from the timeline of events, that Atiyah in late 2005 took over responsibility for al-Qaida's communications with Zarqawi. The relationship between al-Qaida and AQI had now entered a different stage compared to in 2003–4, where conversations between Zarqawi and Abd al-Hadi al-Iraqi in Waziristan had focused on exchange of military and material resources. From 2005, al-Qaida's relationship with AQI focused on "correcting" AQI's behavior and to deal with complaints from other groups and individuals about AQI's behavior within the Iraqi insurgency. Atiyah, who had spent three years in Mauritania studying Islamic jurisprudence, and who had worked as an intermediary between different armed groups during the Algerian Civil War, seems to have been a suitable candidate for communicating with Zarqawi at this stage, especially at a time when al-Qaida needed an intermediary whom Zarqawi respected and listened to.

Zarqawi carried out several provocative actions in the latter half of 2005 which probably alerted al-Qaida and highlighted the need for taking control over their affiliate. In a speech published on September 14, 2005, Zarqawi made three declarations: First, he declared "a total war against the Rafidite Shi'ites throughout Iraq, wherever they may be."[33] Second, he declared that "from now on, whoever is proven to belong to the Pagan [National] Guard, to the police, or to the army, or whoever is proven to be a Crusader collaborator or spy—he shall be killed."[34] Third, he threatened the Sunni tribes in Iraq: "We warn the tribes that any tribe, party, or association that has been proven to collaborate with the Crusaders and their apostate lackeys—by God, we will target them just like we target the Crusaders, we will eradicate them and disperse them to the winds."[35]

Another, provocative action was that Zarqawi sought to spread violence to neighboring countries. His group had already been connected to several plots abroad, including an alleged plot to explode a truck bomb that would spread poisonous gas in Jordan in April 2004, and a plot against the NATO summit in Turkey in June 2004. In a speech published on May 1, 2004, Zarqawi took responsibility for the plot in Jordan, although he denied the part about the poisonous gas.[36] But on November 9, 2005, Zarqawi's group carried out a coordinated suicide attack against three hotels in Amman, Jordan, which killed fifty-seven people, many of them Palestinians attending a wedding reception. The attack was badly executed and was carried out without coordination with the al-Qaida leadership in Pakistan.[37]

Thus, we can assume that al-Qaida in Pakistan held internal discussions which led to the letter written by Atiyah to Zarqawi and dated December 11, 2005.[38] It is not clear where al-Qaida leaders were based in December 2005, but it is likely that the main mid-level leadership that Atiyah met with was in North Waziristan.[39] It is also likely that Atiyah communicated with Sheikh Saeed at this stage and received specific instructions regarding what to tell Zarqawi.[40] It is unknown if bin

Laden was involved in the discussions, because there is a long gap in Abbottabad communications between December 2004 and August 2007.[41]

Atiyah's criticism of Zarqawi in December 2005 can be summarized in the following six points [paraphrased from Atiyah's letter]:

- First, you must take the advice of your senior leaders. Do not make a comprehensive decision without consulting with bin Laden and Zawahiri, and with other groups in Iraq, especially Ansar al-Sunnah. Examples of such issues: (1) announcing a war against the Shia, (2) expanding the war to neighboring countries, and (3) conducting "large-scale operations whose impact is great."

- Second, you should consult not only with al-Qaida leaders and Iraqi mujahidin groups, but also with Sunni scholars in Iraq in general, "even if they are religiously unorthodox at times, or even hypocritical …" [He does not mention any names here, but he does later on, see point 5].

- Third, please send your messengers to Waziristan, so they can consult with us. This is more important than sending brothers to bomb hotels in Amman.

- Fourth, strive to win over the people. Respect the religious scholars and shaykhs, be kind to them. Avoid killing any of them, "no matter what."

- Fifth, do not be zealous about the al-Qaida name, you must work with all the mujahidin brothers. Invite them to unite with you, or al-Qaida under Shaykh Usama. You need everyone, including: The Muslim Brothers, the Council of Muslim Ulama, and the distinguished men of the community, clans, and tribes. You can skip obvious traitors, such as Muhsin Abd al-Hamid [An Iraqi Kurd who served as the 42nd Prime Minister of Iraq], although "killing him is not appropriate now." But you need to get along with some of the people of Harith al-Dari, and the tribal leaders.

- Sixth, concerning foreign activities, I advise you to not expand it until you have reviewed it with us, and the brothers here, we have some ideas and conceptions. Do not repeat the mistake of the Amman hotels bombing, where there was a lack of precision in the execution.

The two letters sent from al-Qaida to Zarqawi in 2005 strongly suggest that al-Qaida's leaders were worried about the way things were going in Iraq and sought to actively influence Zarqawi's group.[42] But al-Qaida had difficulty communicating securely with Zarqawi, and Zarqawi himself was slow to send delegations to meet with al-Qaida in Pakistan (he promised to do so in early 2006, in response to Atiyah's December 2005 letter, but the delegation got delayed for unknown reasons). Therefore, al-Qaida decided to try and send their own representatives to Iraq. By April 2007, Atiyah revealed in internal communications with Ansar al-Sunnah that al-Qaida had tried to send at least three representatives to Iraq: two had been arrested, and the third one—a reference to Atiyah himself—had been prevented from going.[43] Al-Qaida's efforts at sending individuals to Iraq seem to have intensified after January 2006, when a delegation from the Kurdish group Ansar al-Sunnah visited al-Qaida in Waziristan.[44]

The Ansar al-Sunnah Delegation

In January 2006, a delegation from Ansar al-Sunnah (AAS) visited Waziristan and met with Sheikh Saeed. Abd al-Hadi al-Iraqi was also present in the meetings, and this seems to be the last, confirmed activity he participated in with al-Qaida in Waziristan before he left the area for Iraq (he was arrested with his family in Gaziantep, Turkey, on October 16, 2006).[45] The AAS delegation was comprised of Abu Dardah, who was the dominant speaker, and a certain Abu Muhammad, who had previously visited Waziristan in 2004. The delegation held several meetings with Sheikh Saeed and Abd al-Hadi, which were recorded onto at least fifteen audiotapes totaling almost ten hours. There was also a short four-minute reply from Zarqawi about a month later on February 27, 2006.

In their introduction, the AAS representatives talk about how their relationship started with Zarqawi in 2002. Abu Dardah explains that AAS had a camp in Kurdistan. Zarqawi came and visited them for four days, and then, "through the brothers, they went down into Iraq, and linked up with an organization in Iraq of Kurdish and Arab brothers in Mosul and Baghdad."[46] AAS formed a presence inside Iraq in Mosul, Kirkuk, and Baghdad, and this is when they changed their name to Ansar al-Sunnah Army.

The other AAS representative, Abu Muhammad, continues the story in Tape 3. He says he was in Baghdad at the time Zarqawi came in 2002.[47] Zarqawi's original intention was to open a jihadi front in the Levant. So he started gathering weapons and worked for a year, until the American invasion. He settled in Mosul for a while, and worked with AAS in Mosul for about three months [in 2003], and he did not announce the formation of his own group yet. Then, he disappeared [and re-appeared in the Battle for Fallujah in April 2004].

In Tape 6, entitled "Our differences with Abu Musab," Abu Dardah talks about the origins of the differences between AAS and Zarqawi: in the beginning, they hoped that Zarqawi would join hands with them, and this was before he formed the group Tawhid wal-Jihad.

> [Zarqawi] asked the brothers for help, and they helped him ... he asked them to teach him how to make vehicle-borne Improvised Explosive Devices (IEDs), and the brothers sent him a person who taught him to make vehicle-borne IEDs, and also, in the beginning, when the Jordanian Embassy bombing happened [in Baghdad, on 7 August 2003], he had asked for a brother from us, and these brothers, they went and blew up this embassy for them, and it was a suicide operation. In the beginning, it was like this. ... he would come, he knew us, and we knew him. We could not imagine that he would suddenly announce the Tawhid wal-Jihad group.[48]

In retrospect, Abu Dardah was able to rationalize why Zarqawi had announced the formation of al-Tawhid wal-Jihad. He knew Zawahiri did not agree with the AAS working method, because in October 2000, when they visited Afghanistan and met with al-Qaida and other groups, they had presented their slow and gradual approach [to revolution], and Zarqawi had disagreed with them. Here is how Abu Dardah described "the origin of the difference" between him and Zawahiri:

> [Zarqawi] believes that the Iraqi arena is a battlefield (*sahat ma'raka*) that comes with people and money and settling of scores with the Americans. And that he has no role in the matter of preparation, and building people [i.e. cadre], etc. He only gathered people, and sent them to battles, they either get martyred, or they win. If he wins, he wins, if they are killed, they are killed, and if he does not succeed in the battle, he moves to another area and fights [there].[49]

Abu Dardah says that in contrast to Zarqawi, the AAS method is to build up an entity (*kayyan*) in Iraq with support among the Sunni people. Abu Dardah's opinion seems closer to the opinion that Ayman al-Zawahiri expressed in the leaked letter from July 2005, minus the "international" part about spreading to other countries and liberating Jerusalem. Abu Dardah blames Zarqawi for not "providing any convincing answers" to why he had to form Al-Tawhid wal-Jihad in the first place. He says that the questions to Zarqawi increased after Zarqawi joined al-Qaida in October 2004. However, Zarqawi never gave a convincing answer; he would only say that his entity was approved by the "Shaykhs of the Arabian Peninsula."[50] It is not clear if he here refers to bin Laden, Yusuf al-Ayeri, or others. Abu Dardah claims that al-Tawhid wal-Jihad was originally founded based on a fatwa from Sheikh Yusuf al-Ayeri, the Saudi al-Qaida leader killed on June 2, 2003.[51] However, according to Truls Tønnessen, al-Tawhid wal-Jihad was formally announced on April 26, 2004, after the US withdrawal from the first battle for Fallujah.[52] It is not clear if Abu Dardah refers to historical correspondence between Zarqawi and al-Ayeri before the latter was killed in June 2003, or if he conflates Yusuf al-Ayeri with someone else. Zarqawi had many contacts among Shaykhs on the Arabian Peninsula through his religious advisor, Abu Anas al-Shami, who knew scholars such as Salman al-'Awda and Safar al-Hawali.[53]

Abu Dardah claims that after Zarqawi joined al-Qaida, the policy of AAS was to work within the new reality and to try and get closer to Zarqawi's group. AAS held several meetings with them, where senior figures Abdul Hamid and Abu Abdullah al-Shafi'i participated. He says it was hard to discuss with Abu Musab, so instead they tried to influence those around him such as Abu Anas al-Shami, but the latter was killed on September 16, 2004, and many of Abu Musab's staff were killed in the Abu Ghraib prison raid on April 2, 2005. After the prison raid, AAS says they continued the sessions with Zarqawi.

By now, Zarqawi and AQI have lost Fallujah, and the Iraqi insurgency has become increasingly polarized, owing to disagreements over the Iraqi elections in early 2005. One thing that annoyed AAS was that Zarqawi was recruiting Iraqis from other groups. He "offered them money and cars to come and fight with him."[54] Furthermore, Zarqawi commanded the Arab foreign fighters (*al-muhajirin*), many of whom were new to Iraq and had no experience fighting.

AAS says their policy was initially to not open a front with the Americans, but Zarqawi disagreed, and he opened the Fallujah front [in April 2004], after AAS specifically advised him not to do it. They also advised him against the second Fallujah battle, starting November 7, 2004. After the defeat at Fallujah in November 2004, AAS claimed that the "unity project" with Abu Musab continued. There was a last, private session between Abu Abdullah al-Shafi'i and Zarqawi. After that, there were sessions with others. Abu Abdullah wanted them to reach an agreement on a program (*manhaj*) or vision (*ru'ya*).[55]

Abu Dardah then jumps back to mid- or fall 2004, to talk about how Zarqawi's pledge to al-Qaida was another annoyance for AAS. Zarqawi announced to AAS in advance that he is pledging allegiance to Shaykh Osama, and that he would announce it after some time (*ba'd fatra*), and send the Sheikh a letter. The AAS Emir, Abu Abdullah al-Shafi'i, was very surprised and said to him, "You surprised me … we were supposed to consult with each other. We've had these meetings for 4–5 months, 1–2 meetings per month, to get closer, and then you throw this to the side and give me a new thing, and it's no longer my matter alone."[56] AAS interpreted the bay'a as a mere power play on part of Zarqawi. By attaching himself to al-Qaida's name, he could pressure the other groups in Iraq to join him, and if they refused to join, he could slander them, accusing them of being against Osama bin Laden.

On Tape 6, Abu Dardah talks about their specific problems with Zarqawi's group. His complaints can be divided into five topics: First, AQI entered battles that they had no chance of winning, like Fallujah, and others. Second, AQI targeted the Iraqi police, or police recruits, and tribes who often overlap with police, and this turned the tribes against them. Third, AQI targeted civilians on a large scale, which seems to have started after the Iraqi elections in early 2005. Fourth, AQI made extensive use of suicide bombings as a tactic, a practice that was also criticized in public by the highly influential Jordanian Salafi-jihadi scholar Abu Muhammad al-Maqdisi.[57] Fifth, AQI's policy of rejection toward the other Sunni groups. AAS believed one should talk with the other groups and treat them kindly, even the non-Salafi ones, such as the Islamic Party, the Association of Scholars, the National Dialogue Council, and the Sunni Endowment.

Abu Dardah goes on about other topics until Tape 16, which is about the proposed solutions. The tapes make it clear that AAS's problems with Zarqawi started already back in the spring of 2004, when Zarqawi announced al-Tawhid wal-Jihad without AAS's knowledge, and it continued after Zarqawi's bay'a to bin Laden in October 2004. Moreover, in late 2004 or in 2005, AQI started attacking AAS's local allies, such as the local police forces in Mosul.

Toward the end of the sessions with al-Qaida, Abu Dardah proposes three solutions:

1) The general solution is "change or reform (*taghyir aw islah*)" of the internal methodology (*al-manhaj al-dakhili*) and external policy (*al-siyyasa al-kharijiyya*) of AQI.[58]
2) Al-Qaida needs to send a person to Iraq to study the issue, and to study the reality. He needs to remain for several months. He needs to have Sharia and military competence, and he needs to take control over AQI and to initiate reforms.
3) Bin Laden must write a special letter to Ansar al-Sunnah Army, blessing the group and blessing the work and approach of the group.

In early 2006, a "few days before" January 29, 2006, Atiyah sent a letter to Sheikh Saeed, informing him that he had reconnected with Zarqawi, and that Zarqawi had sent several messages answering to Atiyah's December 11, 2005, letter and a more recent letter. Atiyah confirms in this correspondence that he has started planning to go to Iraq:

> Regarding the departure of this poor servant to their side, it is in the planning process. I ask God for assistance. I informed our brother [Zarqawi] about the issue, and he became very happy. We are coordinating now, so don't forget us in your prayers.[59]

After Sheikh Saeed received Atiyah's report, he sent two letters to Ansar al-Sunnah dated January 26 and 29, respectively. The first is a personal letter from Ayman al-Zawahiri to the AAS leader Abu Abdullah al-Shafi'i, written before the Ansar al-Sunnah delegation visited Waziristan. Zawahiri writes to the AAS Emir that "the Shaykh [bin Laden] has directed me to follow up on the case of unification with you." He continues, "do the brothers in the Ansar al-Sunnah Army agree, in principle, to unite with Jama'at Qa'idat al-Jihad," and he asks Ansar to send a representative to Pakistan to "complete" the matter. At the end of the letter, there is an addendum [probably added by Sheikh Saeed] saying that they understood from the Abu Dardah delegation that Ansar agrees to unity in principle, but that they first want "reform" (*islah*) of Al-Qaida in the Land of the Two Rivers. The letter indicates that Ayman al-Zawahiri was formally in charge of al-Qaida's dealings with Iraq, and especially with what would become al-Qaida's main "project" over the next few years, namely to forge unity between AAS and AQI.

The second is a letter from the "Special Committee of Qa'idat al-Jihad for following the affairs of the Mujahidin in Iraq," which is most likely a committee led by Sheikh Saeed, because the letter refers to the meeting with the Abu Dardah delegation. The letter states that "we have taken a blessed step toward reforming the situation (*islah al-wad'*) and toward reaching for the better, by sending an honorable brother and a virtuous shaykh, you know him very well." This sentence is probably a reference to Atiyah's planned travel to Iraq, given that Atiyah around the same time confirmed that Zarqawi had approved his travel to Iraq.[60] Atiyah's mission is not clear. The Abu Dardah delegation wanted someone to "take control" over AQI and "initiate reforms," while Zarqawi described it more like a fact-finding mission, as he wrote in one of his letters to Atiyah: "How I hope that you [Atiyah] will come so that I can inform you of the details of the work."[61]

After the January 2006 correspondence between Atiyah, Zarqawi, and Sheikh Saeed, Atiyah continued to communicate with Zarqawi, and on February 27, 2006, Zarqawi recorded a short reply to answer Abu Darda's accusations against him. The reply was ultimately found in bin Laden's house in Abbottabad, together with the other Iraq-related files from this period.[62] Zarqawi said the following:

> Abu Dardah is telling different things than what I told. There are two different stories, so who should you believe? Abu Dardah merely heard the news and transmitted them, but I lived through the details of the events. And when I disagree with him, that's in the events that I lived through, I was an eyewitness, but he only heard about it, and I think there is a big difference between the two. (…).[63]

Zarqawi does not provide any specific evidence to back up his version of the story, so it is hard to know which version is true (al-Qaida leaders in Pakistan presumably had the same problem—this is why al-Qaida tried hard in 2006–7 to send several "fact-finders" to Iraq to investigate, but they ultimately failed to reach Iraq). After this file, there is a gap in the chronology of Abbottabad documents and the next letter we have from Atiyah is from about a year later, in March 2007. In this letter, he confirms that Zarqawi in the end kept his word about sending a delegation to al-Qaida, and the delegation reached al-Qaida around April 2006.[64] We shall return to this correspondence shortly. First, several dramatic events took place in Iraq.

On June 7, 2006, Zarqawi was killed, and Abu Hamza al-Muhajir and Abu Omar al-Baghdadi took over leadership of al-Qaida in Iraq, now known as the Mujahideen Shura Council (*Majlis Shura al-Mujahidin*). The Mujahideen Shura Council was an umbrella organization established by Zarqawi in January 2006 which was dominated by al-Qaida in Iraq and included a number of smaller Sunni Iraqi insurgent groups. Abu Hamza al-Muhajir (aka Abu Ayyub al-Masri or Karim) was an Egyptian with historical ties to the senior al-Qaida leadership in Pakistan. Abu Omar al-Baghdadi was an Iraqi whose real name was Hamid Dawud Mohamed Khalil al-Zawi. He was a former police officer from the Anbar province in Iraq who joined the insurgency after 2003, and who later joined forces with Zarqawi's group. Bin Laden indicated in a speech that neither he nor the other senior al-Qaida leaders in Pakistan knew Abu Omar al-Baghdadi personally.[65] In Abbottabad communications, they mostly communicate directly with Abu Hamza al-Muhajir.

Bin Laden issued several speeches after Zarqawi's death, where he talked about the importance of fighting the Americans and of rejecting the Iraqi regime and the democratic system in Iraq. His message in these speeches is that whoever allies with the government, including the tribes in Iraq, must expect retaliation from the mujahidin. He thus seems to come out in defense of Abu Musab al-Zarqawi, defending him against slander that AQI kills innocent Iraqi civilians. He claims that Zarqawi had clear instructions to attack Americans, and that attacks on the Iraqi people, such as tribes and the like, was only because they allied with the enemies in the plot to kill the Iraqi Sunnis.[66] It is not clear if bin Laden had been informed yet of the Abu Dardah delegation's visit to Waziristan.

In October 2006 there was another seminal event, namely the announcement of the establishment of the Islamic State in Iraq (ISI). Ayman al-Zawahiri later confirmed in internal communications that AQI had decided on announcing an Islamic State in Iraq without consulting with al-Qaida beforehand.[67]

Relations between al-Qaida and the Islamic State in Iraq

The announcement of the Islamic State in Iraq provoked almost universal condemnation from leading Salafi scholars and from other Sunni Muslim insurgents in Iraq.[68] On April 4, 2007, the Kuwaiti Shaykh Hamid al-'Ali issued a fatwa concluding that ISI is not a true Islamic state, and he asked them to withdraw the declaration. On May 2, 2007, an umbrella organization called the "Jihad and Reform Front" (JRF) was established in Iraq, seemingly as a counterweight to al-Qaida in Iraq. The JRF was formed by Iraqi insurgent groups that refused to join the Islamic State, and had support from Qatar. Some of the core groups in JRF were the Islamic Army, the Mujahidin Army, and a breakaway faction of Ansar al-Sunnah led by Abu Wa'il and Muhammad al-Juburi.[69] ISI later, in a letter to al-Qaida written in April 2010, blamed the AAS for having known about the conspiracy to establish the JRF, but failing to warn ISI of its establishment. They also accused the AAS leader, Abu Abdallah al-Shafi'i, of being against negotiations with ISI and of being willing to support the JRF, had it not been for internal resistance in his group.[70]

But before these major public controversies, on March 15, 2007, Atiyah sent Sheikh Saeed a new batch of correspondence from an unknown place (Atiyah is currently trying to reach Iraq, but probably only managed to reach the Baluchistan province of Pakistan, or Iran). His correspondence covers four topics. The first topic is his recent correspondence with Ansar al-Sunnah, who is continuing their accusations and complaints against the ISI. Atiyah's advice at this stage is to continue communicating with them and advising them, but let us "not rush to accept any of the accusations and lawsuits … and many of them do not stand up to scrutiny." The second topic is about groups in Lebanon who want to become part of al-Qaida, while the third topic is his correspondence with a group called the Kurdistan Brigades, who have recently joined the Islamic State in Iraq. The fourth topic is Atiyah's latest correspondence with Abu Hamza al-Muhajir, who defends himself against Ansar al-Sunnah's accusations.[71]

Two weeks later, Atiyah again writes to Sheikh Saeed and gives him an update on the situation. This letter confirms that Sheikh Saeed previously asked Atiyah to write "letters of firm guidance" to Abu Hamza al-Muhajir and Abu Omar al-Baghdadi.[72] We do not know exactly what prompted this order from Sheikh Saeed, but one could guess that the establishment of the Islamic State in Iraq in October 2006, without al-Qaida's permission, played a role. Bin Laden at this stage had not yet reacted publicly to the establishment of ISI. His first message commenting on the internal divisions in the Iraqi insurgency was issued in October 2007, a whole year after ISI was announced.[73]

Atiyah says he is worried about the ISI now, that he "fears for their political mistakes," and that the latest sermon of Abu Omar al-Baghdadi contained "clear errors." He is referring to a speech by Abu Omar al-Baghdadi issued March 13, 2007, in which Abu Omar outlined the current policies of the ISI, including specific sharia prohibitions.[74] Atiyah's assessment of the speech is as follows:

> [Al-Baghdadi's latest speech indicates that] they are extremist, and it implies that they are deeply entrenched and in a hurry..!! And it alienates and lacks wisdom. I wrote to them myself and admonished them, and used strong words against them. I fear that if they continue in this manner and method, they will corrupt and alienate people, who could be won over by enemy after enemy. And they will give the enemies and opponents an opportunity to exploit [the people].[75]

Atiyah writes in the same letter that groups in Iraq have used chlorine gas in operations, and that he is skeptical of it and needs Sheikh Saeed's guidance. He refers to the chlorine gas attacks that started around October 2006 and continued through March 2007 that were publicly denied by the ISI:[76]

> I expressed to them [ISI] my opinion that such matters are dangerous and require centralization and the permission of the senior leadership, because they may be difficult to control and may harm people, and what may happen is distortion of our image, alienation of us, and so on … They have stopped doing it now, but it would be best if you—my brother Adnan [Sheikh Saeed]—would study this issue with your experts and giving us a clear constitution on it that we can tell our brothers about![77]

In April and May 2007, Osama bin Laden received various letters of criticism and warnings about the Islamic State in Iraq. A letter from the newly established Jihad and Reform Front dated May 22, 2007, asks bin Laden to disavow the ISI.[78] There is also another letter to bin Laden from an anonymous person, who appears to be an old acquaintance from the 1980s Afghan-Soviet war, telling him in a similar manner about the "mistakes" of the ISI and questioning whether bin Laden is informed of the reality in Iraq.[79]

Around mid-2007 (after March 28, but before August), there is a letter to Sheikh Saeed conveying more news from Atiyah.[80] Atiyah complains that he is alone in advising and correcting the ISI, and that he needs help from senior al-Qaida leaders. He believes there is a strong conspiracy in Iraq against ISI, and he is afraid that ISI might succumb to their enemies if they continue to make internal policy mistakes. But Atiyah also complains about Ansar al-Sunnah, that they keep making the same accusations, and that ISI has different versions of reality, and it is hard to know which one is true. Overall, Atiyah's report indicates that he is frustrated with both parties, but that he is willing to give ISI the benefit of doubt.

The next correspondence from Atiyah is by the end of July 2007. At this point he confirms that he is still trying to reach Iraq: "And regarding the travel of Mahmud (Atiyah) to his Tablighi uncle, the matter is very strange. Every time I organize and strive—either, the road is not good on our side, or I receive signs from there, saying the road is not good and the entry points …"[81] Around the same time or later, Abu Hamza al-Muhajir confirms in a letter to Atiyah that he wants him to come to Iraq and to work as a Sharia official for ISI:

> … I would like to stress that we are in dire need of you, and the matter is critical because we do not have anyone trustworthy who can assume this responsibility before God, i.e. the Sharia responsibility, and I hope that you will make an effort with all your strength [to travel] in this direction, and we are fully prepared for any suggestion you may have.[82]

Al-Muhajir seems to be hinting in this letter to an ongoing conflict with ISI's Sharia judge, Abu Sulayman al-Utaybi, who was publicly fired from his position at the end of August 2007.[83] Al-Utaybi reached Waziristan sometime in October or November 2007. As for Atiyah, he never reached Iraq, but returned to Waziristan around the same time, in October 2007. He later recorded his experiences on audiotape and sent them to bin Laden, but these audiotapes appear to have been removed from the Abbottabad collection.[84]

Bin Laden Gets Involved in the Iraq Issue

On August 17, 2007, Osama bin Laden reconnects with the rest of al-Qaida's senior leadership, including Sheikh Saeed, Atiyah, and Zawahiri, after being cut off from communications for many months. In his letters he refers to the need to respond to Hamid al-'Ali's statement denouncing ISI on April 4, 2007, and more generally, about the need to defend ISI in a public media campaign that should be led by Zawahiri. He also encloses at least five new audio messages, to be published during the fall of 2007, and two written documents for internal discussion within al-Qaida. One of them is called "*Bayyan al-iman* [Statement of Faith]," discussing theological issues, and the other is "*al-mashura lil-ikhwa fil-iraq* [Advice to the brothers in Iraq]."[85] Bin Laden's "Advice to the brothers in Iraq" was sent between Atiyah and Zawahiri, who both commented on the draft and sent it back to bin Laden. Zawahiri's reply, which was the most elaborate of the two, was written on October 18, 2007.[86] It is worth noting that until now, bin Laden has not commented publicly on the establishment of the Islamic State in Iraq. The topic is sensitive, because bin Laden has been criticized both publicly and privately for not commenting on ISI's establishment. The insurgent movement in Iraq had become polarized by increased infighting, so there is one group who wants bin Laden to endorse the ISI, and another group who wants him to denounce ISI and distance al-Qaida from it. His "Advice to the brothers in Iraq" can therefore be interpreted as his draft public reaction to the establishment of ISI that he now seeks to discuss with the rest of al-Qaida's senior leaders.

Bin Laden initially suggests taking a middle position. His advice, in short, is to form a council of *Ahl al-hall wal-aqd* (a representative council of Muslims; and a historical reference in Islam to the council that elects the Caliph), with representatives from all the existing mujahidin groups in Iraq, more specifically from their Shura councils. They will together elect a "reconciliatory Caliph." Meanwhile, he praises and welcomes the efforts of Abu Omar al-Baghdadi and ISI, but refuses to openly take their side, saying instead that "whoever joined them, joined them, and whoever abstained, abstained." And he also praises the unity efforts of other groups, which seems to be a reference to the establishment of the Jihad and Reconciliation front in May 2007 (this is certainly how Zawahiri interprets it, see below). He prefers talking about an "Islamic Emirate in Iraq" rather than a state, and refers to al-Baghdadi as "Emir," but not as "Emir al-Mu'minin [Leader of the Believers]"; the latter title would imply that al-Baghdadi is the superior authority over Muslims in Iraq. Bin Laden acknowledges that al-Baghdadi united with others to establish the Islamic State, but he also downplays the meaning of using the *dawla* [state] label, as he says, establishing a "state" does not have meaning in itself. The important thing is to gather the ranks of the Muslims under one banner, and this is an absolute duty of Muslims that comes before establishing a state. Bin Laden's statements are in line with his later policy to gently try to convince ISI to change their name from state to "Emirate," and to drop the "Emir al-Mu'minin" title, which is also in accordance with advice from Ansar al-Sunnah's negotiator to ISI in around mid-2007.[87]

In his draft statement, bin Laden does not single out any specific groups that al-Qaida should work with, or abstain from working with, in Iraq. He only stresses that all the mujahidin in Iraq should join the Council of *Ahl al-Hall wal-Aqd*, simply because doing so is in accordance with Islam's core tenets. Bin Laden's advice is in line with the speech he recorded to the people of Iraq around this same time, but the speech is even vaguer, only calling for "unity" but without mentioning the formation of a Council of Ahl al-Hall wal-'Aqd, and without mentioning any mujahidin groups by name.

In his internal reply sent a month later, Zawahiri disagrees fundamentally with bin Laden. He says that bin Laden seems to welcome the unity efforts of the Jihad and Reconciliation Front, which is inappropriate because the groups in that front are not Salafi in their approach. He points out that they did not make clear statements on the role of Sharia law in society, but rather, made such generalizations in their statements, "as if they were trying to attract other mujahidin groups to them, such as the Muslim Brotherhood."[88] He is therefore very skeptical of any words that praise them. He also reminds bin Laden that the *Dawla* (state) is a reality here and now, and therefore, it does not make sense to downplay it by saying it is reserved for a later stage.

This latter argument plays into Zawahiri's more fundamental disagreement with Laden's proposal. He says the proposal to form a council of *Ahl al-Hall wal-Aqd* is a dangerous idea, because the other groups will use it as an argument to call for the dissolution of the Islamic State. Zawahiri says that by calling for the formation of the council, bin Laden implies that ISI is merely one of several jihadi groups in Iraq—which is exactly what Hamid al-'Ali argued in April 2007, when he called for the dissolution of the Islamic State. Moreover, Zawahiri thinks that the groups in Iraq will not be able to agree on such a council and will instead enter into "an endless debate" about its size, composition, and so on.[89] Al-Qaida will thus have "lost twice": they will both be responsible for dissolving ISI, and for failing to achieve unity in Iraq.

Zawahiri's attitude is that the situation in Iraq is so polarized that al-Qaida cannot simply take a middle position, because this would be exploited by ISI's enemies in their fight against ISI. His attitude is summed up as follows:

What I see is that we must be very clear in our support for the state and our support for its leader, represented by Abu Omar al-Baghdadi, may God protect him. The establishment of the state has become a reality that cannot be reversed, with God's help. Our statements on this particular issue should be so clear, frank and precise that they cannot be interpreted or taken in any other light.[90]

Zawahiri then gives his analysis of how he understands the current reality in Iraq, further supporting his argument that al-Qaida must give clear support to ISI and to be careful of some of the other groups, in particular the Jihad and Reform Front. He says that the JRF and Iraqi Hamas are getting ready to negotiate with the Americans, to crush the ISI and take power in the Sunni areas of Iraq, allowing American troops to withdraw. Zawahiri ends his letter by quoting from bin Laden's private instructions to him to start a media campaign to defend the Islamic State in public. Zawahiri says that these quotes include clear and good advice, and should be the basis for all of al-Qaida's public speeches regarding Iraq. In other words, he thinks al-Qaida should clearly support the ISI, confirm its legitimacy, and encourage all the other groups in Iraq to unite with them.

In summary, bin Laden gives two messages to al-Qaida in August 2007 regarding the Iraq issue. On the surface, he wants al-Qaida to conduct a public media campaign to defend the Islamic State in Iraq against slander and conspiracies. In private, bin Laden seeks to control the behavior of ISI and to work actively to unite various Iraqi groups. He tells Sheikh Saeed to be strict with the ISI, give them firm guidance, and prevent bad behavior within their ranks. This last point is in line with the policy that was already started by Sheikh Saeed and Atiyah in March 2007.[91] In addition, he proposes that in order to achieve unity of rank in Iraq, the mujahidin groups there should form a representative Shura (*Shura ahl al-hall wal-aqd*), in emulation of how the Caliph was elected during the first Caliphates in Islam. This Shura would ultimately have the authority to elect a Caliph that everyone agrees on. Zawahiri strongly disagrees to this proposal, because he believes that it would be used by ISI's enemies to call for the dissolution of the Islamic State.

Despite the fact that Zawahiri believes defending ISI in public is the only way forward in Iraq, he agrees with bin Laden that al-Qaida needs to give frank and strict advice to the ISI leadership. Zawahiri was especially annoyed when the ISI leader on August 8, 2007, declared war on Iran without al-Qaida's approval.[92] Afterwards, Zawahiri sent a letter to Abu Hamza al-Muhajir, criticizing him for threatening Iran without consulting with al-Qaida first. He says: "You know that Iran is our main route for money, personnel and communications, and there is also the question of the hostages."[93] He also doubts whether ISI is capable of carrying out the threat, given that ISI is allied with groups in Iran (such as the Kurdistan brigades) that are infiltrated by the Iranian regime, and in sum he thinks that announcing a threat in the way ISI did will ultimately cause political losses.

On October 22, 2007, Al-Jazeera published an excerpt of a speech by bin Laden to the Iraqi people, which bin Laden had recorded in August 2007 or earlier, at the same time he drafted the internal advice memo to al-Qaida on how to deal with Iraq. The Al-Jazeera excerpts focused on the parts of bin Laden's speech where he admits mistakes, and calls on all parties to unite. The message excerpts may be read as indirect criticism of ISI's behavior in Iraq.[94] Afterward, al-Qaida's media agency al-Sahab posted the full bin Laden speech on jihadist forums, along with a statement that said that Al-Jazeera distorted the meaning of the original message.[95]

A few days later on November 3, 2007, Atiyah wrote to bin Laden that "yes, we wished that it contained a reference, even if it were a simple, brief, to support the Islamic State in Iraq ..." but all in all, he believed the speech was good, and it did no harm.[96] He revealed that there had been internal discussions in al-Qaida regarding the negative publicity, and how to react to it. Atiyah says he recommended to Zawahiri that nothing needed to be done:

> ... this uproar [on Al-Jazeera] has no effect, and does not harm anything. Rather, I know that many people of knowledge, virtue, and fairness, ... rejoiced over it and will increase their insight, love, and support, because the speech was more like a speech of principles, and it is like a stage that comes just before the stage of complete and explicit support for the Islamic State in Iraq.[97]

Echoing Zawahiri's attitude in how to deal with Iraq, Atiyah recommends that bin Laden in his next speech should give "... clear and complete support for the state and a focus on clarifying and explaining the truth of the conflict, and a call to join the state and unite under its banner, and with necessary recommendations and advice to follow the truth, stay away from sectarianism, and be loyal to God, His Messenger, His religion, and the believers."[98] However, he underlines that there is "no rush" in doing so because we first need to complete the consultation about it.

There is another speech from bin Laden, published on December 29, 2007, that seems to respond to the input he by now had received from other al-Qaida senior leaders. The one-hour audio message is entitled "The way to foil plots," and it is addressed to all the mujahidin groups in Iraq. In this message, he first defends ISI's assassination of Abd al-Sattar Abu Rishah, the leader of the Anbar Salvation Council (a council of tribal leaders who opposed ISI in Anbar) on September 13, 2007. He talks about the Awakening Councils that were formed in a plot by Americans and their allies "to steal the blessed fruit of jihad in Iraq." He says that some "weak-hearted" people joined the Council, such as Abd al-Sattar

Abu Rishah, who was killed by "the lions of Islam" because he was "misled and [was] misleading others," and because he "sold his religion."[99]

Second, he talks about a second "axis" of the American plot, which is to establish a "National Unity Government" sponsored by America and the Gulf countries, to replace the current Maliki government. Some Islamic parties also support this plot, which he calls "high treason."[100] The leader of the Islamic Party is among them. He then says, "The people have also seen other leaders cooperating indirectly through America's agents in the region, particularly the ruler of the Land of the Two Holy Mosques [Saudi Arabia]." This sentence appears to be a reference to the leader of the Islamic Army, as the information that the Islamic Army leader met with the Saudi king was included in Zawahiri's advice to bin Laden in October 2007.[101] Bin Laden continues, saying that the National Unity Government claims they need to form to fight the Shia aggression in Iraq, but the real solution—according to bin Laden—is jihad and "unifying the mujahidin."[102]

Bin Laden then goes on to talk about al-Qaida in Iraq. He says that Zarqawi's group was the first to fight the "criminals" in Iraq, but now the Iraqi mujahidin groups have "betrayed them" by dividing the jihad in Iraq in two parts—an "honest resistance" fighting Americans, and an illegal fight against the "apostate militias." But "God has nothing to do with these divisions," he says, referring to the fact that the Prophet even fought his own cousins. Now, he is candid about his attitude toward the various actors:

> The Islamic Party and some fighting groups support America against Muslims. This is a clear infidelity and an open apostasy. We seek strength from Almighty God. Members of the Islamic Party and those fighting factions should disavow their leaders and correct the course of their parties and groups.[103]

He then praises ISI for their efforts to unite the Iraqi insurgents:

> Here, we should mention the people who were the first on the issue of unity and accord because of the credit they deserve. Muslims were pleased when a number of the Emirs of groups, which are fighting for the sake of God, and a number of chiefs of steadfast and mujahid tribes unified their stand under the banner of monotheism and pledged allegiance to honorable Shaykh Abu-Umar al-Baghdadi as Emir of the Islamic State in Iraq (ISI). (…) May God reward them in the best way. Their accord is a blessed and great step toward unifying the other efforts to form the major group of Muslims.[104]

He says that some groups complained that they were not able to be part of the decision. Bin Laden replies that the brothers "sent you letters and waited for almost two months for your arrival," which seems to be a direct reference to ISI's dealings with Ansar al-Sunnah prior to ISI's establishment.[105] In his October 18, 2007, advice to bin Laden, Zawahiri specifically asked bin Laden to include this information in his public statement about ISI, which is one of several indications that bin Laden, in this case, followed Zawahiri's advice. Bin Laden then recounts the story of how the Prophet's companion Abu Bakr in the seventh century AD formed a Caliphate without consulting other parties, but the other parties nevertheless pledged bay'a to him afterwards, for the greater sake of unity [alluding that the groups in Iraq, mainly AAS, should do the same to the ISI].

Then, bin Laden arrives at the sensitive topic of whether he will endorse ISI's claim to supreme authority over the Sunni Iraqi insurgent movement. He formulates it in the following way: He first talks about the duty to unite, and says that if the exact conditions [of a Caliphate] are not in place, then the duty is to form the "great Muslim group," "… through pledging allegiance to the group that is the most committed to righteousness and truthfulness." He suggests ISI is this group, because he says immediately afterwards: "He who follows the local and global campaigns of infidelity can see that they are primarily targeted against the Islamic State in Iraq (…) I believe that all these ferocious campaigns against the mujahidin in the Islamic State in Iraq are staged because these mujahidin are deeply committed to righteousness and the Prophet's teachings …" Then, bin Laden makes an even clearer statement, saying it is a sin to not swear allegiance to the Emirs of ISI, who have been "recommended by trusted, fair persons." He states that Abu Umar al-Baghdadi was recommended by Abu Musab al-Zarqawi, and Abu Hamza al-Muhajir "is well known by your brothers in Afghanistan."[106] And so,

> refraining from pledging allegiance to one of the Emirs of mujahidin in Iraq after their recommendation by trusted, fair persons under the pretext of not knowing their conduct leads to great evils, one of the gravest of which is obstructing the establishment of the great Muslim nation under one imam, which is a nullifier.[107]

The speech confirms that bin Laden took the advice of Zawahiri and other senior al-Qaida leaders, including Atiyah and Sheikh Saeed, in the fall of 2007.[108] While he was initially reluctant to endorse ISI in public, he ended up issuing a speech containing a clear endorsement. The main reason seems to have been Zawahiri's argument to bin Laden about how a "middle position" on ISI would not work in the polarized environment in Iraq, because it would only strengthen the side that called for the dissolution of the Islamic State. Endorsing ISI seemed therefore to be the lesser of two evils in a situation where al-Qaida lacked clear information about conditions on the ground. Meanwhile, al-Qaida continued an internal discussion about how to bring about unity between ISI and Ansar al-Islam (formerly Ansar al-Sunnah), and the related topic of how to internally reform ISI and what kind of reforms to push for. These discussions were influenced by the arrival of an ISI defector, the former Sharia judge Abu Sulayman al-Utaybi, in Waziristan in October or November 2007.

Al-Qaida Formulates Internal Policies toward ISI

In October 2007, Atiyah returned to Waziristan from either Iran or Baluchistan province of Pakistan, after trying to reach Iraq for the last one and a half years. On November 3, 2007, he wrote the first of several letters to bin Laden about his experiences and about his recommendations for the Iraqi field. Around this same time, ISI's former Sharia judge, Abu Sulayman al-Utaybi, arrived in Waziristan after being fired from ISI. The judge carried with him a series of new accusations about ISI which al-Qaida had to take into account when deciding on their internal policy toward the ISI.

Around January 2008, Atiyah recorded a series of audiotapes for bin Laden where he described his experience trying to go to Iraq. The audiotapes were forwarded to bin Laden on February 4, 2008, along with a letter from Ayman al-Zawahiri.[109] In the audiotapes, Atiyah repeats his previous advice to bin Laden that al-Qaida should endorse the ISI, but he admits that he now has some reservations after hearing the words of the ISI defector, Abu Sulayman al-Utaybi. He therefore needs to qualify his advice. He states that the Iraq war is currently in a stage of "differentiation and splitting" between two sides—the movement striving for God, and the movement striving for other [worldly] purposes. He says the first movement is represented by the Islamic State in Iraq and Ansar al-Sunnah, and the other movement is represented by all of the others, including parties that "pretend to carry the Salafi banner," such as the Islamic Army. He says there has been a "wave of reactions [against ISI]" that started in the Anbar province of Iraq, with the establishment of the Awakening councils and Salvation councils, and it has now spread to the whole country. For this reason, he says, "… before hearing the words of the judge [al-Utaybi], I was calling for support for al-Dawla [the Islamic State]… But now, if the defect is in the state itself, then this requires new words or new research."[110]

He then goes on to cover various topics, including a detailed account of the various actors in the Iraqi insurgency, before returning to his advice about what al-Qaida should do with Iraq in Tape 8. In this tape, which is called "Future expectations for Iraq," he says that he believes jihad in Iraq will continue no matter what, and that it will have overall positive effects for the region. However, al-Qaida still needs to think about what to do in case the ISI got defeated. Atiyah brainstorms four ideas: (1) we should have a strong media campaign to cover up the defeat; (2) perhaps we should think about moving the battle to neighboring countries, like Syria; (3) perhaps we should carry out "decisive strikes" in Saudi Arabia; or (4) perhaps we should stir up trouble between America and Iran, "in order to cover up a collapse in Iraq."[111] He recommends that al-Qaida should investigate the allegations against ISI, continue to give direction to the ISI, and to continue to communicate with Ansar al-Sunnah, and to work for unity between them. He does not see any point in communicating with other groups, except these two, reflecting his earlier view that only ISI and AAS represent the "movement striving for God" in Iraq.

On February 23, 2008, bin Laden reacts to the messages from Atiyah by sending a letter to him, Zawahiri, and Sheikh Saeed proposing solutions for how to reform ISI and to unite ISI and Ansar al-Sunnah. We do not have this letter, but the other al-Qaida leaders refer to it in their replies sent in March and April 2008, giving a good indication of its content.[112] In short, bin Laden suggests that al-Qaida should send a "committee to settle differences" to Iraq, and he suggests it should be led by Atiyah and perhaps including the ISI defector, Abu Sulayman al-Utaybi. He further suggests forming an independent Sharia court in Iraq that would settle disputes between the groups. It seems like the two suggestions are related—i.e., that the al-Qaida committee would ideally also be involved in forming the Sharia court. Atiyah's answer in March 2008 is the following:

> Regarding the idea to send a committee led by Atiyah, the brothers almost unanimously agree that we should avoid it, owing to the dangers it entails, and the roads are not good … Then, the situation there may not be in need of more delegations. We need to monitor our brothers through correspondence, and directions, and questions, and also, by orders … And supporting them with cadre, whenever possible. And to help them to reform and direct them on the right path.

Atiyah then elaborates on a topic he brought up in the January audiotapes, namely, that al-Qaida should plan for what to do, in case the ISI collapses. His advice is now focused more specifically on what to do inside Iraq:

> Thinking about an acceptable policy for integrating our brothers in the Islamic State with Ansar al-Sunnah under a new name, which may serve as a cover for this bitter political issue, for example (…) "The Islamic Emirate in Iraq" … and a

> half-silent change in leadership and responsibilities, etc. And also, changing the title "Amir al-Mu'minin" to something else that's appropriate … !

Atiyah's suggestions mirror suggestions from AAS that were put forward in the internal negotiations between AAS and ISI in September-October 2007. This suggests that al-Qaida was informed of the negotiations before ISI formally informed al-Qaida about them in a letter sent to al-Qaida in April 2010.[113] The AAS deputy specifically asked in these negotiations ISI to consider changing their name, and the title of the Emir, to make the thought of an AAS-ISI unification more palatable for the AAS shura.[114]

Zawahiri replies to bin Laden's proposal around the same time, in a letter dated March 5, 2008. He says,

> Sending someone from here in these conditions would be impossible. Atiyah returned after months of waiting, and he was told by those who promised him (…) In regard to forming a committee to settle differences, it is a good suggestion, but it must be accepted by the various parties, and at least the parties on the correct plan. We will not be able to send an individual from here, but we may ask the brothers there to work on it. (…) And in regard to the suggestion of the court, it is a very good suggestion … in regard to the court's personalities … [he mentions here that the road is too difficult to send Atiyah, and that al-Utaybi cannot be trusted, implying that the court must be established by the Iraqi groups themselves].[115]

Zawahiri goes on to detail his opinion about Abu Sulayman al-Utaybi. He is generally skeptical of Utaybi, because he is "… unknown to us, and we have no information about him, and also we have not received the opinions of the brothers there about him, about why they removed him." Furthermore, Zawahiri says, al-Utaybi's behavior in Waziristan is "not comfortable" because he refused to swear bay'a to al-Qaida; and when he was asked to work on al-Qaida's sharia committee with Abu Yahya al-Libi, "he left after one day" and went to a rival group, the "[Hamud] al-Dhabbah's independent group." Nevertheless, Zawahiri is intent on keeping relations cordial while they investigate the issue, as he says, "And based on a suggestion from the brothers, I have sent a message to Abu Sulayman welcoming him, and assuring him that we have worked on what he said, and I encourage him to cooperate with his brothers."[116]

Zawahiri's advice to bin Laden on Iraq, for now, seems limited to "asking the brothers there to work on [forming a court or committee to settle differences]." His other suggestions dealing with Iraq are unspecific, and are limited to the propaganda aspect—he says bin Laden should continue to call for support to the "Mujahidin in Iraq" with men and money, and "support the parties that espouse the real Islamic trend."[117]

At the same time, Zawahiri also sends a letter addressed to the ISI Emir, Abu Omar al-Baghdadi, which incorporates bin Laden's suggestions, but without mentioning sending anyone from al-Qaida in Pakistan. Here, we gain further details about the court suggested by bin Laden. Zawahiri gives al-Baghdadi the following directions:

> Endeavor to appoint some qualified brothers to form a Supreme Judicial Council and establish a Supreme Sharia Court for Muslims in general, including the Mujahidin, not affiliated with the state or any group, whose mission is to adjudicate disputes through Sharia arbitration, so that justice will prevail, security will be established, and disputes will be eliminated.[118]

In the letter, Zawahiri also reminds al-Baghdadi that they would like ISI to comment on the accusations by Abu Sulayman al-Utaybi.

Finally, there is a letter from Sheikh Saeed to bin Laden regarding bin Laden's latest Iraq proposal. The letter is dated April 16, 2008, but parts of it were written earlier. He says he had a "Shura" with the other brothers regarding the Iraq issue, which probably refers to a recent physical meeting between him, Zawahiri, and Atiyah, which was also mentioned in Zawahiri's letter. His recommendations echo those of Atiyah and Zawahiri: Atiyah should not go to Iraq for security reasons, and al-Utaybi is not suitable, "owing to his differences with the brothers there." Sheikh Saeed provides more details about al-Utaybi's behavior, which "was not reassuring":

> We tasked him to work with the Sharia committee, and a while after, we got to know that he's going to the interior [Afghanistan frontline] through Al-Dhabbah, who has split from us, and when we mentioned that we had agreed that he would be with the Group (*al-jama'a*), and that he has a duty to listen and obey it, he said, "I am with the Group, but I am not obligated to listen and obey it, because I have not given the *bay'a*." And there were no more words between us and him, knowing that he did not give the oath in Iraq, as he had told us.[119]

He also has some specific suggestions regarding Iraq. He says first, we should "give [ISI] military support as soon as possible, by giving good military training to Kurdish brothers and to send them as soon as possible." Second, we should prepare cadre in Waziristan, train them in "Sharia, politics and administration, like you suggested," and send them to Iraq. He mentions a candidate, a 35-year-old Algerian brother, who came six months ago and who swore *bay'a*, so "perhaps he will move there soon." Third, we must "activate" our communication with them, and he says he has appointed "brother Salih al-Mauritani [aka Yunus al-Mauritani]" to carry out this task.[120] Fourth, we should confirm al-Utaybi's accusations by contacting third parties, such as "the Emir of the Kurdish brothers in Iran [likely a reference to Abu Arif al-Shahada]."[121]

Sheikh Saeed's letter seems to conclude the internal al-Qaida discussion regarding Iraq in the spring of 2008. As we heard, Zawahiri sent a letter to the ISI Emir, Abu Omar al-Baghdadi, summing up al-Qaida's recommendations. The correspondence between al-Qaida and ISI Emir in Iraq appears to have become minimal after this. The al-Qaida leaders in Pakistan indicated that the ISI stopped replying to their messages after this, but we do not know the reason. A few formal letters were sent between the two groups until 2010,[122] when Abu Umar al-Baghdadi and Abu Hamza al-Mujahir were both killed in a US airstrike. After this, ISI appointed Abu Bakr al-Baghdadi as the new Emir of ISI, without asking for bin Laden's approval beforehand. After this, Atiyah sent ISI a request for information on al-Baghdadi's background, but, as far as we know, never received a reply.

We do not have any more letters from bin Laden commenting on Iraq after 2008, but we can assume that he accepted the unanimous recommendation by Atiyah, Zawahiri, and Sheikh Saeed to not try and send any more high-ranking al-Qaida members there. Overall, there is a shift in al-Qaida's relationship to ISI at this stage where al-Qaida gives up trying to influence events directly, instead relying on indirect methods such as working through Kurdish groups (presumably, the Kurdistan Brigades) in Iran. From late 2008, bin Laden seems to shift focus to Iran, after receiving an alarming report from his escaped son Sa'd about the dire conditions of the Arabs (including his own family members) in Iranian prisons. The Iran issue takes up much space in bin Laden's communications in the first half of 2009, until Iran gives in to pressure and starts releasing members of bin Laden's family. After this, bin Laden turns his attention to the growing domestic unrest in Yemen, which will be further discussed in Chapter 7.

Concluding Remarks

In January 2007, the United States started a troop surge where they deployed some 20,000 extra troops to Iraq. The first major operation started in Baghdad in February 2007 and continued throughout the year. The operations severely degraded the ISI. As ISI came under increased pressure both from the United States and domestically, in March and April 2007 ISI started targeting Sunnis, including leaders of Sunni mujahidin groups. In May 2007, some Sunni opposition groups supported by Qatar formed the Jihad and Reformation Front to fight ISI. In mid- and late 2007, ISI targeted Anbar tribes. On September 14, 2007, ISI killed the leader of the Anbar Salvation Council, a tribal coalition fighting against the ISI in Anbar. Bin Laden later defended this particular killing in his December 2007 speech where he endorsed the Islamic State in Iraq.

As ISI's security situation deteriorated in 2007, their correspondence with al-Qaida became more irregular. Between July and October 2007, Abu Hamza al-Muhajir sent at least one letter to Zawahiri, which we do not have. Zawahiri replied to Abu Hamza in October 2007, admonishing ISI for threatening to go to war with Iran without consulting al-Qaida first. In November 2007, Atiyah reported that he had corresponded with Abu Hamza, and that Abu Hamza confirmed his commitment to al-Qaida. By now, the ISI defector Abu Sulayman al-Utaybi had arrived in Waziristan, and al-Qaida sent several letters to ISI asking them to comment on al-Utaybi's accusations. But there are no more letters from Abu Hamza al-Muhajir, until he sends a short reply to Sheikh Saeed in April 2008 in which he calls al-Utaybi's accusations "lies and slander." He indicates that he will elaborate in a later message, but it is unknown if he followed up on his words. Around the same time in March 2008, Zawahiri sent a letter of advice to Abu Omar al-Baghdadi, with several suggestions for internal reform. This is the last known letter we have from al-Qaida to Abu Omar al-Baghdadi advising him on internal matters.

In July 2008, Ansar al-Sunnah published a critical booklet called "The Book of Truth" (*sifru al-haqiqa*), telling their version of the story of the Iraqi insurgency.[123] Later in April 2010, ISI's Shura Council sent a letter to al-Qaida in which they contested AAS's version of history and explained in detail why they had fallen out with Ansar al-Sunnah.[124] This letter suggests that communication between al-Qaida and ISI continued in some form after 2008, but we do not know the extent of it. It is also evident that from April 2008, al-Qaida started de-prioritizing Iraq, and some members, like Atiyah, suggested that al-Qaida needed to plan for a scenario where the ISI collapses.

In a letter in May 2010, Zawahiri indicated that he expected the Iraqi battlefield to "spin into a spiral of sectarian and ethnic conflict," and that victory for the mujahidin there was less likely than in Afghanistan.[125] By now, al-Qaida had already turned their attention to other and more promising battlefields such as Yemen and Somalia, which we return to in Chapter 7. By 2010, al-Qaida had also started positioning itself for a future Taliban victory in Afghanistan, but in this process, they had to let go of some of their global ambitions, as the next chapter will show.

5

Al-Qaida and the Taliban

We do not accept that you treat us as guests in the Afghan cause. It is our
cause as well, and we have participated in it for more than twenty years.[1]
—Sheikh Saeed, in a meeting with Afghan Taliban, April 2008

This chapter continues the story about how al-Qaida participated in the war in Afghanistan. While Chapter 2 covered the initial years from 2002 to 2004, this chapter looks at the next stage of the war, when the Taliban became more organized and started taking control over the insurgency. The period covers President Obama's announcement in December 2009 of a timetable for the withdrawal of US troops and the US troop surge in 2010, which prompted different actors to start positioning themselves for a future Taliban victory in Afghanistan.[2] In the midst of these internal contests, al-Qaida were indeed treated as "guests," and al-Qaida's leaders had no choice but to work within the new realities.

The chapter focuses on the political-level interactions between the leaders of al-Qaida and the Taliban. The Abbottabad documents reveal that by 2008, some al-Qaida leaders had started suspecting that parts of the Taliban's senior leadership in Quetta were controlled by the Pakistani Inter-Services Intelligence (ISI). This realization led to an internal debate about how and whether to communicate with the leaders. Bin Laden was disinterested in communicating with Mullah Omar as long as there was no private and trusted line of communication. However, the rest of al-Qaida believed al-Qaida should try to influence their own political standing in a future Taliban-led Afghanistan, regardless of possible ISI influence over the leadership. In 2010, bin Laden ended up writing a few courtesy letters to Mullah Omar, while Ayman al-Zawahiri suggested a more elaborate strategy for how al-Qaida should secure its future in the region. Both of them realized that al-Qaida in the short- to mid-term probably needed to move its globally oriented activities away from Afghanistan and Pakistan.

The Taliban Insurgency Intensifies (2005–7)

The period from 2005 to 2007 is characterized by a marked rise in the Taliban insurgency in Afghanistan, and visible changes in the Taliban's organization— from operating as a loose insurgency to putting in place a central leadership organization called the Rahbari Shura, also known as the Quetta Shura.[3] In other words, in 2005–6 the Taliban started positioning itself more clearly as the superior insurgent authority in Afghanistan. In this section I discuss how the rise of the Taliban's influence led to a renewal of the historical rivalry between Taliban and Gulbuddin Hekmatyar, and how al-Qaida positioned itself in this struggle.

As we recall from Chapter 2, bin Laden at the start of the insurgency in 2002 provided financial support to a number of independent actors, including Hekmatyar's insurgent group, Hizb-e-Islami. The financing seems to have discontinued from around 2004. The immediate reason for this might have been the arrest or disappearance of key individuals involved in delivering money to Hekmatyar's representatives. In retrospect, however, the centralization and intensification of the Taliban insurgency from 2005 onwards might have been another reason for why al-Qaida decided to channel all their support through the Taliban.

Various accounts describe the role of Pakistan, or Pakistani intelligence ISI, in the expansion of Taliban's influence in 2005–6. According to the view of the Afghan intelligence (NDS), "ISI had made a desicion in 2005 to support the Taliban more actively," because Pakistan felt threatened by the consolidation of Karzai's rule, and his relationship with India, between 2003 and 2005.[4] According to Steve Coll, this information was largely ignored by the Bush administration, who preferred to work with Pakistan to hunt al-Qaida inside Waziristan. However, the Pakistanis were getting fed up with working with the Americans, because the military operations in Waziristan were creating blowback effects in the form of terrorism in Pakistan.[5] In March 2006, the United States and India signed a Civil Nuclear Agreement, and the United States handed over operations in Afghanistan to their European NATO allies, signaling they would eventually leave Afghanistan. Both these were moves that might have caused Pakistan to lose trust in the United States as an ally.[6]

In his detailed reconstruction of the early history of the Taliban insurgency, Giustozzi reported that "there is near-universal consensus among the Taliban that 2005 represented a turning point for the insurgency."[7] He attributed this shift to increased levels of funding from multiple sources, corresponding to an observation made by Coll, saying that Saudi Arabia started funding the Taliban secretly from 2005 via the ISI. However, it would be a gross simplification to say that the Taliban resurgence was caused by Pakistani support. It was rather a complex, local effort driven in large part by the Taliban themselves. According to the high-ranking Taliban member Abdul Hai Mutma'in, Mullah Omar himself was actively involved in restarting the insurgency in 2003, by issuing audiotaped instructions to the Taliban's senior leadership.[8] Moreover, Giustozzi documented how the Taliban from 2005 gradually expanded their influence, village by village, in Kandahar and Helmand provinces, responding to popular grievances about the Karzai government and the Americans. But Giustozzi, via high-level Taliban sources, also claimed that much of the funding for this effort came from the ISI: "In part, the increase in violence was the result of more external aid becoming available, with the Pakistani ISI's Directorate S for the first time committing itself to the effort."[9] This happened specifically to disrupt the 2005 Parliamentary elections in Afghanistan. Giustozzi thus supports the Afghan NDS's assessment in 2006 that Pakistan started getting involved in Taliban as a reaction to Karzai's growing influence and India ties.

In 2005, Eastern Afghan insurgents also started to become more organized under the Taliban umbrella, in an organization called "Ijraya Shura" for the East. This represented a challenge to Gulbuddin Hekmatyar of the Hizb-e-Islami, whose fighters started joining the Ijraya Shura because it was better funded than Hekmatyar's own "Shamshatoo Shura."[10] It was in this context that Hekmatyar started positioning himself vis-à-vis the rising Taliban influence in Afghanistan. In 2006, he issued a number of statements and interviews in which he called for jihad against the United States, threatened US officials, and praised Osama bin Laden.[11] In an interview with the Pakistani Geo TV conducted in December 2006, he boasted that he had helped bin Laden and Zawahiri escape Afghanistan.[12] One can interpret Hekmatyar's public statements in 2006, where he uses global jihadist language and claims personal connection to Osama bin Laden, as a strategy to strengthen his position in an internal contest for power over the Afghan insurgency.

The Abbottabad documents support this interpretation. They reveal that in 2007, after Hekmatyar had made a series of public overtures to bin Laden, he also made a private request to bin Laden to help him unite with the Taliban.[13] In mid- or late 2007, bin Laden received a letter from an Arab middleman nicknamed Uthman al-Shihri, who uses a Saudi nickname and who appears to work for Hekmatyar Al-Shihri claims that he is involved in negotiations to unite the ranks of Taliban and Hekmatyar's party, Hizb-e-Islami. In his letter, he describes Hekmatyar's eagerness to unite, but claims he is unable to convey direct messages between Hekmatyar and Mullah Omar because the US and Pakistani intelligence are in the way. He also claims that the Taliban officials he talked to expressed opposition to joining "the Qutbis and Mawdudis"—a disparaging reference to Hekmatyar's Muslim Brotherhood background. He therefore asks bin Laden for help in uniting Hekmatyar and the Taliban, because he believes bin Laden may have some influence over Mullah Omar:

> You should write to Mullah Muhammad Omar, and tell him about the duty to unite, and tell them to discard their beliefs about the Qutbiyyin and the Mawdudis, and tell him that Hekmatyar is in the trenches, and fighting jihad, and the enemies are looking for him, etc. And my Sheikh, you know the people's hearts and you can [convince them].[14]

He claims that many former members of Abdul Rasul Sayyaf's party, *al-Ittihad al-Islami*, joined Hekmatyar, and that they want unity in Afghanistan. He has noticed that bin Laden tends to promote Taliban in his speeches as the supreme authority in the Afghan insurgency. His advice to bin Laden is clear: "I say, do not take sides with anyone and do not join a party. It is necessary to write a letter to them all, and to call for unity within Afghanistan, and to sign with your name."[15]

The Saudi intermediary encloses a letter from Hekmatyar personally, which contains the same message, but in a slightly more lecturing way, revealing Hekmatyar's own power ambitions. Hekmatyar asks al-Qaida to stop calling on Hizb-e-Islami's members to join the Taliban. He believes Mullah Omar is not the right authority to lead an Islamic Emirate, and he thinks the groups should unite now to fight jihad, and later decide on who should lead a future Islamic Emirate in Afghanistan. His letter ends with a reminder to bin Laden that they previously had an agreement to pay Hizb-e-Islami a monthly amount of 50,000 USD.[16] The letter from al-Shihri also reminds bin Laden of the important logistical role played by a Hizb-e-Islami network in Kabul, referred to as the "Kabul University Group," in suicide attacks in Kabul carried out jointly between al-Qaida and HIG.

The Afghan war at this time, in mid-2007, is expanding rapidly and the Taliban are consolidating their power over the insurgency. This likely prompted an actor like Hekmatyar to seek assistance from bin Laden in "uniting" with the Taliban. Despite being an inferior actor compared to the Taliban, Hekmatyar is only interested in "unity" on his own terms. He wants to diminish the Taliban's influence and create his own version of a joint Taliban-Hizb-e-Islami insurgent group where he is able to yield more direct power as a commander. Quite possibly, he also envisions himself as a candidate to lead a future Islamic Emirate in Afghanistan. In this context, it makes sense that he is trying to solicit Osama bin Laden's support.

Hekmatyar likely felt threatened by the increasing influence of foreign intelligence agencies, primarily Pakistan's ISI, over the Taliban's senior leadership, a point which he alluded to in his letter to bin Laden. Over the next few years, the Taliban-affiliated Haqqani network would also rise up to challenge Hekmatyar's Hizb-e-Islami (also known as Hizb-e-Islami Gulbuddin or HIG) on an operational level in Kabul and Eastern Afghanistan. While HIG had traditionally played an important role in supporting suicide attacks in Kabul, from 2008 this task became dominated by the Haqqani network. The first high-profile attack was the suicide attack on the Kabul Serena hotel, on January 14, 2008, and it was followed by a wave of so-called "complex attacks" in Afghanistan from 2009 onward.

Al-Qaida, of course, had an ambivalent relationship to Hekmatyar. Bin Laden and Hekmatyar had cooperated during the Afghan-Soviet war in 1979–92, but bin Laden's political support to Hekmatyar ended when the latter entered the Afghan Civil War in 1992. Therefore, it is no surprise that bin Laden ignored Hekmatyar's request for support in 2007. Bin Laden's policy since 2002 had been to support Taliban and Mullah Omar as the supreme leader of the Afghan insurgency, which was a direct continuation of his policy toward the Taliban in the late 1990s. Al-Qaida's challenge was that they had no way of contacting Mullah Omar directly, and were forced to deal with Taliban leaders whom they viewed with suspicion.

The Conflict between the Quetta Shura and Dadullah Front (2007–8)

At the same time as the Taliban was strengthening its military position in Afghanistan, the movement suffered a severe blow—the killing on May 11, 2007, of its most famous military commander, the infamous, one-legged Mullah Dadullah. In al-Qaida and jihadist mythology, Dadullah was known for his bravery and uncompromising dedication to jihad, while among Taliban rank and file, he was most of all known for his brutality.[17] After 2001, he became one of the most powerful figures within the rising Taliban insurgency. He was among the first commanders to establish a large-size Taliban force in Helmand province, the Dadullah Mahaz ("Dadullah Front").[18] When Taliban reorganized and started expanding in 2005, Dadullah became the overall leader of its Military Commission, akin to the position of a Minister of Defense.[19]

Throughout history, Dadullah had repeatedly provoked the rest of the Taliban with his behavior, and had several times been subject to internal sanctions in the Taliban.[20] In the spring of 2007, another such event happened, when Dadullah's group kidnapped the Italian journalist Danielle Mastrogiacomo and two Afghans accompanying him. Dadullah wanted to use the hostages to pressure the Karzai government to free his brother, Mansour Dadullah, and other imprisoned Taliban. In the course of these negotiations he killed the two Afghan hostages. After this incident, Taliban's Ulama Council ruled that the killing was unlawful, and Mullah Omar sent Dadullah an audiotape, insisting that Dadullah stop killing Afghan civilians and stop acting on his own. Dadullah's independent behavior had by now provoked others in the Taliban too, including Mullah Baradir, the day-to-day leader of the Taliban, whose distaste for Dadullah was well known within the Taliban rank-and-file.[21]

Then, on May 11, 2007, Mullah Dadullah was killed in Helmand in a military raid led by British Special forces.[22] The killing led to rumors among Dadullah's men in Helmand that senior Quetta Taliban leaders had betrayed Dadullah's position in order to get rid of him.[23] The rumor reached al-Qaida's senior leader Sheikh Saeed, who had a cordial relationship with Mullah Mansour Dadullah (aka Mullah Bakht or Akhtar Muhammad), who is Mullah Dadullah's brother. In September 2007, Sheikh Saeed met with Mansour in an unknown place, and the meeting was filmed and turned into a propaganda video for al-Sahab entitled "Meeting between Brothers." This was a rather unusual video, because it is the first example of a propaganda video showing a meeting between two high-ranking officials of al-Qaida and Taliban, respectively.[24]

The video was in line with al-Qaida taking a more visible role in the Afghan insurgency from 2007 onward, exemplified most clearly in the May 2007 release of another propaganda video naming Sheikh Saeed as the "Emir of al-Qaida in Afghanistan."[25] There seems to have been a political motivation behind the announcement, because Sheikh Saeed was already the 'general manager' ("no.3") of al-Qaida, and as far as one can tell from the Abbottabad documents, his responsibilities did not change after May 2007. Moreover, there were no internal references in Abbottabad documents to an organization called "Al-Qaida in Afghanistan," neither before nor after 2007, but there were references to individual fighting groups. However, just a month before the announcement of Sheikh Saeed's ostensible new title, on April 27, 2007, news broke that Abdul Hadi al-Iraqi, the previous Taliban-appointed Emir of foreign fighters in Afghanistan, had been arrested and transferred to Guantánamo.[26] Abdul Hadi had quit as Emir of the frontline back in 2004, but this was not common knowledge to the public.[27] To the contrary, he was widely described as a "top al-Qaida leader" in the media at the time of his arrest. His arrest thus created a perception in the media that al-Qaida currently did not have an Emir for the frontline in Afghanistan. For al-Qaida, who were operating in a competitive environment in Waziristan, it was imperative to fill this vacuum before anyone else did.

Other Abbottabad correspondence describes this competitive environment in detail. Various al-Qaida leaders reported to bin Laden in the spring of 2008 about a handful of independent-minded "Emirs" operating in Afghanistan. They claimed to work for al-Qaida and Osama bin Laden, but in reality they operated their own, independent groups.[28] They included a Saudi nicknamed "Hamud al-Dhabbah [Hamud the Slaughterer]," who, according to Zawahiri, enticed new recruits to join him by saying, "Whoever wants coffee, communications, and operations, he must go to al-Dhabbah!"[29] The point which caused most consternation to al-Qaida was that these commanders were exploiting al-Qaida's name to attract money donations from the Gulf, which they then used to strengthen their own, independent fighting groups. After the public announcement of Abd al-Hadi's arrest in April 2007, al-Qaida might have worried that one of these rogue commanders would hijack the Emir position and exploit it for propaganda purposes, which in turn would put al-Qaida in a dilemma of either staying silent, or having to reveal publicly that the Arab frontline in Afghanistan was fraught with internal dissent.[30] This may explain why al-Qaida in May 2007 made a highly visible and public announcement of Sheikh Saeed's appointment to lead "Al-Qaida in Afghanistan." Those who knew al-Qaida well made a mockery of the announcement, as they knew Sheikh Saeed was not a frontline commander, but an office cleric.[31] But as we shall see later, Sheikh Saeed turned out to be just the type of leader that al-Qaida needed in Waziristan, where symbolic power and diplomatic skills turned out to be more important for al-Qaida's survival, than fighting.

Returning to Mullah Mansour, he probably had his own motivations for meeting with Sheikh Saeed in the fall of 2007. He appeared to be running his own public relations campaign at that time, designed to strengthen his candidature as the new commander of the Dadullah front, and to attract the attention of Arab donors by adopting global jihadist rhetoric. The most infamous example is a video released on October 3, 2007, where he claims to have trained two hundred suicide bombers ready to strike the West, complete with footage showing groups of masked men dedicated to targeting various regions of the world.[32] Needless to say, none of these "suicide bombers" ever showed up in a plot to target a Western country. In the meeting with Sheikh Saeed in September 2007, Mansour Dadullah leveled some serious accusations against the rest of the Quetta Shura Taliban. He also insisted that Sheikh Saeed met with two men who were imprisoned by Mansour's group. Mansour accused them of being "spies" who had given away Mullah Dadullah's position to the Americans, on orders from high-ranking Taliban leaders. Sheikh Saeed later reported to bin Laden:

> We have received confirmed news from Hajji Mansour Dadullah that some of the Taliban leaders (Mullah Baradar, Mullah Obaidullah, Mullah Akhtar Mansour, and others) participated with the Americans in killing Mullah Dadullah. (…) We met with the imprisoned, after the request and insistence of Mullah Mansour on this, and they confessed before us what was previously mentioned, and Mullah Mansour asked us for your advice in this strife, and we had previously advised him to raise the matter to the Commander of the Faithful, so he said that the problem is that there is no line for him except through these leaders …[33]

By now, several versions of the story of Dadullah's killing were circulating in the media. In Western media, the story about the alleged conspiracy against Dadullah was well known, but there was also an entirely different version of the story, circulated by the London-based newspaper *The Times*, and which relied on anonymous "defence sources."[34] This story claimed that Great Britain and the United States had used advanced signals intelligence techniques to track Dadullah's brother, Mansour Dadullah, after he was released from jail in Kabul in return for the Italian hostage Mastrogiacomo. After spending some time in Pakistan, Mansour Dadullah had subsequently led the Afghan coalition forces to Dadullah's position inside Helmand. While the exact details are hard to verify, parts of the story, including the involvement of the British Special Boat Service (SBS) in the raid on Dadullah, and the existence of a US signals intelligence unit in Afghanistan called "Task Force Orange," have later been corroborated by other sources.

We might never get the full truth about Dadullah's killing. But the point here is that the internal strife in the Taliban between the Dadullah Front and the Quetta Shura put al-Qaida in a delicate position. Al-Qaida at the time was ideologically closer to the Dadullah Front than the Quetta Shura. At the same time, al-Qaida's overall policy was to endorse Mullah Omar's overall authority within the Taliban, in spite of having limited information about Mullah Omar's actual whereabouts or status within the movement. If al-Qaida endorsed the Quetta Shura, they risked supporting an ISI-influenced faction of the Taliban, but if they endorsed the Dadullah front, they risked causing further schisms in the Taliban which would weaken the jihad as a whole. In the end, al-Qaida chose a middle path, but the case illustrates that al-Qaida leaders had different attitudes about how to deal with the risk of Pakistani ISI influence—bin Laden being a hardliner, while others, such as Zawahiri and Sheikh Saeed, being slightly more pragmatic.

We do not know exactly when al-Qaida started communicating directly with the Quetta Shura. In November 2007, Sheikh Saeed reported to bin Laden about his meeting with Mansour Dadullah, and in his next letter, sent sometime before December 17, 2007, he informed bin Laden that a high-ranking Taliban delegate (presumably from the Quetta Shura) had visited him and delivered a message from Mullah Omar, but that it was "of suspicious accuracy." Bin Laden reacted strongly:

> I am saying to you, it is very important to find out the truth of that delegate and deal with them based on your finding. I am not going to hide it from you, the majority of the delegates are following same path of that man who surrendered our honorable brother, may God set him free [probably a reference to Mansur Dadullah[35]]. You need to mention this when you start dealing with them, because it is vital, and these people have no shame in allowing the apostate state intelligence to lead them.[36]

On February 4, 2008, Zawahiri wrote to bin Laden that the Mansour Dadullah case had "developed a little." Mullah Omar sent an audio message asking Mansour to hand over the spies to a third party, Baitullah Mahsud in Waziristan, to be interrogated by a neutral party. However, Mansour refused and instead killed the spies. As a consequence, the Taliban expelled him from the organization. Mansour Dadullah's expulsion from the Taliban was made public on December 31, 2007.[37]

Zawahiri revealed in the letter that he had personally prepared a letter to Mullah Omar, but he and Sheikh Saeed decided not to send it, because they did not have a trusted way of communicating with Mullah Omar. Zawahiri believed there is a secure way through Mullah Omar's personal assistant, Tayyeb Agha, once they managed to reconnect with him. Zawahiri also said that he and Sheikh Saeed asked advice from the old al-Qaida ally, Sheikh Muhammad Yasir, who " … advised us in these circumstances to restrict our letters to regular niceties and only emphasize our commitment to listen and obey, because we are not sure how letters get delivered, who receives them, or who copies them."[38]

In March 2008, Atiyah reported to bin Laden that a Taliban *kumisiun* for Waziristan had come to visit them to coordinate the upcoming fighting season. According to Giustozzi, commissions (*kumisiun* in the singular) are "executive organs tasked with implementing policies decided by the Rahbari Shura."[39] This is the first confirmation in the Abbottabad documents that

Quetta Shura Taliban had sent such a committee to meet with al-Qaida in Waziristan. It may have happened earlier without being reported, but it may also be a reflection of the Quetta Shura's desire to take more direct control over the insurgency, which at this time was growing bigger each fighting season. The main purpose of the meeting was presumably to coordinate the future operations of all the fighting groups in Waziristan. Al-Qaida used the occasion to inquire about their status within the Taliban amidst international pressure on the Taliban to "separate" from al-Qaida. Atiyah concluded after the meeting:

> We found them to be good and honest people, God knows best, and we saw nothing in their words and emotions except good things, love, and counsel. … the important thing is that we sat together, and we saw that in general, our thoughts regarding the matters of Waziristan and elsewhere were identical. We agreed with them on points of work for this [fighting] season, in the interior and elsewhere …[40]

Moreover, the commission confirmed that rumors of a split in the Taliban over al-Qaida were "absolutely baseless."[41] Atiyah and Sheikh Saeed agreed with the Taliban commission that they would send a message to Mullah Omar via the official delegation. In this context, Atiyah suggested to bin Laden to write a test message containing no sensitive information, to see if it goes through without being tampered with:

> And would it be possible, dear Shaykh, to send from your side a letter to Amir al-Mu'minin, and to ask him to answer it, in order for you and us to see: Will it reach him in a complete form, securely and accurately? [We will see this] by way of his answer, of course. The letter is suitable for our wish to denounce things, and to discover what is there, and how the man is doing, regarding strength and freedom and free choice … and how is the road to him, etc.[42]

Around the same time, in early March 2008, Zawahiri sent a new letter to bin Laden asking for advice on how to proceed with the letter to Mullah Omar.[43] Sheikh Saeed also offered his thoughts on the case. On April 16, 2008, he sent a letter to bin Laden stating that Taliban between January-February 2008 had sent a delegation to al-Qaida to explain the Mansour Dadullah case to them, and to ask them to not interfere further in the case (this delegation is most likely different from the Taliban *kumisiun* for Waziristan, which visited al-Qaida in March or early April 2008):

> Prior to [Mansour's] capture [by Pakistan, on February 11, 2008], a delegation from the Taliban came to us. Their task was to explain to us Mansour's big

mistake, in capturing the spies and then killing them without trial, and especially after the order came from our friend [Mullah Omar] to release them or surrender them to the Shura. They had a cassette tape with them with the voice of our friend. We listened to it and concluded that it was his voice, and he said in it, that "he does not believe what Mansour is saying and his accusations that most of the leaders of the Taliban are agents of America." (…) He said that he has fired Mansour from his position, and he will never be able to return to it, and that Mansour has "approached apostasy (*iqtaraba min al-ridda*)." We are astonished by this harshness from our friend towards Mansour, he did not hear [Mansour's] version, and he did not solve the issue through the judges. This increases our belief that our friend is not in a natural situation, and possibly, and as a minimum, they are isolating him from any type of information except their own.[44]

Sheikh Saeed then proceeded with the quote that introduced this chapter:

… we told them that we do not accept that you treat us as guests in the Afghan cause. It is our cause as well, and we have participated in it for more than twenty years. We will continue in our jihad, God willing, until the return of the Islamic Emirate. You should discuss with us the important matters. And the critical matters that you are not able to discuss with us, you should at least inform us about them and explain the reason for your decision. The delegation was kind and understanding.[45]

Sheikh Saeed then refers to the same rumor that Atiyah had heard earlier, namely that there was an effort by foreigners, "Great Britain and others," to divide the Taliban, and convince them to abandon al-Qaida. Sheikh Saeed has a more pessimistic take on events than Atiyah:

On another note, one of the trusted, Afghan brothers relayed to us that there is talk among the Taliban to expel al-Qaida from the Afghan cause. Many offers have been made to them, from Great Britain and others, in the same vein. And some of them support it. We discussed this matter with the Shura here, and concluded that we should expect the worst, and that we must expand our relations with the sincere Taliban commanders from the original Taliban and whoever joined them—the likes of Haqqani, and the son of Yunus Khalis, and Ustaz Yasir. And we should continue our friendly relations with the Taliban Shura, until it becomes apparent that they are against our principles, and we would like your opinion on this.[46]

Sheikh Saeed also refers to the visit by the Taliban military *kumisiun* for Waziristan "just a few days ago." Like Atiyah, he says that they came to coordinate military operations inside Afghanistan, and to ask al-Qaida to only cooperate with officially appointed commanders. He confirms that they talked about whether there was an anti-al-Qaida current within the Taliban, something they strongly denied.

In his letter Sheikh Saeed is optimistic—he confirms that Pakistan in the spring of 2008 eased the pressure on groups in Waziristan, in order to strengthen the jihad in Afghanistan. He believes their motivation is as before, to "create problems for the Americans and the agent [Karzai] government" whom Pakistan sees as aligned with India. Additionally, he thinks that Pakistan now has an additional motivation which is to quell the growing Tehrik-e-Taliban Pakistan (TTP) insurgency within Pakistan.[47]

This confirms other analysis saying that Pakistan pursued a divide-and-rule policy with the TTP.[48] They sought to support those parts of the TTP who were willing to only fight jihad in Afghanistan, but not in Pakistan. One can suspect that Pakistan's renewed focus on uniting the ranks of the jihadist movement in Waziristan in spring 2008 contributed to strengthening the cooperation between Quetta Shura Taliban and al-Qaida. It might be related to the Taliban's decision to appoint a military *kumisiun* to coordinate insurgents in Waziristan prior to the 2008 fighting season, although we do not know exactly when this commission was formed.

Pakistan's covert support to the jihad in Afghanistan in some ways benefited al-Qaida. Al-Qaida's main priority was the same as Pakistan's—unity of rank and fighting Americans in Afghanistan—and now al-Qaida seemed freer to pursue these goals without having to waste energy on fighting the Pakistani Army inside Waziristan. However, Sheikh Saeed's optimism was short-lived. In 2008, the United States started intensifying their drone strikes on Pakistan's Tribal Areas, specifically targeting mid- and high-level al-Qaida leaders. The first, high-ranking victim of this new campaign was Abu al-Layth al-Libi killed on January 29, 2008, but al-Qaida did not yet foresee the massive toll the drone war would have on al-Qaida's mid-level leadership. It took another year or two before al-Qaida started reacting to the drone threat and implemented measures to mitigate it, before realizing in late 2010 that it was impossible to avoid the drones and that al-Qaida's only option of survival is to evacuate Waziristan.

In May 2008, bin Laden provided his input to al-Qaida's discussions of the Mansour Dadullah case. His answer reveals a cynicism toward Afghanistan, which might well have been partly the result of his practical experiences in dealing with various shady Afghan leaders over the last twenty years. Bin Laden dismissed outright Sheikh Yasir's assessment that the Quetta Shura Taliban are "generally good people." Instead, he says, they are "hypocrites" and "not trustworthy," and he refuses to deal with them. He writes,

> The issue is not an assassination of one man [Mullah Dadullah], despite the sacredness of Muslims' blood, but it is the beginning of the assassination of the true jihadi stream that refuses hypocrisy in the faith of God. You, the brothers, and Mahsud are symbols of this stream; therefore, you should watch out for the hypocrites. ... The brothers said that they will reserve judgment in dealing with them until they prove to be not trustworthy. I have no doubt that they showed that they are not trustworthy by trying to release the accused ones and they confirmed it by ousting Hajj Mansur Dadullah. They also confirmed it once again by refusing to transfer the issue to the justice system, as [Sheikh Saeed] mentioned. (…) Evading justice is a very dangerous thing for their faith and their life. As you remember, some of them, including [Taliban leader] Akhtar 'Uthmani, tried to prevent Tahir [Yuldashev] from being brought to justice in Afghanistan. Based on the above, please make sure to carry out steps that will protect and strengthen the honest stream and weaken the hypocritical stream that represents the ISI.[49]

The fact that bin Laden believed in the conspiracy theory about Mullah Dadullah's killing does not, of course, lend credence to the theory itself. It rather speaks to bin Laden's isolation in Abbottabad. We glean from the Abbottabad letters that the other al-Qaida leaders, including Sheikh Saeed and Zawahiri, were more careful in making rash judgments about the Taliban, while bin Laden sometimes had a tendency to jump to conclusions and to back them up with doctrinarian positions about Sharia and jihad. The Mansour Dadullah case is a good example of this. In his reply to Sheikh Saeed, bin Laden did not comment on the serious crimes that were in fact committed by Mansour Dadullah prior to his expulsion from Taliban, i.e., his refusal to heed Mullah Omar's direct order to send the arrested "spies" to Waziristan for trial, and his subsequent decision to kill the two spies without permission. Each act in itself—killing prisoners, and disobedience to the Emir—was a grave violation of the Taliban's code of conduct, and according to Mutma'in at least, it was not unusual for Mullah Omar to expel disobedient members the way he did with Mansour.[50] Sheikh Saeed's speculation that Mullah Omar "is not in a natural situation" because he did not insist on a Sharia trial seems somewhat unfounded. Likewise, bin Laden's assertion that the senior Taliban leaders were "no doubt" part of a "hypocritical stream" within the Taliban was built upon a view that bin Laden had developed several years earlier. From 1998 onwards, bin Laden's relationship with the Taliban had grown tense due to disagreements over bin Laden's right to issue anti-American propaganda from the soil of Afghanistan.[51] As bin Laden alluded to, there was also an incident in early 2001 when there was a tense conflict between al-Qaida and the Islamic Movement of Uzbekistan, in which the Taliban sided with the Uzbeks.[52] Bin Laden's allegation some seven years later, that parts of the Taliban leadership lack commitment to the true principles of Sharia, was therefore not new.

Bin Laden dismisses Atiyah's earlier suggestion that they should send Mullah Omar a test message through the "hypocritical" leaders in the Quetta Shura. "The condition for corresponding [with Mullah Omar] is a trustworthy intermediary," he says, and this ends the matter for the time being.[53] As far as is known, there is no correspondence between al-Qaida and the Taliban until a year later—around mid-2009, when Zawahiri establishes contact with Mullah Omar's assistant, Tayyib Agha, and sends him a letter commenting on the Taliban's foreign policy. Bin Laden sends Mullah Omar at least two letters, one in September 2010, and another one in December 2010, five months before he is killed.[54] We will return to these in the next section.

Al-Qaida Positioning Itself for the Future (2009–11)

The year 2009 marked a new shift in the Taliban insurgency, because it is the year that Taliban became convinced that the United States will soon leave Afghanistan. President Obama's speech in December 2009, in which he announced a start date for the US withdrawal, served as a final confirmation to both the Taliban and al-Qaida that victory was near. But as previously discussed, the Pakistanis had become wary of the waning US commitment to the war already in 2008. There was considerable international pressure in 2009 on reaching a reconciliation deal between the Taliban and Karzai, and on the Taliban to denounce al-Qaida. These pressures subsequently led to unrest within the Taliban between a faction favoring a negotiated deal and another faction wanting to pursue a purely military solution. The "military solution" did not mean exclusive focus on armed jihad, but rather, a comprehensive political and military campaign aimed at presenting Taliban as the only viable alternative to power in Afghanistan, and to push for direct negotiations between the United States and the Taliban. In 2009, the Taliban's external communications thus shifted toward a more reconciliatory tone, and Taliban started improving their foreign relations with other countries.

In the spring of 2009, a Taliban *kumisiun* again visits al-Qaida in Waziristan. Like a year ago, the purpose is to coordinate the upcoming fighting season with all the Waziristan-based support groups. The commission meets with Sheikh Saeed, and praises his efforts to create the "Mujahideen Shura Council," a joint Shura for jihadists in the tribal areas of Pakistan. The Mujahideen Shura Council was ostensibly an alliance between three Pakistani commanders (Hafiz Gul Bahadur, Maulawi Nazir, and Baitullah Mahsud), but al-Qaida claimed in internal communications that the Shura was led by Sheikh Saeed, with Abu Yahya al-Libi as the deputy.[55] This "Shura" appears to have been an initiative by Mullah Omar, and there were rumors that the Haqqanis were also involved in its creation, but the facts remain unconfirmed.[56] The purpose of the Shura is to unite the ranks to fight jihad in Afghanistan, which is in line with the general policy of Afghan Taliban, but its purpose is also to "defend" North Waziristan from the Pakistani Army's incursions into tribal territories. Sheikh Saeed and Zawahiri both reported in August-September 2009 that the Waziristan-based mujahidin were carrying out many attacks on the Pakistani Army in North Waziristan, and TTP also carried out terrorist attacks in Pakistani cities, to put pressure on the Pakistanis to leave them alone.[57]

The Taliban *kumisiun* in spring 2009 delivered to Sheikh Saeed yet another "suspicious-looking" letter from Mullah Omar.[58] Al-Qaida's suspicion that parts of the Taliban were under the control of ISI, and that they were using Mullah Omar's name in their communications, thus persisted. Al-Qaida at this time was still waiting for a direct line to open up with Mullah Omar's personal assistant, Tayyib Agha. That line seems to have opened up around mid-2009, when Zawahiri sent Tayyib Agha a letter "… containing a warning to him, a reminder, and a discussion about Iran, the UAE, and about some of the expressions they use."[59] We do not have this letter, but we can guess the main content based on Tayyib Agha's answer which came about a year later in June 2010.[60] In this letter, Tayyib Agha defended the Taliban's decision to establish a relationship with "some countries and parties that agree with us on opposing the [Americans]," and he also defended the Taliban's decision to establish relationships "even with the fighting enemy" to "stop the war or entering a treaty," and he says this was a direct order from the Commander of the Faithful "owing to the presence of such relationships with them in the past." Tayyib Agha remarks that al-Qaida did not object to these relationships in the past, "so why are the brothers worried today?" He also states that the Taliban will not abandon "the treaty agreement and its articles and content."

One is left to speculate on the exact content of Zawahiri's original letter to Tayyib, but as a minimum, Zawahiri probably criticized the Taliban for establishing relations with certain foreign countries such as Pakistan, the

UAE, and Iran. As for the "treaty" that Zawahiri criticized, the most probable interpretation is that it refers to a peace treaty between Pakistani militants and the Pakistani government—of which there were several in 2009—that was endorsed by Mullah Omar.[61] For example, prior to the formation of the Mujahideen Shura Council in February 2009, Mullah Omar was quoted in some media, urging the TTP to stop attacking Pakistani security forces. Even if al-Qaida supported the Mujahideen Shura Council, they probably would have objected to this type of black-and-white statement, given that al-Qaida and TTP were in a direct battle with Pakistani Army in Waziristan and elsewhere, and that as a minimum, they needed to fight the Pakistani Army in self-defense.

In late 2009, the Taliban indicated in public messaging they would be willing to negotiate directly over a US withdrawal. In a statement sent to media on December 4, 2009, they said that the Taliban has "no agenda of meddling in the internal affairs of other countries and is ready to give legal guarantees if foreign forces withdraw from Afghanistan."[62] The message that a future Taliban state will be of "no harm to other countries" had been repeated in Mullah Omar's public messages since at least 2008,[63] but this time, the Taliban were more explicit.

By the end of 2009, al-Qaida mid-level leaders have sensed a change in the Taliban over the last year, and start thinking about how to strengthen what they call the "sincere" or "honest" Taliban—those who believe that "armed jihad" is the only way to win the war in Afghanistan, and who reject any form of negotiated solution with the United States or Karzai. Zawahiri thus wrote the letter to Tayyib Agha in mid-2009 as a start. Bin Laden throughout 2009 appeared to be uninterested in trying to write a letter to Mullah Omar, and perhaps for this reason, al-Qaida's Sharia official Abu Yahya al-Libi sent a letter to bin Laden on January 24, 2010, reminding him of the importance of reconnecting with Mullah Omar. Al-Libi told bin Laden that he had noticed recently in the Taliban's official statements "the use of terms and phrases that were not customary or known among them," and that statements issued in Mullah Omar's name were "very far from his style, method, and tone, and it may be that the Shura Council has the authority to issue statements in its name."[64] Abu Yahya does not state explicitly what he thinks, but it seems that he is worried about the "hypocritical stream" in Taliban gaining too much influence. So he suggests to bin Laden to open up a direct line of communication with Mullah Omar:

> What I see, our honorable Sheikh, is to activate the relationship between you and the Commander of the Faithful through correspondence, which God willing will be easy. This will have a good effect on their souls, and make them feel your closeness to them and your adoption of their cause. It would be nice if

you would communicate with them, remind them, and strengthen their resolve, as there will be great good in that, God willing.[65]

On May 16, 2010, Zawahiri writes a letter to bin Laden where he gives his thoughts on how al-Qaida should position itself with the Taliban. He writes, under a paragraph called "Entrenchment [*al-tamakkun*] in Khorasan,"

> I think that we have to enable the base of jihad in Khorasan, and the conquest is approaching with God's help, and our entrenchment in Khorasan requires us to make its people and righteous people our supporters and backers, especially the Taliban and their loyal leaders, headed by the Commander of the Faithful, may God protect him.

> And that we deal with them with wisdom and reason before emotion and enthusiasm. And that we approach them gradually, and there is no harm in using some of the cunning that is permissible by Sharia, from not showing all matters, and arranging means of movement and communication that are not apparent, and reducing the display of the real presence until it appears much less than its reality, ...

> And following an educational approach with the Taliban in particular and the Afghans in general, which produces generations of ideological Mujahideen leaders, and other means that I ask God to open up for the Mujahideen, so that they balance between the necessity of preserving their fortress in Khorasan, and continuing their work in it and outside it.[66]

Zawahiri's plan is generally the same approach that al-Qaida has always had to the Taliban, namely, to try and gradually convert them to their own ideology and to concentrate on networking with what they call the "sincere stream," individuals who are closer to al-Qaida ideologically and who might influence the direction of the movement at large. In addition, Zawahiri now adds that al-Qaida should pursue a population-centric policy in Afghanistan where al-Qaida will educate a new generation of "ideological mujahidin leaders"—presumably through militant training camps, religious schools, institutes, and the like.

Zawahiri then discusses some possible future scenarios for Afghanistan. The first is that the Taliban takes power in Afghanistan after negotiating a deal with the Americans to restrict al-Qaida's activities within the country. Zawahiri writes that he does not think the Americans would accept this solution, but if he were an American advisor ("and thank God I am not") this is what he would advise, as it would be a worst-case scenario for al-Qaida's future in the country. He suggests that if the above happens, al-Qaida should basically do what they did prior to 2001. They should work with the Taliban to gradually gain their trust and, at the same time, continue pursuing their global agenda in secret, and through the regional affiliates, who are not under Taliban's authority.

> … we should continue some of the means of secret organizations in continuing our work in a way that does not explicitly contradict the orders of the Commander of the Faithful. … At the same time, our brothers in other regions, that are not under the authority of a government, must continue the rest of our [global jihadi] message which we cannot declare or practice.[67]

In his May 2010 letter to bin Laden, Zawahiri discusses other options for Afghanistan's future, including the possibility that Taliban takes power in Afghanistan by force. He assesses that this is the best option for al-Qaida, because it would forge a close alliance between al-Qaida and the Taliban against the rest of the world. But regardless of what will happen, Zawahiri sees a future for al-Qaida in Afghanistan under Taliban sponsorship, working slowly to gain more ideological influence within the Taliban through training, education, and networking with their ideological allies within the movement. The scenario is similar to how al-Qaida worked with the Taliban in the 1990s, the difference being that al-Qaida now has "regional affiliates" in the Middle East and North Africa that can presumably carry out the globally oriented work that the Taliban does not want to be associated with Afghanistan.[68]

On May 31, 2010, Zawahiri sent a second letter to bin Laden, elaborating among other things on the importance of Afghanistan for al-Qaida's future. He thinks Taliban will soon return to Afghanistan in which case it will be important, as a "fortress of Islam and a shelter for Muslims and immigrants."[69] He says victory in Iraq and Afghanistan is essential for the jihadist movement, but Afghanistan is more important, because it is more likely, while Iraq— although strategically more important—"… is expected to spin in a spiral of sectarian and ethnic conflicts."[70] His remarks are made in context of a wider discussion in al-Qaida around this time on whether al-Qaida should focus on staging new international terrorist attacks against the United States, or continue their support to the wars in Afghanistan and Iraq. Bin Laden favors the former solution while Zawahiri favors the latter, because Zawahiri is convinced that the United States is weakening fast as a consequence of these wars, and that it is only a matter of time before the Taliban wins the war in Afghanistan.

On June 19, 2010, Atiyah informs bin Laden that they have restored their line of communication with Tayyib Agha, and he sends bin Laden Tayyib Agha's letter defending the Taliban's decision to have foreign relations and to enter "pacts" with the "fighting enemy," as discussed previously.[71] About three weeks later, on July 8, 2010, Atiyah writes a new letter, and tells bin Laden about al-Qaida's recent contact with a messenger from Tayyib Agha. The messenger said that Mullah Omar wanted to meet with bin Laden, and that he had an important oral message for bin Laden to be delivered in person. Al-Qaida answered that the request was impossible as it was in violation of the strict operational security procedures around bin Laden. Sheikh Saeed suggested instead that the two leaders should communicate via audio recordings.[72]

The Abbottabad collection gives no further indication of what the "important" message from Mullah Omar was in early July 2010, or if the two leaders succeeded in communicating via audio. In the 2010 fighting season the Taliban was under renewed and strong military pressure from the US "surge,"[73] and at the same time, the Quetta Shura Taliban were losing power internally to other actors, such as the Haqqanis and the Peshawar Shura.[74] In this context, one could speculate if Mullah Omar, or someone acting in his name, wanted to reach out to bin Laden to encourage him to issue public speeches to help strengthen internal cohesion among the Taliban and help redirect financing streams from the Gulf towards Quetta. According to one source, Tayyib Agha in 2010 was specifically put in charge of collecting money donations from the Middle East on behalf of the Taliban.[75] He was also responsible for setting up the first Taliban delegation to Qatar in 2010, which later turned into a permanent Taliban representation in Doha.[76] This context provides a background for understanding Tayyeb Agha's increased correspondence with al-Qaida in 2010, especially a letter to bin Laden dated August 28, 2010, in which al-Qaida is asked to minimize their presence in Afghanistan, which we will return to below.

First, we need to discuss another contextual factor, which is that around June 2010, the Pakistanis reached out to al-Qaida and TTP in Waziristan in order to convince them to stop attacking inside Pakistan. Despite the formation of the "Mujahideen Shura Council" for Waziristan in February 2009, groups such as TTP had continued fighting the Pakistani army and had carried out a large number of terrorist attacks in Pakistani cities.[77] It can be noted also that the Pakistan intelligence leadership (via "Shujah Shah" as al-Qaida calls him) sent al-Qaida several messengers in 2010—one of them at the start of July 2010—the same time as Mullah Omar's messenger came to Waziristan with the "important message." This is what the Pakistani intelligence said, according to Atiyah's description:

What was noteworthy this time [start of July 2010] was that they also inserted Hamid Gul into the meeting, and Fadl-al-Rahman Khalil [leader of Harakat ul-Mujahidin] attended as an advisor. They sent a message saying, "Give us some time, a month and a half or two. We are trying to convince the Americans and pressure them to negotiate with al-Qaʻida, and to convince them as well that negotiating with the Taliban without al-Qaʻida is of no use. Just wait a little bit. If we are able to convince the Americans, then we (meaning the Pakistanis themselves) have no objection to negotiating with you and sitting down with you."[78]

Atiyah's letter illustrates that both al-Qaida and TTP are independent actors in Pakistan who try to influence the situation by playing other actors against each other, and by threatening and using violence in a strategic manner. They are neither pawns of the Pakistani intelligence, nor irreconcilable extremists who only know violence, but they do represent a clear "jihadist" stance. After describing the various negotiation processes, Atiyah sums it up by saying to bin Laden:

> As you know, this is just talk! So are the Pakistanis serious, or are they just playing with us? We must be cautious and ready and aware. We must maintain our focus and determination. Of course, they are in a difficult position, as well, and they see their lords and masters, the Americans, in an extremely difficult position, too. This is a government mired in hypocrisy, but there is refuge in God.[79]

Atiyah sums up his opinion to bin Laden: "We will take advantage of any genuine opportunity for a truce with the Pakistanis so that we can focus wholly on the Americans. This is clear. Yes, there may be difficulty in it for many of our Pakistani brothers, [but we will try to convince them]."[80] In other words, there is general alignment in the interests of al-Qaida and parts of the Pakistani establishment—they both want the jihad to focus on fighting in Afghanistan, at least for now.

In August 2010, bin Laden told Atiyah that he agreed to Atiyah's proposal to move al-Qaida senior members out of Waziristan and lay low for a while. He says that military operations in Afghanistan should focus on "special large operations"—presumably, a reference to the complex suicide attacks that the Haqqani network was known for. The campaign seemed to be a strategic adaptation to shape the battlefield in Taliban's favor in Afghanistan, to pave the way for a military solution to the conflict, which may also include direct negotiations (not for peace, but surrender and withdrawal) between Taliban and the Americans. Bin Laden supported this strategy.[81]

On August 28, 2010, Atiyah reported to bin Laden that a letter had arrived from Mullah Omar via Tayyib Agha. While we cannot be completely sure, it appears that this might be an unsigned and undated letter that was found in Abbottabad and released by the Office of the Director of National Intelligence (ODNI) in 2015, under the nondescript heading "Undated letter re Afghanistan."[82] The letter is addressed to "My dear brother," and it asks him for three things: first, to establish "the bases" in the neighboring country, meaning Pakistan; second, to "not announce a responsible official (*mas'ul*) for the country in the future"; and third, that "you, and the officials who are known among you, avoid showing your presence in the country, now and in the future, although your participation in *jihad* will continue with the mujahidin as before."[83]

The sentence that most clearly suggests this is a letter from Mullah Omar is the request to the "brother" to not appoint a future *mas'ul* for Afghanistan. The Arab group that in the past had been most candid about having an official responsible for Afghanistan was al-Qaida. As we recall from earlier, al-Qaida appointed Sheikh Saeed as Amir for "Al-Qaida in Afghanistan" in May 2007, and Sheikh Saeed was killed on May 22, 2010, just two months before Atiyah forwarded the anonymous letter to bin Laden. Another fact that suggests the letter is from Mullah Omar to bin Laden is that the letter matches correspondence from bin Laden addressed to Mullah Omar one month later, on September 25, 2010. This letter is addressed to the "Emir of the Faithful" [Mullah Omar's title] and contains a short message saying that "we hear and obey in what you mentioned for we are your soldiers and we are with you heart and soul in supporting the great religion of God."[84]

Bin Laden probably viewed the Mullah Omar letter with suspicion, because it was in the same format (printed on a computer and with no signature) as the purported Mullah Omar letters that Sheikh Saeed had flagged in the past as being "of dubious accuracy." However, since the letter was delivered through Tayyib Agha, which was a channel that al-Qaida trusted, bin Laden could hardly ignore it. He thus sent a standard reply of "we hear and obey," but more interestingly, al-Qaida also appears to have heeded several of Mullah Omar's requests. Al-Qaida never appointed another Emir for Afghanistan, and al-Qaida's al-Sahab media agency largely stopped issuing propaganda where al-Qaida's presence in Afghanistan was mentioned.[85] This meant that al-Sahab also had to cancel a planned release of a propaganda video about the Bagram attack on May 22, 2010, which they did. Atiyah reported to bin Laden in June 2010 about the German-Turkish fighter Bekkay Harrach's leading role in that attack and described him as a former member of al-Qaida's External Operations cell. Coincidence may have derailed al-Sahab's video project, but it was conspicuous that al-Qaida never announced Bekkay Harrach's "martyrdom," and that his "martyrdom" finally was announced more than six months later by the Islamic Movement of Uzbekistan, describing him as an IMU member.[86] One can now guess, based on the Abbottabad documents, that this had to do with the new media restrictions that the Taliban imposed on bin Laden in August 2010.

On November 5, 2010, bin Laden sent a second message to Mullah Omar. This message was not styled as a response, which suggests it was sent on bin Laden's initiative. The message concerned a topic that bin Laden had been preoccupied with since at least mid-2010, namely the issue of "shedding Muslim blood." The gist of the message is that bin Laden wants Mullah Omar to issue a public speech where he reminds Taliban that it is not permissible to "shed Muslim blood" and one must especially avoid targeting mosques and public markets. He refers to "many new reports [of such attacks] recently," and reminds Mullah Omar that such attacks are not permissible according to Sharia. He concludes, "Muslims in general, and the mujahidin in particular, need to hear you cautioning them on the serious matter of shedding Muslim blood unjustly."[87]

The year 2010 was an extremely bloody one in both Afghanistan and Pakistan, with many suicide attacks targeting mosques, weddings, and public gatherings. In addition, there was an uptick in attacks in Pakistan targeting Shia religious sites and gatherings. Bin Laden's letter to Mullah Omar may have been prompted by bin Laden's sincere desire to stop this negative trend, seen as extremely damaging for the reputation of the jihadist movement. He had recently given the same type of advice to the leader of AQAP, Nasir al-Wuhayshi, in Yemen (discussed in more detail in Chapter 7). At the same time, bin Laden's words to Mullah Omar appeared to be a bit like preaching to the choir, as the Afghan Taliban were well aware of the danger of shedding blood unjustly, and had warned about it in their own propaganda and code of conduct for years already.[88]

Bin Laden's letter to Mullah Omar may in fact have been prompted by another, unrelated incident. On October 31, 2010, the Islamic State in Iraq carried out a highly controversial attack on the Cathedral of Sayyidat al-Najat in Baghdad, where they massacred forty-seven worshippers. In the aftermath of the incident bin Laden received a letter of criticism from someone named "Shuayb," and in response, bin Laden instructed both Atiyah and Zawahiri to issue short statements on the topic of avoiding unjust bloodshed, and to make it a priority. Moreover, he instructed Atiyah to inform "Shuayb" that he had written about the issue to Mullah Omar. The context thus suggests that bin Laden's last letter to Mullah Omar was part of a larger effort by al-Qaida around this time to correct their image abroad, and especially in the Middle East. This topic will be further elaborated in the next chapter.

In November and December 2010, Ayman al-Zawahiri wrote two letters to bin Laden to comment on the letter that Mullah Omar sent to bin Laden in July 2010, which bin Laden replied to with a short message saying, "We hear and obey in what you mentioned." Zawahiri offered the following analysis:

> Regarding our friend's letter to you, a thought appeared to me, which is that this letter may have been prompted by the fear of these brothers of the expansion of Al-Qaida and its growth by the grace and power of God, and that they see that bearing the burden of this huge body is too much for them, and their energy is insufficient for it, and exposes them to problems with many parties. ... Therefore, they are content with protecting those who flee to them, and they do not go beyond that.[89]

Zawahiri thinks that because of this attitude, Taliban might pressure al-Qaida in the future to deny their connection to other groups. Therefore, he recommends to bin Laden that al-Qaida should announce the affiliation of al-Shabaab in Somalia as soon as possible, so that the Taliban cannot pressure them to deny their connection to al-Shabaab in the future. In another letter, Zawahiri speculates further on why Taliban said what they did:

> This time, another possibility occurred to me, which is the economic possibility, meaning that our brothers [in the Taliban] expect that things will go their way, but they fear the difficult economic situation they will face, and they know that any party's cooperation with them is conditional on abandoning people like us, and therefore they proposed this solution, which satisfies their consciences and opens the way for them—as they think—to development, and I think that they should be left until they realize the facts themselves, because they do not learn from the experiences of those who came before them, such as Sudan and others.[90]

Zawahiri says that there is a worst-case scenario, which is that "[they] want us to be nothing but silent and inactive refugees."[91] He then proposes a work plan to ensure al-Qaida's survival in the region in the future, which is more detailed than the thoughts he presented in March 2010. He now says that first, al-Qaida should continue their *da'wa* and training of the jihadist movement in Pakistan so that Pakistan's tribal areas will continue to be safe bases. Second, he proposes that al-Qaida should influence the Afghan Taliban to become more receptive of al-Qaida's ideology, through educating the local youth "through military, religious and cultural courses," and working with our "loyal friends" in the movement. As examples of "loyal friends," he mentions Sheikh Haqqani and Professor Muhammad Yasir, who have been mentioned in other Abbottabad correspondence as well, and some commanders in Eastern Afghanistan, some of whom have ties to al-Qaida going back to the 1989 Battle for Jalalabad, and who were allied with bin Laden after 1996. Third, he says al-Qaida should move away from "the center" (probably a reference to North Waziristan), and to minimize visibility in general. Al-Qaida should stop specifying their place in their official media. Al-Qaida should stop having permanent training camps, centers, and guest houses, but continue supporting the jihad in Afghanistan, and to have mobile training facilities. These suggestions mirror the request in the presumed Mullah Omar letter to bin Laden in August 2010, and indicate that Ayman al-Zawahiri took the letter seriously and was ready to heed at least some of Mullah Omar's orders.[92] Fourth, Zawahiri suggests strengthening al-Qaida's links with groups outside Afghanistan and Pakistan, both by strengthening communications with the affiliates and by adding new groups to their affiliate network.[93]

We do not know what bin Laden replied to Zawahiri, but in a draft document commenting on events in late 2010–early 2011, bin Laden wrote some lines which sound like they were meant for Zawahiri:

> Regarding what you mentioned about the possibilities for the next stage and the pressures of the Tayyib [Agha] group on us, I think that if that is the case without there being another arena to which we can go, then the [fighting] brothers will remain with them, and we and the brother leaders will be outside Afghanistan in Pakistan, for example, even if it requires that we disappear as we are now, in exchange for the officials remaining far from the pressure of the people (*al-qawm*).[94]

Although it is never stated explicitly, it seems that al-Qaida by late 2010 had now given up the hope of finding an alternative way of communicating with Mullah Omar, far from the eyes of the ISI or their agents. As we recall, their only hope for such communication was through Mullah Omar's secretary Tayyib Agha, but when al-Qaida finally received a message from Tayyib Agha in mid-2010 it was in the same "suspicious" format as the letters they had previously received from various Taliban delegations to Waziristan. Al-Qaida decided to work within these new realities while looking for other opportunities to continue the "global jihad."

Concluding Remarks

Al-Qaida's correspondence with the Taliban leadership picked up in 2009–10, when both Taliban and al-Qaida started positioning themselves for a future Taliban takeover of Afghanistan. In 2010, al-Qaida established a line of communication with Tayyib Agha, a long-time secretary and confidant of Mullah Omar whom the al-Qaida leaders trusted. In August 2010, Mullah Omar sent bin Laden a letter asking al-Qaida to keep a low profile in Afghanistan, and al-Qaida appears to have heeded this request. The content of Mullah Omar's message to al-Qaida conformed to the "hardliner" line within the Taliban that wanted to continue the armed jihad, but that also wanted to position themselves as a real, political alternative to the Afghan regime. This required that the Taliban distance themselves from al-Qaida, at least on the surface. Al-Qaida had little choice but to answer politely, but simultaneously plan for how they could achieve a better position in the future. Al-Qaida was not ready to give up its "global jihadi" agenda, but the leaders realized they had to work within the realities of Afghanistan.

The strategy proposed by Ayman al-Zawahiri in late 2010 was in some ways a continuation of how al-Qaida had dealt with the Taliban pre-2001, but there were some notable differences. First, al-Qaida should make full use of Pakistan's Tribal Areas and strengthen the "jihad movement" there to function as a secondary base for al-Qaida. Second, al-Qaida should actively educate Afghans and insert them as loyal elements into the Taliban's future organization. Third, al-Qaida should minimize their overt presence in the region, and instead, work through their regional affiliates in the Middle East and North Africa, and work to strengthen al-Qaida's global network. We do not know what bin Laden thought about this strategy at the time, but the Abbottabad documents suggest he was preoccupied with larger questions, such as what kind of organization al-Qaida should be in the future, and how to organize the next stage of al-Qaida's confrontation with the United States. Bin Laden also devoted considerable time to following political developments in Yemen.

Then the Arab spring happened, and it took everyone by surprise, including al-Qaida. Bin Laden's initial reaction was that the spring revolutions were a good omen and a political opportunity for al-Qaida. Based on drafts found on bin Laden's computer, he saw the Arab Spring as proof that the United States had finally been so weakened that it had been forced to withdraw its influence from the Middle East:

> While we were fighting in Afghanistan and draining the head of the infidels, it became weak to a degree that enabled the Muslim nation to regain some of its self-confidence and courage. It also removed the overwhelming pressure to not revolt against the agents of the US. As this pressure gradually vanished, the people started their revolutions.

Bin Laden's final directions regarding jihad in Afghanistan are also a fitting way of summing up this chapter:

> We got what we wanted from the Afghanistan front, by shattering the prestige of the world's main infidel, and though we will continue our jihad there, yet we should give our main attention to the Muslim nation's revolution that should be illuminated with the creed of monotheism in order to reinstate the rule of the Caliphate.[95]

External Operations 2008–11

I acknowledge that it is important to strike America and Europe in their own homes, but we must also realize that the battle in Afghanistan and Iraq is extremely important.[1]
> —Ayman al-Zawahiri, in a letter to bin Laden in May 2010

In 2010, al-Qaida was divided on how much time and resources the organization should spend on targeting the United States. At the start of the year, bin Laden sent out a letter to the other senior leaders, arguing that al-Qaida needed to re-focus all its efforts on striking inside the United States because the wars in Iraq and Afghanistan were not sufficient to deplete US resources and force its withdrawal from the Muslim world. Ayman al-Zawahiri disagreed, saying the wars were working and that it was just a matter of time. He observed that throughout history, empires had fallen due to costly wars abroad, and not due to terrorist attacks in their own homes.[2] In an argumentative style rather typical of Zawahiri, he turned bin Laden's own words against him: "Abu Abdullah [bin Laden] has previously mentioned that Iraq is the most important battlefield of jihad in this era, and that the battle with America and the West will be decided … on the battlefield, not in their own homes."[3]

These discussions must be seen in the context of a broader discussion that took place around the same time about al-Qaida's policies toward their regional affiliates, primarily in Yemen, Algeria, and Somalia. The discussions about al-Qaida's external operations thus took on two dimensions, one pertaining to al-Qaida "Central" and its External Operations office in Pakistan, and the second pertaining to al-Qaida's affiliates and what kinds of operations and targets they should prioritize. In the letter exchanges between the al-Qaida leaders in Pakistan, these two dimensions are sometimes hard to tell apart, which is partly a reflection of the different views on "external operations" that existed within al-Qaida. Nevertheless, I will attempt to separate the two. In this chapter, I continue the history of al-Qaida's External Office in Pakistan, while the next chapter will mainly deal with al-Qaida's policy toward the regional branches.

In Chapter 3, I talked about how al-Qaida's external operations office experienced a lull in activities in 2007. The most disruptive event was Rashid Rauf's arrest in Pakistan in August 2006, which led to the unraveling of Abu Ubaydah al-Masri's external operations network in Pakistan and in the UK. An unrelated incident, which may also have affected external operations, is that in the spring of 2007 there was a major crisis internally in the jihadist movement in Iraq, which preoccupied much of the al-Qaida leadership's attention. Abu Ubaydah al-Masri briefly appeared in the Abbottabad documents in 2007, but only in "carbon copy" on Atiyah's communications with Iraq and various new jihadist groups in the Levant and Gaza. This suggests that Abu Ubaydah was either inactive because of deteriorating health, or distracted by the Iraq crisis, or both. However, he still had some assistants working for him, such as a man nicknamed Saleh al-Somali (aka Abu Salih, Abd al-Hafiz) who took over External Operations from 2008 onward.

While Saleh al-Somali tried to restart al-Qaida's external operations, Germany-based volunteers had started traveling to Waziristan. The first group of significance came in 2006, and they included individuals who became part of the so-called "Sauerland plot" in 2007.[4] In this first group, there was also a Moroccan-German individual named Bekkay Harrach, who used the nickname Abu Talha al-Almani. While many of the Germans joined a Turkish-speaking group in Waziristan called Islamic Jihad Union, Harrach ended up joining al-Qaida, and this could simply have been owing to his Arabic language and cultural background, or because, as Sheikh Saeed recalled later, "he came with the intention of a martyrdom operation."[5] Harrach ended up working in al-Qaida's External Operations under both Abu Ubaydah and Saleh al-Somali.[6] He became the most visible face of al-Qaida's anti-Western propaganda in 2009, but in reality he played only a minor role in operations. The most important of Saleh al-Somali's assistants in Waziristan was Rashid Rauf, who managed to escape from Pakistani jail in December 2007. Rauf was involved in meeting and training various Western recruits who came to Waziristan in 2008–9, some of whom were later sentenced in Europe and in the United States on terrorism charges. In addition to Rauf, the American-born Adnan al-Shukrijumah (aka Ja'far al-Tayyar, Tufan) worked in al-Qaida's external operations office in this period. Abbottabad documents reveal that he was a rather colorful personality who did not contribute substantially to al-Somali's work, in spite of having a 5 million USD bounty on his head. The fact that he was a "most wanted terrorist" by the FBI was seen by al-Qaida as a liability, because it meant he could not move around in Pakistan. But what disqualified him from being promoted in al-Qaida in the end might simply have been his lack of skills.[7]

Overall, the chapter argues that al-Qaida's External Operations deteriorated under Saleh al-Somali's command, especially after November 2008 when Rashid Rauf was killed in a drone strike. After Rauf was killed, al-Somali lacked experienced personnel and resources, which led to experimentation with other, and more low-cost methods of terrorizing the West. This included what Atiyah referred to later as "psychological warfare" in the form of propaganda videos featuring the Moroccan-German Bekkay Harrach, and the scaling down of terrorist attacks to using everyday items, such as knives and gas canisters, as weapons.[8]

Bin Laden was unimpressed with al-Somali's performance and already in mid-2009, he requested that Atiyah replace him. The problem was that there were no other candidates, because *all* of al-Qaida's experienced external operations cadre had now been arrested, killed, or died of natural causes.[9] This dire situation changed somewhat in January 2010 when one of al-Qaida's Sharia officials, the young and multi-talented Yunus al-Mauritani, wrote to bin Laden and proposed a new plan to revive al-Qaida's External Operations work. Al-Mauritani subsequently became a favorite of bin Laden's, and was appointed in mid-2010 to be in charge of attacking "American interests abroad," including an ambitious plan designed by bin Laden personally to attack oil tankers in the Strait of Hormuz. But this attack plan is only a small part of the story about al-Qaida's External Operations office in this period. The most surprising discovery from Abbottabad documents is the diversity of opinions that existed among al-Qaida leaders in 2010 on the very topic of "external operations." As I will argue, this calls into question the definition of al-Qaida as a group dedicated to targeting *the West*, or "the far enemy" per se. While it might have been true in 2001, ten years later the picture became more nuanced.

External Operations under Saleh al-Somali (2008–9)

When Saleh al-Somali took over as External Operations chief in early 2008, al-Qaida enjoyed a relatively stable sanctuary in North Waziristan. This sanctuary was about to be targeted in a massive campaign of drone strikes that had been approved by the Bush administration, and that continued in full force after

President Obama took office in January 2009.[10] The first high-ranking victim of this drone campaign was Abu al-Layth al-Libi, who was killed at the end of January 2008. However, in 2008 al-Qaida probably did not realize yet the carnage that was about to hit the organization. Only in the spring of 2010 did al-Qaida's leadership order a full review of their own security situation in Waziristan, which resulted in a report recommending that al-Qaida leave North Waziristan.[11] The US drone campaign in 2008–9 can be seen as part of the reason for why al-Qaida initiated an internal review process in 2010, which led to a policy of moving more of al-Qaida's operational activities outside the Afghanistan-Pakistan region. But in 2008, there was still a window of opportunity for al-Qaida to try and revive the terrorist campaign against Europe that Rashid Rauf had previously helped design in 2004–6.

Little is known about the man known as Saleh al-Somali, including his true identity. He was appointed as al-Qaida's external operations chief sometime after Abu Ubaydah's death around January 2008, and in March the same year he wrote bin Laden a letter outlining his ideas and plans for external operations work.[12] Al-Somali reveals in the letter that he worked "for a little while" with the previous chiefs, Hamza Rabia and Abu Ubaydah al-Masri, and that he gathered his knowledge from conversations with them, and from bin Laden's public speeches. He then outlines his interpretation of al-Qaida's external operations strategy: to prioritize hitting the United States, preferably inside America, and preferably "economic and military targets" as well as targets that lead to "general terror" (*ra'ab 'amm*), such as large crowds of people. As a second priority, he talks about targets related to the "international system that America controls," such as the UN, oil, and gas, and his third priority is US allies, which he divides into "layers," with the top layer at this stage being "the UK, Denmark, Canada and France." Al-Somali admits in the letter that al-Qaida's external operations activities suffer from a defunct Documents Forgery Office, which means in practice that they have to rely on operatives entering Pakistan on short-term visitor visas.[13]

After sending his initial report to bin Laden in March 2008, Saleh al-Somali set out to fulfill his "vision for the work." According to a progress report he wrote a year later, this vision included carrying out an "operation" by the end of 2008; re-establishing an organizational structure to support the work; and networking with other groups so that they could "carry out parts of this assignment."[14] We now know quite a bit about this activity in 2008, through the court cases of several al-Qaida recruits arrested in Europe and the United States in 2009 and 2010. The three most serious plots, which all had confirmed links to Saleh al-Somali, were the "Manchester plot" in the UK in April 2009, the "New York City

Subway plot" in the United States in September 2009, and the "Jyllands-Posten plot" in Norway and Denmark in July 2010. The targets of these plots reflected al-Qaida's old strategy of attacking the United States and the UK, alongside a new target—Denmark, because of the Muhammad cartoons affair going back to late 2005. Bin Laden issued two speeches in April 2006 and January 2008, respectively, directly threatening the cartoonists. More importantly, after his January 2008 speech he issued an internal order to al-Qaida's senior leaders to stage attacks on Denmark. Zawahiri followed up the order in March 2008, by writing letters to the al-Qaida Emirs in Iraq and Algeria, urging them to target Danish interests at the first available opportunity.[15] It is likely that Saleh al-Somali also received the order to attack Denmark around this same time.[16]

Al-Somali was joined in the external operations work in 2008 by a small group of individuals. In internal al-Qaida communications, these are referred to as Rauf, "Anas," and "Tufan" in addition to some "new brothers," whom we know from other communications included the German-Moroccan Bekkay Harrach.[17] We know very little about "Anas," except for the fact that he was an experienced operative who was killed sometime before Rashid Rauf in November 2008. As for the other individuals, they affected the External Operations work in different ways.

Rashid Rauf was undoubtedly the most important of Saleh al-Somali's assistants, owing to his previous experience with al-Qaida's external operations from 2004 to 2006. He managed to escape from Pakistani jail in December 2007. His escape from jail was an embarrassing affair for Pakistani authorities, who later conducted an internal investigation of the incident.[18] The investigation concluded that Rauf's escape was in all likelihood staged after Rauf bribed, or got help from, some of the police officers who were watching him. Rauf was related by marriage to powerful clerical families in Pakistan, including to the family of Masood Azhar, the founder of Jaysh-e-Muhammed (JeM), a Pakistani militant group that was established in 2000 primarily to fight against India in Kashmir. JeM has a large network and resources in Pakistan, so the fact that Rauf managed to escape from jail is perhaps not too surprising.

From 2008, Rauf appears to have been based in North Waziristan, and often accompanied Saleh al-Somali when the latter met with Western recruits.[19] Between meeting recruits, Rauf found the time to write down a series of reports about his experiences and ideas for future work. These reports were discovered by German police in 2012, during the arrest and prosecution of a Turkish-German individual who had trained with al-Qaida in Waziristan.[20] It transpired later that this individual had been in contact with Yunus al-Mauritani, who in mid-

2010 was recruiting a team of international operatives for his newly proposed external operations project, which we will return to below. This suggests that Rauf's reports were part of the "library" of training and preparation literature that was kept by al-Qaida's External Operations office in Waziristan, and that was presumably used to train new operatives.

While al-Somali and Rauf were trying to revive al-Qaida's terrorist campaign against Europe in 2008, the American-born Adnan al-Shukrijumah was working alongside them with related activities. US authorities described al-Shukrijumah as a "most-wanted terrorist" with a 5 million USD bounty on his head, but the Abbottabad documents suggest that the reality was a bit more complex.[21] Internal al-Qaida correspondence in 2009–11 contains references to a certain "Tufan" who worked off and on with al-Qaida's External Operations, and because he fits the description of al-Shukrijumah, I have concluded that they are probably the same person.

Adnan al-Shukrijumah was born in Saudi Arabia and grew up in Florida, United States. He was an old al-Qaida associate from the early 2000s, and he might have met or worked with Khalid Sheikh Mohammed at some point. In December 2004, bin Laden proposed him (using his old nickname, Ja'far al-Tayyar) as a candidate to lead part of al-Qaida's external operations work, and more specifically, the effort to carry out a terrorist attack inside the United States.[22] It seems that Al-Shukrijumah was not taken onboard at this stage, because his name does not appear in any plots until 2008, when he became part of Saleh al-Somali's External Operations team.

Some of the recruits who were connected to the Najibullah Zazi plot in the United States in 2009 claimed they met with Shukrijumah in South Waziristan in late 2008, and that it was Shukrijumah who "convinced them to carry out an attack in the US."[23] It seems clear that Shukrijumah at the time was in charge of basic training for English-speakers who wanted to fight in Afghanistan, but it is not clear if he was also in charge of staging terrorist attacks in the US. The Abbottabad documents indicate that when Shukrijumah met Najibullah Zazi and the other members of the "New York City Subway plot," he did not enjoy the full trust of al-Qaida's senior leadership and was in the process of being "tested" by al-Qaida to perhaps take on more responsibilities in the future.

In August 2009, when al-Qaida discussed appointing a new external operations chief other than Somali, 'Tufan's' name came up: Atiyah wrote to bin Laden about Tufan, that " ... he has flaws and we all agree he is not suitable for this work as we had tried him, although he is now on Abu Saleh's [al-Somali's] work team."[24] In late December 2009, after al-Somali was killed, Sheikh Saeed wrote to bin Laden that there were two candidates to take over—Yunus al-Mauritani and Tufan (calling him Muhibullah). Tufan had positive and negative sides, making him on the one hand "the most suitable person" for the position, and on the other hand "not suitable at all" owing to his personality, and the fact that he was wanted by the Americans and therefore was unable to move around. In March 2010, Sheikh Saeed reported that he had come up with a solution where Yunus would first train a team that would form an external operations cell abroad, while Tufan would stay in Waziristan as a manager of a downsized external operations office there. One reads between the lines that this was not really a promotion, because al-Qaida was about to move all important and sensitive work out of Waziristan.

In August 2010, bin Laden specifically asked Atiyah for a candidate that would specialize in carrying out attacks inside America. Bin Laden wanted this activity to be completely separate from Yunus al-Mauritani's task to attack American targets abroad. Tufan's name came up again. Atiyah, who had been promoted to al-Qaida's general manager after Sheikh Saeed's death, started by expressing his relatively positive opinion of Tufan: "God willing, he is fit to supervise a major operation inside America, or work inside America in general, but we have some comments on the brother, …"[25] Atiyah then elaborates on Tufan's personality flaws, which are in line with what Sheikh Saeed had said in letters to bin Laden earlier: in short, Tufan is the kind of person who "asks for large sums of money to carry out operations," he has a "boasting personality," and he has a hard time concentrating on one thing. By now, Ayman al-Zawahiri had also been able to contribute to the discussion. Al-Zawahiri is rather negative toward Tufan, saying that "he doesn't enjoy trust in the organization," and complaining about his lack of focus in his work. However, Zawahiri is open to the idea of "testing him" to see if he has changed since the last time Zawahiri dealt with him—he does not specify when.[26] Atiyah sums up his conclusion to bin Laden: "For this reason [we] were cautious and tried to gradually employ him and give him the opportunity. But he has good qualities … The result is that this brother in my opinion now is perhaps suitable for this job." He further says: "This is preliminary information, if we want some deliberation—and this is what I see and advise because we have a session with brother Tufan after Eid [September 9–10, 2010], God willing, to discuss his work with us and the projects he proposes"[27]

We do not know what happened during this meeting "after Eid," and whether the results of the meeting were reported to bin Laden. But at the end of September 2010, bin Laden sent a short, but clear message to Atiyah: "With respect to the work in America, Brother 'Tufan' is not appropriate."[28] Shukrijumah was killed by Pakistani forces in South Waziristan in 2014, but it is unknown what his role was at that time. He obviously stayed in the Tribal Areas, perhaps maintaining contact with Zawahiri after bin Laden and Atiyah were killed, but we do not know. There are no indications that al-Qaida had an active External Operations Office in Pakistan's tribal areas after 2011, suggesting that the office was discontinued after bin Laden and Atiyah were killed. Zawahiri, as was mentioned previously, did not believe External Operations were essential to al-Qaida's war against the United States.

The main terrorism case in the West connected to Shukrijumah is the case in which he was indicted along with Najibullah Zazi's co-conspirators, namely the plot to attack the New York City Subway in 2009. Court documents reveal that the plotters visited Waziristan in late 2008 and met with al-Shukrijumah, al-Somali and Rauf. Al-Shukrijumah might have been the deputy of Saleh al-Somali at this stage, but we do not know if he had any responsibilities besides providing basic training to English-speaking recruits, which is also used by al-Qaida as a way of vetting future operatives. Court documents make clear that it was al-Somali and Rauf who were in direct contact with Zazi after he returned to the United States in 2009. Zazi was apparently arrested after e-mails to him from Waziristan were intercepted by US signals intelligence, but he also engaged in suspicious behavior before that, like buying large quantities of hydrogen peroxide in his hometown in Denver, Colorado.[29]

After Rauf was killed in November 2008, Saleh al-Somali lacked experienced personnel and resources for his external operations team. This is clear from the status report that he sent to bin Laden around April 2009, where he outlined how he had managed to achieve his goals so far.[30] The report was written after Najibullah Zazi returned to the United States in January 2009, but before Zazi had started to buy bomb-making materials.

In the report, al-Somali sums up what he achieved under each of the three goals he had set back in 2008. The first goal was to "carry out an operation," presumably in the West. To achieve this goal, he says he sent "a number of brothers" to Britain, Russia, and Europe. He says there were two types of plots. The first type was made up of brothers whom al-Somali had known for some time, and in whom he "had confidence." He says he sent one team of brothers to Russia, and the other to the UK. In Russia, they were to strike at the US Embassy or a gas pipeline, and in the UK, he said they could strike any target they saw fit. He says he does not know what happened to either of these groups. The second type of plot was that he trained a number of "new brothers," superficially and "in a hurry" before their visas expired. He also does not know what happened to these brothers. Shortly before he wrote the report, he says he heard about some arrests in the UK, which is a reference to the "Manchester plotters," but he does not yet know if they belonged to him. Two other plots connected to al-Somali were revealed after he wrote the letter—the New York City Subway plot in September 2009, and the Jyllands-Posten plot in July 2010.

Regarding the second goal, to set up an organizational structure for external operations work, he says there is a need to create a documents forgery office and improve other aspects of work, including communications and weapons manufacture, but he has not managed to create any of the necessary structures yet. He talks about setting up offices abroad, to avoid surveillance of communications in Pakistan, and they discussed places such as Iran, Somalia, and Turkey. He says they "backed off the idea" of an office in Iran, owing to "financial costs and other considerations." It is not clear what these "other considerations" would be, but in the spring of 2010, that attitude had certainly changed. On April 14, 2010, Sheikh Saeed told bin Laden that he planned to send Yunus al-Mauritani's external operations team to Iran, and in mid-May, Zawahiri told bin Laden they had received a message from the Iranians saying that al-Qaida could operate in the country, doing "coordination and collecting money and other things," on two conditions: that al-Qaida avoids using official border crossings, and that they do not work with any Iranian citizens.[31] The plan to send Yunus to Iran was later vetoed by bin Laden, and possibly also hampered by other developments. Yunus remained in Baluchistan, Pakistan until he was arrested in Quetta in September 2011.

Returning to Saleh al-Somali's progress report in April 2009, it was overall not very impressive. Al-Somali ended up talking more about what should be done, than what had actually been done, since his last report. Al-Somali's lack of qualified personnel and material resources had led to experimentation with other, and more low-cost methods of terrorizing the West. This included what Atiyah later referred to as "psychological warfare"; a series of threatening al-Sahab videos in German designed to influence the Federal elections in Germany on September 27, 2009.[32] The campaign was a bleak reflection of bin Laden's proposed strategy in mid-2004, when he had asked Hamza Rabia to attack countries before their elections in order to sway the election result, in the hope of replicating what had happened after the Madrid bombings. The most memorable video is one where the Moroccan-German operative Bekkay Harrach speaks for al-Qaida dressed in a Western-style suit and tie. These experiments obviously did not work—Angela Merkel's party won the 2009 elections and German troops stayed in Afghanistan until 2021.[33]

Another terrorist tactic introduced by al-Somali around this time was to "guide the brothers towards new methods like using the simplest things like household knives, gas tanks, fuel, diesel, and planes, trains as cars as killing tools."[34] These ideas were presented to bin Laden in private almost a year before *Inspire Magazine*, issued by al-Qaida's branch in Yemen, started introducing the tactic in their official propaganda. This type of thinking is somewhat reminiscent of Abu Mus'ab al-Suri's theory of "individual operations (*al-'amal al-fardi*)," introduced to the jihadist movement in early 2005. We know that the *Inspire Magazine* editor was directly inspired by al-Suri, but we do not know exactly where al-Somali got his ideas from.[35] In February 2010, Sheikh Saeed indicated to bin Laden that he was familiar with al-Suri's theory of "individual resistance," and he even suggested it as a way forward for al-Qaida.[36] However, Sheikh Saeed and al-Suri were conceptual thinkers, while al-Somali was more tactically oriented. His suggestion to downscale terrorist operations in the West, and to make use of everyday household items rather than trying to build bombs, was probably a pragmatic adaptation caused by the fact that al-Qaida did not have time or the resources to give new recruits bomb-training in Waziristan in 2009. The other reason was to decrease the chance of operatives being arrested, in other words, an adaptation to European counterterrorism measures which had tightened considerably since the London bombings in 2005.[37]

Bin Laden was not very impressed by Al-Somali's progress at this stage. We do not know if it was because of the progress report or other information, but in any case, sometime between April and August 2009, he wrote Atiyah a letter asking if al-Somali could be replaced as external operations chief, due to "his weakness in this position."[38] We do not have this letter, but we have Atiyah's reply on August 22, 2009. He says that after Rauf and Anas were killed, there were no good candidates. The only other candidate is the above-mentioned Tufan (Adnan al-Shukrijumah), but "he is not suitable," judges Atiyah. For now, Atiyah suggests that he himself will work together with al-Somali to run external operations, until another suitable candidate shows up. But a few months later in December 2009, Saleh al-Somali is killed in a drone attack in Waziristan.

Renewed Discussion about al-Qaida's External Operations

Al-Somali's death in a drone strike in December 2009 prompted an internal discussion in al-Qaida about the future of the external operations office.

The discussion seems to have started in late December 2009 with a letter from Sheikh Saeed to bin Laden, informing him of the death of al-Somali, and Saeed suggesting two candidates for a replacement, namely the Saudi-American Adnan al-Shukrijumah, or a younger candidate from Mauritania named Yunus al-Mauritani, who had joined al-Qaida a few years ago as an assistant Sharia official.

Bin Laden wrote an answer to this letter, which we do not have, but it included as a minimum a proposal to step up al-Qaida's external work activities against the United States. On January 25, 2010, Atiyah and Sheikh Saeed wrote bin Laden a letter back, giving specific advice on how to organize al-Qaida's external operations work.[39] They also enclosed a thirty-two-page proposal by Yunus al-Mauritani on how to revive the organizations' external operations. Yunus' proposal is, in short, to form a network of "sleeper cells" abroad, who will work from several countries and regions such as the Sahel, and to avoid having an identifiable geographical base.[40]

Al-Qaida's mid-level leaders are divided on how to best use Yunus' talents. Atiyah and Abu Yahya al-Libi think that he should be promoted to deputy head of al-Qaida's Sharia committee, assisting Abu Yahya al-Libi with his legal research. Sheikh Saeed, on the other hand, thinks that Yunus should be sent to Yemen to assist AQAP, in addition to arranging "a branch for external work there."[41] After this specific set of recommendations for how to use Yunus' talents in al-Qaida, Atiyah continues with a general recommendation for how to design al-Qaida's external work in the future. He seems here to not talk about the "al-Qaida branches" but mainly, what al-Qaida's external operations department in Pakistan should look like. The question of what type of external work the branches should engage in was introduced at a later stage in the context of discussing the way forward for al-Qaida in Yemen (more on this in Chapter 7).

Their recommendations for al-Qaida's external operations department in Pakistan reflect al-Qaida's weakness at that stage. Sheikh Saeed observes, "Our current circumstances do not allow for heavy spending on external or internal work, but we must adapt our capabilities and our stage."[42] He suggests keeping the office, with a "simple administration" that could exploit opportunities that might arise, in the form of suitable "brothers," "whose personal and financial circumstances allow them to travel and move well."[43] The observation indicates that al-Qaida has meager finances to spend on external operations—which is also hinted at in other letters from this period—and that they are still lacking a documents forgery office. He further suggests to "maintain and develop the [explosives] workshop," "activating remote work via the Internet," and "working through the proposed Turkey office" which will be "launched soon, God willing."[44] But Atiyah's main message to bin Laden is that al-Qaida should be happy with the progress of their work, even if they have not been able to carry out a large international terrorist attack, and that they need to work within their current capabilities. Their suggestions for how to use Yunus' talents in al-Qaida indicate that they want to prioritize al-Qaida's core tasks of doing Sharia research and supporting the regional branches.

Yunus al-Mauritani, on his side, suggests helping bin Laden revitalize External Operations through a four-step plan: The first and most urgent step is to move the activity out of Waziristan to a suitable third country. The second step is to build up a capacity and basically, form a network of "sleeper cells" in different locations, working under civilian covers, which in the long run is meant to finance the external operations work. He mentions North Africa and Sahel as suitable bases to set up commercial activities, drawing from his personal experiences from living in these areas. The third phase is to start operations, in the form of terrorist attacks, and the fourth phase is something he calls "octopussing" or branching out. The initial core team will be small; around three to five people, and there will be a "research and study center" that will function as a cover for international terrorist planning. He mentions the targets as the "coalition countries, headed by those who harm the Prophet."[45] He mentions at the end of the letter a plan for communication that preserves the secrecy of external operations by hiding where the attacks actually came from, or giving the impression they come from many different places. This last strategy is designed to avert the US military strategy post-9/11 of attacking physical sanctuaries associated with al-Qaida.

In his correspondence, al-Mauritani reveals some details about himself: he is from the group al-Mourabitoun in West Africa, and he used to work with Mokhtar Belmokhtar, the infamous leader whose group in 2013 attack the In Amenas gas facility. Yunus spent time with both AQIM and with the "Nigerians," probably a reference to Boko Haram. He traveled in the region, and went back and forth across the African continent and to the Middle East over many years. Around 2006, he was hiding in the desert with AQIM, and he was wanted in Mauritania. Around this time, he spent some time in Iran. He went to Pakistan at least twice, and the second time, it seems he came to stay. We do not know how he connected with al-Qaida, but by January 2010, he was a trusted member of al-Qaida's Sharia committee. Al-Qaida's mid-level leadership has only good things to say about Yunus, and they stress to bin Laden that he is multi-talented and could fill many positions: He knows Islamic Law (Sharia), history and poetry, spycraft and covert operations. The only negative thing they could think of is that he is young and lacks experience in al-Qaida.

A few weeks after this correspondence, on February 15, 2010, bin Laden replies to the above suggestions with a long letter arguing for why it is essential for al-Qaida to carry out international terrorist attacks against the United States. He starts by reminding his staff of al-Qaida's main goal: "That America stops its evil actions against us such as supporting the Jews, and leaving the Muslims and their affairs alone, so it will be easier for us to establish a true Islamic state."[46] He acknowledges that while fighting in places such as Afghanistan is a legal duty, he stresses that "we have the right to stop this war from its main source, because we need to stop it as fast as possible, and this is by way of the American people."[47] He continues by outlining why international terrorism should be a prioritized activity of al-Qaida, and sums it up with a paragraph in bold:

> One of the most important actions of the organization is operations that directly affect the security and economy of the American people as a whole. Operations inside America and targeting oil abroad, especially the countries that export it, are among the strongest and fastest that affect the people and make them put pressure on politicians.[48]

In the letters to Atiyah and Yunus on February 15, 2010, bin Laden explains why he has decided to get involved in external operations at this stage, and why he was not directly involved in previous years. He writes to Atiyah:

> Owing to my carefulness in regard to this matter, I avoided going over the plans of the external operations [i.e. being part of the command chain]. But when the issue was delayed and some problems occurred in managing the external operations, I found myself forced to take part in this matter.[49]

And he wrote in a separate letter to Yunus:

> I received your kind letter, so I read it and was pleased with what it included about the importance of external work and your valuable suggestions for its advancement. I have long felt what you talked about, about the necessity of focusing on this department and developing it. However, the brothers were complaining about the lack of cadres in this field. Praise be to God who brought you, and I hope that the Almighty will May God grant you success in cooperation with the responsible brothers to advance external work.[50]

The above quoted paragraphs suggest that bin Laden saw Yunus' arrival in al-Qaida as an opportunity to realize ideas about external operations that he had for a long time, namely, to carry out spectacular, international terrorist attacks that would cripple the US economy. He alluded to the same thoughts in his letter to Hamza Rabia in 2004, which is the only other evidence we have in Abbottabad documents of bin Laden's direct involvement in external operations. The question remains whether bin Laden in early 2010 had a "renewed" interest in targeting the United States, or whether Yunus' proposal in early 2010 simply prompted bin Laden to grasp a long-awaited opportunity.

The answer is not necessarily either-or. We know from previous communications that bin Laden tended to jump onto opportunities when they arose. After the United States invaded Iraq, bin Laden said that Iraq was the most important battlefield for the jihad movement. After a Danish newspaper published a series of Mohammed cartoons in 2005, there was a strong reaction around the Muslim world, but al-Qaida held a relatively low profile, except for one speech issued by Osama bin Laden in 2006, in which he declared that those who insult the Prophet should be killed.[51] However, when the same newspaper re-published the Mohammed cartoons in early 2008, bin Laden ordered al-Qaida's external operations department, as well as the "al-Qaida affiliates" in Iraq and Algeria, to carry out an attack on Denmark, and on June 2, 2008, al-Qaida operatives carried out an attack on the Danish Embassy in Islamabad, killing six people.[52]

When al-Qaida's leaders discussed the way forward in 2010, Yunus suggested to prioritize countries that insulted the Prophet, and Zawahiri wanted to prioritize the battlefields in Iraq and Afghanistan. By now, bin Laden expressed that he had changed his mind about these causes. Bin Laden specifically wrote to Yunus, in response to his suggestion to attack countries that insult the Prophet: "[While I said this in the past, now] I give more weight to this: That it is not possible to deter the aggressors by scattered efforts, in a time when our powers are limited."[53] In other writings bin Laden makes it clear that he wants to start a "new phase" for al-Qaida taking into account the strength of the United States, which makes it impossible for the jihadists to establish a permanent Islamic state. Bin Laden then presents a refined version of the "far enemy doctrine" that al-Qaida developed in the late 1990s, which suggests that before an Islamic State can be established, al-Qaida first has to weaken the United States through international terrorist attacks. In addition, al-Qaida should concentrate on supporting active "frontlines" that already exist (i.e., in Iraq and Afghanistan), but avoid opening new ones—an argument which directly affects al-Qaida's policies toward the regional affiliates, further discussed in Chapter 7. One could say that bin Laden's re-engagement with al-Qaida's external operations in 2010 was prompted on the one hand by the opportunity offered by Yunus al-Mauritani's talents, and on the other hand by the failure of the jihadist movement to achieve its goals in the decade after 9/11.

Bin Laden's letter about external operations in mid-February 2010 included an order to appoint Yunus as the new chief of external operations, and to have him start recruiting a small team and train them before finding a sanctuary abroad. Bin Laden received replies from the other senior leaders—from Sheikh Saeed on February 17 and March 8, and from Zawahiri many months later, on May 16 and 31. Sheikh Saeed's reply is, as always, polite:

> Regarding what you wrote about the subject of external work and its importance and the importance of striking the enemy in his own home, we support your opinion one hundred percent and may God reward you for the convincing evidence and matching examples that you have kindly provided, which has increased our conviction and made the priority and importance clear to us and we will exert our efforts to achieve that, God willing.

However, Sheikh Saeed goes on to suggest that al-Qaida has limited capabilities, and that the group should prioritize the "frontline work" in Afghanistan and elsewhere. He then comments on bin Laden's suggestion to ask AQAP to attack Americans instead of fighting the Yemeni regime: in practice, he says, this is impossible because AQAP are under direct attack from the Yemeni regime. Therefore, al-Qaida must continue fighting both "near" and "far" enemies in places like Yemen. It is, in this context, that he suggests that perhaps al-Qaida should adopt the theories of Abu Mus'ab al-Suri: " ... we see that it is inevitable for us to confront both groups [i.e. both the near and the far enemy] as long as we have places where they are united, or to wage a war of individual resistance (*al-muqawama al-fardiyya*) as Abu Musab al-Suri wrote."[54]

Sheikh Saeed further says, " ... it is true what you mentioned that hitting them in their own home has a greater and faster impact, but hitting them abroad also has a great impact in draining them, especially economically ...."[55] This argument was later echoed by Ayman al-Zawahiri. He also says that al-Qaida currently does not have money in their budget to spend extra on external operations, as " ... 80% is spent on work inside Afghanistan and Pakistan, ... and I see that we cannot reduce it in favor of working in the enemy's home."[56] On the other hand, he says, we should keep a "miniature" version of the external operations department in Pakistan, led by Adnan al-Shukrijumah, and to carry out the project proposed by Yunus, which is to train a small team of cadre and move abroad as quickly as possible. In addition, Sheikh Saeed proposes to work through the planned "Turkey office" of al-Qaida, which was discussed earlier (we do not know if the office materialized).

At the end of March 2010, Yunus sends bin Laden a detailed plan for his activities,[57] and responds to a detailed proposal from bin Laden, in which bin Laden suggested a project to target oil tankers in the Hormuz strait. Yunus is positive to the plan, but says that it needs "time and cells that educate and refine its ambitions before it sets off ... Therefore, I hear and obey what you have ordered, and the matter requires a long time, and we will put it in its place, God willing, within the general context of the plans, as I will provide it to you, if God wills."[58]

Yunus also mentions, in his end-of-March 2010 correspondence, that he found a promising, Europe-based Moroccan recruit, describing him as follows:

> we found a Moroccan brother who is understanding and aware, residing in Europe, and specializes in electronic mechanics. He is in his final year of university, and all that remains for him is the practical applications [year], and he was born on 15-6-1981.

This "Moroccan" was among a number of jihadists from Germany and Austria that Yunus managed to recruit in Waziristan in 2010. Some of them were from a group called the German Taliban Mujahideen. The intention seems that they were going to be "sleeper" or logistics cells for al-Qaida in Europe. There are at least two groups that were arrested in 2011. The first is comprised of two individuals named Maqsood Lodin and Yusuf Ocak. In German court documents, their names are spelled as "Maksud L." and "Jusuf O." They were caught with a large collection of al-Qaida documents, infamously concealed in a porn video in an encrypted file called "Sexy Tanja."[59] It is from this case that we have the Rashid Rauf reports about the planning of the London bombings on 7/7 and 21/7, and of the Transatlantic plot in 2005–6.

The second cell is also interesting. They were known as the "Dusseldorf cell" and according to German media, Yusuf al-Mauritani's promising "Moroccan recruit" was among them: he is named Abdeladim el-K.[60] Bin Laden also referred to the "Moroccan" in one of his letter drafts.[61] His full name was revealed in a US court case in November 2011 as Abdeladim El-Kebir, and he was arrested on April 29, 2011.[62] In a letter from April 2010, Sheikh Saeed tells UBL:

> As for sending some brothers to study, it takes time, and the brother Abu Al-Baraa Al-Maghribi [El-Kebir], whom Sheikh Yunus told you about, we asked him to do that and he promised it while we were researching it here, and forgive us for the delay in all matters[63]

According to one Abbottabad document, Yunus' intention for "the Moroccan brother" was to lead al-Qaida's documents forgery office. In other words, he was not going to be involved in terrorist attacks in Europe, but to have a civilian "cover" and work in a support activity. The Moroccan was also supposed to start recruiting people, including a pilot or pilots, and also some people who could study in universities. Yunus describes these activities as belonging to the "second stage" of his plan for al-Qaida's external operations.[64]

In April 2010, Sheikh Saeed confirmed to bin Laden that Yunus had started his activities, and that they were working on setting up a safe house in Iran to be an initial base for external operations. He writes: "We decided that the course would be in Iran, and therefore we sent a sum of money with Yas [a Kurdish brother trusted by al-Qaida] to find a place there, that would be at the disposal of Sheikh Yunus."[65]

Sheikh Saeed was killed in a drone strike in North Waziristan on May 22, 2010. Atiyah took over the work responsibilities for him and continued communicating with bin Laden regarding Yunus' progress. Around this time, Ayman al-Zawahiri also managed to send his opinions through, after being cut off from al-Qaida communications for several months. Zawahiri suggests that al-Qaida should prioritize the wars in Iraq and Afghanistan, rather than international terrorism:

> I acknowledge the importance of striking America and Europe in their own homes, but we must also realize that the battle in Afghanistan and Iraq is extremely important. Abu Abdullah has previously mentioned that Iraq is the most important battlefield of jihad in this era, and that the battle with America and the West will be decided—and only God knows the unseen—on the battlefield, not in their own homes.[66]

Zawahiri essentially makes a similar argument as Sheikh Saeed did earlier. While he is more direct and frank in his feedback, and strongly encourages bin Laden to continue focusing on fighting the Americans in Afghanistan and Iraq (but especially Afghanistan, as this battlefield has most promise of succeeding), he does not object to any of the specific plans that were agreed upon between bin Laden and Sheikh Saeed, such as sending Yunus al-Mauritani to a foreign country to set up an external operations office there.

On July 6, 2010, bin Laden sends Atiyah a letter, granting Yunus the authority to "work" in the regions of al-Qaida's branches in Algeria and Yemen, and he ordered Atiyah to inform the Emirs in those regions to cooperate with Yusuf upon his arrival. He also ordered the AQIM Emir to allocate money from his budget, "which may amount to two hundred thousand Euros during the next six months," to finance Yunus' activities. This example indicates that there was a close link between al-Qaida central and AQIM, with the former exercising authority over the latter.[67]

Around the same time, on July 6, 2010, bin Laden writes Yunus a letter asking him to "concentrate on America" rather than on countries that insulted the Prophet, such as Denmark; and to concentrate specifically on a project proposed earlier by bin Laden to strike oil tankers in the Gulf.[68] A few months later, on September 26, 2010, bin Laden writes Yunus another letter clarifying that he needs to focus on operations targeting the United States, but outside the US homeland. He says:

> I would like to explain to you the separation of the work inside America, with the project of sinking the oil tankers, it is owing to the fact that each of the two branches is extremely large, extremely important, and extremely critical, and in order to make both of them succeed, is that they remain separate, so in case there was any leakage of critical information, it would not affect the other project.[69]

We do not know if al-Qaida ever found a candidate to carry out the other, "extremely critical" project of striking inside America. Bin Laden wrote to Atiyah around the same time, on September 26, 2010, that Adnan al-Shukrijumah was "not suitable" for that particular task, and al-Qaida at the time appears to have had no other candidates. On the other hand, we know that al-Qaida's branch in Yemen was already targeting the United States and had almost succeeded twice—with the so-called "Underwear bomber" on December 25, 2010, and with the "printer bombs" on US-bound cargo planes in July 2010. As far as we know, these attacks were not coordinated with senior al-Qaida leaders in Pakistan.

Throughout the fall and winter of 2010–11, Atiyah continues to report to bin Laden about the progress of Yunus' travels. On September 29, 2010, he confirms that Yunus has left North Waziristan, and in November he reported that Yunus "continues to be in the frontiers area on the Baluchistan side." The last communication from Atiyah is from April 5, 2011, less than a month before bin Laden was killed in the Abbottabad raid.

> Regarding Shaykh Yunus, he is fine, and I sent to him your latest letter, and God willing he received it. A month ago, he wrote to me and told me that he might go to Somalia directly if he can make the arrangement. ... He and his friends decided that going to Iran and staying in it is not appropriate ... Just to remind you, Shaykh Yunis has three Syrian brothers, one Tunisian, and one Algerian (who used to live in Germany) with him.[70]

In the end, Yunus al-Mauritani was arrested in the city of Quetta, Baluchistan, on September 6, 2011, by Pakistani security forces. He was allegedly held in US detention in Bagram, Afghanistan for two years before being handed over to Mauritania where he was sentenced to twenty years in prison. We do not know what happened to the rest of al-Mauritani's team in Quetta, but given that they were all relatively new and inexperienced recruits, it seems likely that the team disintegrated after their leader was arrested.

Concluding Remarks

This chapter presented two broader arguments about al-Qaida and international terrorism in the decade after 9/11. First, the chapter described the demise of al-Qaida's external operations branch in Pakistan in 2009–10. While it is commonly argued that the War on Terror weakened al-Qaida's ability to attack the West, this chapter adds more details about how al-Qaida's own leaders reacted to the various threats they were facing. The drone war forced al-Qaida to downscale its external operations campaign in Waziristan to a minimum, and it pushed al-Qaida's chief of external operations to suggest a terrorist strategy of simple attacks using household items. In 2010, when Yunus al-Mauritani was tasked by bin Laden to revive the external operations work, he had to start from scratch, recruiting and training his own personnel among newly arrived recruits with no prior experience. It is significant that the first stage of al-Mauritani's "work plan" was to find a secure base for al-Qaida's external operations abroad, outside Afghanistan, and Pakistan. Iran was initially considered as a suitable destination, but for unknown reasons, the destination was later changed to Somalia. In retrospect, bin Laden's plan to revive external operations in 2010 was extremely vulnerable, because it relied too narrowly on one talented individual, supported by a team of inexperienced new recruits.

The second argument presented in this chapter is that by 2010, it was almost only bin Laden who still believed that international terrorist attacks should be a prioritized activity for al-Qaida. Ayman al-Zawahiri and practically all the other senior leaders believed that al-Qaida should prioritize the wars in Iraq and Afghanistan, as these were the most effective way, as they saw it, to weaken the United States. No one was against the idea of carrying out new terrorist attacks against the United States, but also, no one, except for bin Laden, believed such attacks to be essential. It was no surprise, therefore, that the first thing Ayman al-Zawahiri did after bin Laden was killed was to tell Muslims living in the West that "you are only responsible for yourself," meaning in practice that al-Qaida had adopted a low-cost strategy of "inspired" rather than top-down organized attacks.[71] This choice seems to have been a compromise between ideology and practical realities. Zawahiri could not abandon international terrorism completely, because al-Qaida supporters saw it as an essential feature of the group's *manhaj* (method) that had been developed by Osama bin Laden in the 1990s. However, the practical reality was that in 2011, Zawahiri had neither the resources, nor the interest in, developing al-Qaida's external operations branch further. Moreover, the Arab Spring revolutions had opened up new opportunities for al-Qaida to experiment with Islamic state-building in the Middle East. Al-Qaida's transition from a group focused on *jihad* to a group focused on *governance* will be further explored in the next chapter.

A New Phase for Al-Qaida

I would like to consult with you on a matter that has appeared to me to be very important, which is changing the name of al-Qaida.[1]
—Osama bin Laden, draft of a letter to Atiyah (August 2010)

The Abbottabad letters reveal that in mid-2010, Osama bin Laden thought about changing the name of al-Qaida. He drafted a two-page text outlining his arguments, added a list of new name suggestions, and pasted it into a draft letter to Atiyah.[2] We do not know if the letter was sent, but bin Laden's idea of a name change did not come out of the blue. In mid-2010, al-Qaida had entered a "new phase of correction and development," as bin Laden put it, and needed to review their past mistakes.[3] In his draft, he wrote that one of al-Qaida's weaknesses was its name. "The name al-Qaeda expresses a military base with some fighters in it, without indicating our broad concern for uniting the Ummah," he argued. One of the new suggestions was "*Jama'at i'adat al-Khilafa al-Rashida* (The group to restore the rightly guided Caliphate)."[4]

Bin Laden's thought about a name change in 2010 is in itself a superficial event in al-Qaida's history. As far as we know, it was never discussed internally, and quite possibly, the draft letter never left bin Laden's computer. On the other hand, the event carries symbolic value, because it serves to illustrate one of the main conclusions in this book, namely that al-Qaida had changed fundamentally in the decade following 9/11. The leaders in Pakistan had by 2010 realized that al-Qaida needed to expand its popular support base and to have something concrete to offer the people besides jihad. In short, al-Qaida needed to start thinking of itself as a physical political entity, a "center with regions,"[5] which would ultimately lead to the restoration of the Caliphate.

The change in al-Qaida's thinking came about through a series of internal discussions among the senior leaders in Pakistan. In this chapter I trace the origins of these discussions and argue that political opportunities that opened up in Yemen and Somalia in 2009 pushed al-Qaida to change in two significant ways. First, al-Qaida went from being an organization focused solely on *jihad* to being an organization focused on *governance*. Second, it went from being a dispersed network of regional "affiliates" in the 2000s to adopting more of a centralized organization model in 2010. The challenge for al-Qaida, as we shall see, is that they did not have sufficient personnel to put in place a functioning bureaucracy at the central level. When the Arab Spring opened up new opportunities in 2011, al-Qaida's lack of organizational resources caused it to become sidelined by ISIS, which by 2013 had a far stronger and more effective bureaucracy in place.

The origin of these internal discussions can be traced back to a letter of advice that bin Laden wanted to send to the AQAP leader, Nasir al-Wuhayshi, in January 2010. The letter of advice was spurred by geopolitical developments in the Gulf region. In January 2009, Saudi and Yemeni jihadists had joined together in Yemen to re-establish al-Qaida on the Arabian Peninsula (AQAP), and in spring 2009, there was an escalation of domestic unrest in Yemen, with a secessionist movement starting an insurgency in the South, on top of the ongoing Houthi rebellion in the north of the country. In the midst of these developments, Nasir al-Wuhayshi sent al-Qaida several letters, declaring optimistically, "If you ever wanted Sanaʿa [the Yemeni capital], today is the day!"[6] Bin Laden appears to have received at least one of al-Wuhayshi's letters in January 2010, and this prompted him to write a draft response which caused an internal discussion in al-Qaida. Al-Wuhayshi was eager to use the political opportunities caused by domestic unrest in Yemen to capture territory for his group, but bin Laden preferred a more cautious approach, focusing on first fighting the "far enemy," America.

Bin Laden's thoughts about Yemen in early 2010 seemed in some ways similar to his advice to the Saudi jihadi movement in 1996, as outlined in the now-infamous "Declaration of Jihad against the Americans Occupying the Two Holiest Sites."[7] In both cases, bin Laden wanted to discourage local Islamist rebels from starting a violent revolution against the "near enemy." He believed, correctly as it turned out, that such an attempt would be suicidal because the rebels did not have enough popular support. Bin Laden's proposed solution, in 1996 as well as in 2009, was to concentrate on fighting the "far enemy," the United States. But the similarities between the two cases were only superficial. In the 1990s, there was a physical US troop presence in Saudi Arabia, which had been widely condemned by a group of Saudi scholars known as the Awakening (*Sahwa*) Movement.[8] Yemen in 2009 was different. There was no overt US military presence and no *Sahwa* legitimizing jihad against a foreign occupier.

As we shall see, bin Laden's suggestion that AQAP should only attack the United States, while a number of "infidel" actors were contesting for control over Yemen's territory, fell on deaf ears. However, it sparked an internal discussion in al-Qaida in the spring of 2009 on two topics: whether al-Qaida should revive its international terrorist campaign against the United States, as discussed in Chapter 6; and what advice al-Qaida should give to AQAP in Yemen.

When these discussions began, al-Qaida was at a crossroads. Al-Qaida had failed to control events in Iraq, where the local al-Qaida affiliate had descended into *takfirism*—an ideology that makes excessive use of *takfir*, i.e., the act of declaring a Muslim an infidel, to legitimize violence against other Muslims. At the same time, geopolitical events had opened up a number of new opportunities. In 2009, two new groups joined the al-Qaida orbit—a resurrected Al-Qaida on the Arabian Peninsula (AQAP), made up of old al-Qaida affiliates from Saudi Arabia and Yemen, and al-Shabaab in Somalia. The latter group sent a pledge of allegiance to al-Qaida in 2009, but did not officially become an al-Qaida affiliate until 2012.[9] However, the Abbottabad documents suggest that the group was treated internally in al-Qaida as an affiliate from 2010, which is why I refer to it as an affiliate in this chapter. In addition, there was al-Qaida in the Islamic Maghreb (AQIM), which had been with al-Qaida since 2007, but where communications had been recently restored after being infrequent for the past two years.

Somewhat ironically, it was al-Qaida's Iraqi affiliate, the unruly Islamic State in Iraq (ISI), that had paved the way for these new opportunities. ISI's visibility and status within the Iraqi insurgency, and bin Laden's public endorsement of the group, changed the image of al-Qaida from international terrorist organization fighting America, to an organization which advocated the establishment of Islamic states across the Muslim world. This new image attracted old and well-established jihadi groups, such as al-Shabaab in Somalia, to join al-Qaida in 2009. The other affiliates in Algeria and Yemen were likewise driven in part by the desire to establish an Islamic state in their region and looked to ISI as a role model. Symptomatic of this fact is that already from 2009, both al-Shabaab and AQAP started using the ISI black-and-white banner depicting the "Seal of the Prophet" in their official propaganda.[10]

After the al-Qaida leadership started discussing what to do in Yemen, in mid-2010 the Taliban placed restrictions on al-Qaida in Afghanistan. The Taliban was expecting victory in Afghanistan soon and was preparing both militarily and politically for the takeover. As we heard in Chapter 5, al-Qaida realized that they would probably not be able to pursue their globally oriented agenda from Afghanistan in the future. The narrowing down of options in Afghanistan encouraged al-Qaida to start paying more attention to the regions. Thus, what started as a discussion about the way forward for al-Qaida in Yemen had by mid-2010 broadened into a more principled discussion about al-Qaida's future. The discussion was not so much about what kind of organization al-Qaida should be, because this had already been defined by the affiliates: Al-Qaida should be a center with regions, which would be the foundation for the restoration of the Caliphate. The discussion was rather about how al-Qaida should implement its global jihadist ideology within these new realities. In a highly symbolic move, Atiyah suggested to bin Laden in January 2010 that al-Qaida should adopt the Islamic State in Iraq's "Seal of the Prophet" banner as a general symbol for al-Qaida.[11] Bin Laden, as we have heard, thought instead about scrapping the al-Qaida name altogether. While these suggestions came to nothing, they nevertheless illustrate the crisis of identity that al-Qaida was going through.

After tracing the origins of the discussion of a "new phase" in al-Qaida, I look at the broader context of al-Qaida's regional affiliates, especially in Algeria and Somalia, and how they interacted with al-Qaida during 2009–10. These regions influenced al-Qaida's central leadership by asking a set of principal questions related to their military and communications strategy: Should we try to take control over territory? Should we declare an Islamic State? Should we declare our official affiliation with al-Qaida? What enemy should we prioritize? And can we make truce with "infidel" countries? I argue that the various needs and questions posed by the regions pushed al-Qaida to have an internal discussion about principal questions related to governance and state-building. This led al-Qaida in the end to formulate a general policy, drafts of which were circulated internally and to the regions during 2010.[12]

The development of a general policy for the regions tends to get lost in Western security narratives that only focus on the international terrorist threat from al-Qaida. A far more profound development is that al-Qaida—which had always been a "non-territorial" organization (i.e., an organization that was not interested in conquering territory for the purpose of establishing an Islamic State)—in 2010 finally started talking about governing their own territories. In retrospect, this was a prescient move, owing to the gradual weakening of traditional state authorities in the Middle East and North Africa over the 2000s, which ultimately found its expression in the Arab Spring uprisings in 2010–11. On the other hand, al-Qaida was far too late in realizing the importance of building "jihadist" state institutions, and the central leadership was so weakened by 2011, that the governing project was impossible to carry out in practice. When the upheavals happened, the Islamic State in Iraq was much better positioned to seize the opportunity, because the organization had been building their "Islamic State" brand since 2006 and had an unprecedented access to human resources inside Iraq, due in large part to the "de-Ba'athification" policy pursued during the first year of the US occupation.

The Origin of the "New Phase" Discussion

In July 2010, bin Laden wrote a fifty-seven-page letter to Atiyah where he explained his new vision for al-Qaida, described as a set of principles to guide al-Qaida's future work. Bin Laden put many of his original thoughts into the vision, but it also incorporated input from other senior al-Qaida leaders, given in various letter exchanges over six months from January to June 2010. In this section I discuss how the "new vision" originated in 2009 as a direct reaction to domestic unrest and political opportunities opening up for al-Qaida in Yemen.

The origin of the new vision is not explicitly stated in Abbottabad documents, but the first dated reference to internal al-Qaida consultations can be found in a letter from Sheikh Saeed and Atiyah to bin Laden in January 2010.[13] In this letter, they confirm that they received bin Laden's consultation on two topics, "external operations" and Yemen. As I argued in Chapter 6, bin Laden's advice on external operations was probably prompted by the death of Salih al-Somali in December 2009 and the need for al-Qaida to make a decision regarding the future of the External Operations Office in Waziristan.

As for Yemen, it seems to have been prompted initially by bin Laden's observations about the deteriorating security situation in the country. During 2009, the AQAP leader, Nasir al-Wuhayshi, sent letters to al-Qaida, but it is not clear if these letters reached bin Laden. We know that one letter reached bin Laden around January 2010, because it prompted bin Laden to write a draft response to al-Wuhayshi. In this letter, al-Wuhayshi painted a dramatic picture of events in Yemen. He indicated that "the political conflict is deteriorating, and the situation of the country is about to fall apart" and that AQAP needed to position themselves in order to beat their competitors to power. Al-Wuhayshi described AQAP's main competitors as the Muslim Brotherhood, the "Communists" [referring to the rebel movement in South Yemen, aka the Southern Movement] and the Houthis, who together with their external state sponsors have "depleted the country, economically and militarily."[14] AQAP thus needed to make a principled decision about the way forward. Should AQAP join the fight against the Ali Abdullah Saleh regime in Yemen, or should they lay low and risk a "Communist" or Houthi takeover? Should they declare an Islamic State, or should they work in secret? These questions were of fundamental importance to Osama bin Laden, who was of Yemeni descent and who had been invested in the cause of the Islamist revolution in Yemen since the end of the Afghan-Soviet war in 1989.

Around January 11, 2010, bin Laden asked the other al-Qaida leaders for input on what al-Qaida should do in Yemen, and three weeks later on January 31, he sent them his own thoughts on the subject in a draft letter of advice to Nasir al-Wuhayshi.[15] Al-Qaida's leaders reacted to these letters separately. The Abbottabad archive contains both their default thoughts about Yemen, and their refined thoughts about Yemen after reading bin Laden's policy suggestions.

The first reaction was sent from Sheikh Saeed and Atiyah on January 25, 2010, before they received bin Laden's thoughts on the issue. They say that they received a letter from Nasir al-Wuhayshi in December 2009, which bin Laden appears to have not read yet. They summarize the letter as follows:

> Their assessment of the situation of the Yemeni government is that it is in its weakest condition due to the many fronts that have been opened against it by the Houthis and the Southern Movement, with the economic situation deteriorating to its worst state. (…) Their position on what is happening between the Houthis and the government is to lie in wait and watch, and they believe that the ongoing battle is in their interest because it will lead to the weakening of both parties and the depletion of their strength. This prepares the conditions for the Mujahideen to a greater extent, and their intervention will be when the situation of both parties reaches the brink of collapse.

Afterwards, Sheikh Saeed and Atiyah gave their initial advice for the way forward in Yemen. They advocate a hands-on and proactive strategy:

> we must support them from here from the center (*al-markaz*) in a strong way; Politically, morally, with jurisprudential and legal guidance, expertise and experiences (…) one of the most important things that we care about very much is: communicating with them and finding the appropriate and smooth channels for communication, via the Internet and on land (…) and it is necessary to issue explicit instructions and directives to the brothers there to consult us and refer to us in all their important matters.[16]

Furthermore, they recommended leaving the Houthis and the Southern Movement alone as much as possible, and internally in Yemen, they should concentrate on "Crusader targets" as well as selective strikes on security targets, especially Yemeni intelligence. Externally, they should focus on the United States, and they should also form a "rear base" for the revolutionary movement in Saudi Arabia. Their advice reflected what AQAP had already been doing during the first year of their existence, including attempts to assassinate the Saudi Prince Mohammed bin Nayef in August 2009, and to bomb Northwest Airlines Flight 253 from Amsterdam to Detroit in December.

As for Zawahiri, his initial view on Yemen, which came much later in May 2010, was that al-Qaida was far away and not in a position to influence events directly. His advice was that bin Laden should primarily support AQAP with propaganda and incitement to jihad.[17]

Before receiving these initial inputs, bin Laden provided his own thoughts on the matter in the form of a draft letter of advice to Nasir al-Wuhayshi. He suggested that AQAP should enter a truce with Yemeni authorities and only concentrate on attacking the United States. He also appears to have suggested that AQAP should postpone declaring an Islamic State in Yemen, because this would attract unwanted attention and hostility and lead to the state's rapid demise. Bin Laden's perspective on Yemen was derived from his intimate experiences with failed Islamist revolutions in the 1990s and 2000s, especially on the Arabian Peninsula. Bin Laden had supported Saudi revolutionaries in the 1990s, but had cautioned them against starting a premature violent campaign. Saudi revolutionaries finally started a violent campaign in 2003, amidst the fervor surrounding the US invasion of Iraq, but the movement's popular support was still too weak, and by 2008 most of its members had been killed or arrested.[18] The few members that were left fled to Yemen and re-established AQAP along with a group of bin Laden's Yemeni associates. In other words, there was a direct, historical connection between the failed al-Qaida-revolution in Saudi Arabia to the rise of AQAP in Yemen in 2009. And now that AQAP was about to make the same mistake as in the past, it is unsurprising that bin Laden threw his full weight behind advising AQAP.

Bin Laden's proposal for a truce between AQAP and the Yemeni government might have looked like this, based on a segment found in one of bin Laden's undated drafts:

> The opinion on the issue of Yemen is that we move towards a truce and non-escalation with the government, and that the door remains open with the scholars and tribal sheikhs, on the condition that we will not target anyone inside Yemeni territory, whether from the government or others, (...) and that they do not hinder the activity of the brothers in leaving Yemen and devote themselves to foreign work in the coordination given to Sheikh Yunus [al-Mauritani], and

inform them of that. If the state does not respond or breaks the covenant, we will remain in our project to focus on the head of global disbelief [America] and fight the government only in a case of self-defense … The condition is that the truce is inside Yemen, so if we are expelled from Yemen, we will do whatever we want[19]

The rest of al-Qaida's leaders answered both individually and in the form of a joint statement between February and May 2010. Sheikh Saeed provided the first and most detailed individual feedback. In a letter to bin Laden on February 17, 2010, he said that in practice, it is impossible for AQAP to only fight the United States without fighting the regime, because the United States will pressure the Yemeni government to fight AQAP, "as is the reality now in Pakistan, Algeria, and Iraq, and as is expected and has happened in Yemen and Somalia."[20] Sheikh Saeed says that "it is inevitable for us to confront both groups as long as we have places where they are united, or to wage a war of individual resistance as Abu Musab al-Suri wrote."[21] The other al-Qaida leaders, including Ayman al-Zawahiri, also rejected bin Laden's proposal for a truce.[22]

In April 2010, there was a Shura meeting between four senior leaders (probably Sheikh Saeed, Atiyah, Abu Yahya al-Libi, and Yunus al-Mauritani) discussing Yemen and other topics, which we will return to below. Prior to the April 2010 Shura, other seminal events had happened which required thorough discussion and consultation, and this is probably what prompted the al-Qaida leaders to hold the Shura session. A key event was that the Somali group al-Shabaab had requested to join al-Qaida. They had submitted a formal pledge of allegiance in December 2009, but in April 2010, al-Shabaab was still waiting for an answer. Moreover, by now al-Qaida had received a long letter from the Islamic State in Iraq, defending ISI's decision to not unite with the Kurdish group Ansar al-Sunnah. Finally, there was the question about the way forward for al-Qaida in Yemen. In sum, in the spring of 2010 the discussion about al-Qaida's policy in Yemen was expanded into a discussion about al-Qaida's policy toward the regional affiliates, and a more principled discussion about what type of group al-Qaida should be in the future.

Al-Shabaab Becomes a Topic of Discussion

Parallel to al-Qaida's initial discussions about Yemen, in March 2010 a letter arrived from Mukhtar Abu al-Zubayr, the leader of al-Shabaab in Somalia.[23] The group was in a transitionary phase and urgently needed al-Qaida's advice on two matters, "the issue pertaining to the announcement of the state and the issue of joining the brothers."[24] Al-Shabaab had waited for an acknowledgment of their oath of allegiance (*bay'a*) to Osama bin Laden for several months. In his letter, the al-Shabaab leader complained about the lack of communication with al-Qaida, and the lack of coordination between the regions.

The letter may be a key source to understanding why bin Laden in mid-2010 developed a comprehensive strategy and a new vision for al-Qaida. Al-Shabaab in 2009 was in a position to establish and run a functioning Islamic State in a region of strategic importance to al-Qaida, owing to its geographical proximity to Yemen and AQAP. However, it required that al-Qaida take the lead in running the state—unlike in Iraq, where the Islamic State in Iraq had been self-sufficient and had largely excluded al-Qaida from their decision-making processes. The entry of al-Shabaab into al-Qaida was thus a golden opportunity, but it required that al-Qaida changed focus from "jihadism" to governance and state-building. The end result, as I will argue, was bin Laden's new vision for al-Qaida which included general policies as well as specific instructions to each of al-Qaida's three active regions: Algeria, Yemen, and Somalia (Iraq was theoretically included, but there was no active communication between the two in the fall of 2010).

Bin Laden's initial reaction to the message from Somalia was that he suggested appointing Atiyah to be an overall coordinating official for all of al-Qaida's regions.[25] Sheikh Saeed's answer on April 14, 2010, indicates that he had indeed started thinking about how al-Qaida should relate to the regions, suggesting the historical Caliphate as a model to emulate.

> It is in our thought, and the thought of all the brothers in the other regions that here, we are the center and the leadership (*al-markaz wa al-qiyada*), and that the other regions are the regions and they are the ones that follow the center, and for example in the days of the Caliphate there was the headquarters of the Caliphate and the other regions were subordinate to the headquarters of the Caliphate.

However, Sheikh Saeed had some reservations about appointing Atiyah to the proposed position, which was partly related to matters of internal hierarchies (he says that the "official for the regions" should not be a separate position, but rather a function attributed to the deputy of the "General Manager," i.e., himself), and partly related to Atiyah's personality which Sheikh Saeed described as having "a little harshness" in it.[26]

The same month, al-Qaida's senior leaders minus Zawahiri held a Shura which resulted in four written opinion pieces about Yemen, Iran, Somalia, and Iraq, which were submitted to bin Laden.[27] As mentioned, the Yemen discussion was prompted by bin Laden's proposal at the end of January 2010, that AQAP should enter into a truce with the Yemeni government. The Iraq discussion was prompted by a letter from the Islamic State of Iraq's Shura Council, where they defended their decision not to unite with the Kurdish group Ansar al-Sunnah; while the Somalia discussion was prompted by the latest letter from the al-Shabaab leader Abu Zubayr, where he asks if al-Shabaab should officially join al-Qaida.

The Shura's advice for Somalia revolves around policies for the future Islamic State there, including advice on how to build an educational system and carry out "judicial, political and executive reforms." As a curiosity, the al-Qaida Shura wanted to recommend up front "to put girls' education on the list of priorities, even in the primary stage at least, to repel the false and wrong propaganda of hostility against us," apparently in reference to the negative publicity resulting from the Taliban's ban on girls' education during the 1990s. Furthermore, the al-Qaida Shura stipulated that they will take an active part in developing the new Islamic State in Somalia, although this point seems overly ambitious given the limited resources of al-Qaida in Waziristan:

> [We will advise them to carry out] reforms in the enactment of administrative systems for issues related to the economy, internal and external politics, the Hisbah system and its ethics and issues, enjoining good and forbidding evil, the army and other things, and all matters and the like are completed for them from here little by little.[28]

Finally, the Shura gives bin Laden their recommendations on the specific questions asked by al-Shabaab—should they declare their allegiance to al-Qaida, and should they declare the establishment of an Islamic State? The Shura's recommendation, in short, is to conceal their unity with al-Qaida and to "establish the pillars of the state" without announcing it explicitly.[29]

As for Yemen, the Shura advised that they were not against the idea of AQAP declaring an Islamic State. They thought it would be useful to declare a state even if it did not last long, because it would allow AQAP to build and consolidate support among the tribes. It can be noted that the Shura's advice to declare a state in Yemen was probably not motivated by ideology in itself, but by an assessment of the political benefits such an announcement would have in the local context in Yemen, where AQAP needed to compete for popular support with other ideology-based movements such as the Muslim Brotherhood and the "Communists" (the Southern Movement). Their argument is that declaring a state would better position AQAP for a power takeover in Yemen in case Ali Abdullah Saleh's regime is ousted from power.

The al-Qaida Shura unanimously advised bin Laden that AQAP should not seek a truce with the Yemeni government. Instead, they formulated an alternative to the truce strategy, which was relatively close to bin Laden's original view. They agreed that AQAP should be advised to focus on targeting the United States, and to avoid becoming absorbed in a purely local battle against the regime. However, AQAP needed to put just enough pressure on the Yemeni regime so that they in turn would leave al-Qaida alone: "We need to proceed with them using the same approach we adopted with the Pakistani Army, in a gradual confrontation as much as possible."[30] Their recommendation is to not open a front with them, but AQAP should defend themselves in case they get attacked.

In May 2010 Ayman al-Zawahiri entered the internal al-Qaida discussion, after being cut off from communications with the rest of al-Qaida for several months. About Yemen, he echoes the opinions of the others, that a truce between AQAP and Yemeni authorities is not appropriate. He says that at this stage, the most important thing is to incite the Yemeni population to jihad, and to advise AQAP to not escalate their confrontation with the Yemeni regime.[31] Zawahiri also offers his thoughts on al-Qaida's overall strategy. He says we should focus on consolidation (*al-tamakkun*) of al-Qaida's sanctuary in Afghanistan with the Taliban (as detailed in Chapter 5), and if we are restricted by the Taliban, let the other regions "continue our message [meaning the war against the Americans]," and he repeats his advice regarding Yemen that the main priority now should be incitement to jihad in Yemen and to advise AQAP "to remain steadfast in confronting the government and the Crusaders, and not to rush into battles that they cannot withstand."[32]

At the end of May 2010, Zawahiri sends bin Laden another letter with an update, based on the last communications he received from bin Laden, some of which dated back to January 2010. He says regarding Yemen,

> I have summarized my opinion in the previous letter, and after reviewing your letters, I would like to add that the truce offer is not appropriate, and will have a bad moral effect on the brothers and supporters everywhere, and they will consider it a surrender by the brothers, just as the Houthis surrendered. I also add what I emphasized previously about the very, very, very important role of Abu Abdullah's [bin Laden's] speeches for Yemen, and I insisted on the request with great urgency that a month not pass without a word about Yemen or a mention of Yemen, and God is the Grantor of success for all good.[33]

While Zawahiri was writing this letter, a significant development happened with AQAP in Yemen. On May 25, 2010, a US airstrike mistakenly killed a

Yemeni tribal leader, Jabar al-Shabwani, which led to a tribal uprising against the Yemeni government and the United States. To exploit the popular anti-US sentiment and to recruit tribal militants, AQAP launched a campaign of violence against the Yemeni regime, including a number of attacks on the Army and police. At the same time they continued to target foreigners in Yemen, including Western diplomats. Overall, however, AQAP's actions contradicted the advice that al-Qaida was in the process of sending them. One of the members of al-Qaida's Shura council wrote about this dilemma to bin Laden around June 2010:

> [Regarding Yemen], I see, and God knows best, that we will have to wait a little while to consult on the subject ... so that we may make a decision in light of the recent events, the killing of the leader of the Shabwa tribe [Jabir al-Shabwani] and his companions, and people carrying out bombings and attacking government facilities in various places in Yemen. Because, to interfere with Basir [al-Wuhayshi] now that he's on the frontline, in our opinion, it may cause him a shock because he expects that the conditions are now more available than before for work.[34]

He also argues against a solution where AQAP enters into a truce with the Yemeni regime, as he believes this would create internal splits in AQAP. He indicates that the AQAP leaders are strongly opposed to a truce and would not accept it.[35]

To summarize, the internal al-Qaida discussions in the first half of 2010 revolved first around AQAP's military strategy in Yemen, and from March 2010 around state-building in Somalia and around al-Qaida's general policy toward the regions. During these discussions, it becomes clear that al-Qaida has become a different type of organization. From advocating an agenda of "global jihad," it has morphed into an "affiliate network" with a weak central command and regional affiliates in Iraq, Algeria, Yemen, and Somalia, in addition to an active "frontline" in Afghanistan.[36] The affiliates struggle with some of the same issues and principal questions, and during 2009–10, they independently reached out to al-Qaida's senior leadership in Pakistan for guidance. In Algeria, AQIM had grown and now included a group of Libyans, who wanted to open a frontline in Libya. In Somalia, al-Shabaab had repelled the Ethiopian invasion and was positioning itself for governance, in competition with other Islamists and nationalists. And in Yemen, AQAP was on the verge of plunging into a civil war.

The Somali and Yemeni groups both had strong incentives at the time for declaring an Islamic State, as they believed it would rally supporters to their cause and enable them to establish a strong geographic base from where to expand. The Algerian case was a bit different: the expansion of the group into other regions had created internal tensions that needed to be resolved by a higher authority. Specifically, during 2009 there was a group of Libyans in AQIM that wanted to open a front against the regime of Muammar Gaddafi in Libya. This created an internal dispute in the group, and AQIM wrote to al-Qaida to ask for advice. Abu Yahya al-Libi advised in December 2009 that they should not open a front in Libya at this stage, but rather carry out specific operations against Western targets if the opportunity arises.[37] His advice foreshadows al-Qaida's general policy toward the regions in 2010, which is to limit frontline fighting to Afghanistan and Iraq only.

Although their local contexts were different, the Algerians and Yemenis in 2009 were faced with the same principal question, namely, of whether to expand their local and regional wars. And if not—what should their current strategy be? As for the Somalis, they were one step ahead—having won the war against Ethiopia, they were now ready to establish an Islamic State, but what kind of state should it be? Specifically, the Somalis wondered whether it should be an "al-Qaida-state." In December 2009, al-Shabaab sent al-Qaida in Pakistan a video of the group pledging allegiance to Osama bin Laden, and in the spring of 2010, they were eagerly waiting for the reply. In the same period, al-Shabaab sent a delegation to AQAP in Yemen which seemed to be part of a wider outreach effort to increase their capabilities and get in touch with al-Qaida.[38]

Bin Laden initially disagreed with the rest of al-Qaida on what advice to give to AQAP in Yemen. Bin Laden specifically wanted non-escalation and a truce, while the rest of al-Qaida's leaders advised against a truce. The al-Qaida leadership was then overcome by the rapidly changing events in Yemen, caused by the accidental killing on May 25, 2010, of a popular tribal leader by a US airstrike. To exploit popular sentiment, AQAP immediately started escalating their battle with Yemeni security forces, which is the exact opposite of what the al-Qaida leadership had wanted, but they had not yet submitted their advice to al-Wuhayshi. In the fall of 2010, it thus became extremely hard for bin Laden to convince AQAP to stop their escalation. The most sober assessment in this period was probably made by Zawahiri, who already in May 2010 had concluded that al-Qaida was too far away to control events in Yemen, and the best they could do would be to issue public propaganda supporting AQAP.

Bin Laden wrote his revised letter of advice to the AQAP leader, Nasir al-Wuhayshi, at the end of August 2010, which is further discussed below. But before this, al-Qaida's leadership suffered a dramatic loss on May 22, 2010, when al-Qaida's General Manager, Sheikh Saeed, was killed in a US drone strike. Atiyah stepped up to fill his position. Probably to prepare Atiyah for his new role and fill in any blanks he might have, bin Laden in July 2010 sent him a full outline of his new vision for al-Qaida, based on the previous rounds of internal discussions. This new vision includes a comprehensive strategy for all of al-Qaida's regions and is later referred to internally as the "general guidelines" to be distributed to al-Qaida's regions.

Bin Laden's "New Vision" for al-Qaida

In July 2010, bin Laden outlined his new vision for al-Qaida in a fifty-seven-page letter to Atiyah. He introduces and explains his topic as follows:

> We are in the process of a new phase, to evaluate jihadi action and develop it from what it was in the previous period, on two axes: the axis of military action, and the axis of media publications, provided that our work in these two axes is broadly comprehensive, including the center and the regions.[39]

Bin Laden signals at the outset that his aim is to present a comprehensive vision for an al-Qaida organization that includes the center and the regions. It is the first known example of bin Laden using such terminology, underlining that a shift in al-Qaida's thinking had indeed taken place. He states in the letter that he had previously sent part of the new vision to Sheikh Saeed, prior to the latter's death in a drone strike on May 22, 2010. Overall, however, it appears that bin Laden's shift to thinking of al-Qaida as a center with regions is quite recent, supporting the hypothesis that it happened after AQAP and al-Shabaab joined al-Qaida's organization in 2009–10. Additionally, bin Laden reveals that his thinking of a "new phase" was motivated by al-Qaida's failures in Iraq.[40]

> After the war expanded and the Mujahideen spread out in many regions, some of the brothers became involved in fighting against local hostility, and there was an increase in the mistakes that occurred as a result of a defect in the calculations of the brothers planning the operations, or as a result of something that happened before implementation. In addition, some people expanded on the issue of *Al-Tatarrus* (using human shields), which led to the deaths of some Muslims.[41]

One can assume, based on the context of July 2010, that now that al-Qaida has added two new affiliates (AQAP and Al-Shabaab) and has become involved in supervising them directly, bin Laden sees the need to conduct a study of the "lessons learned" throughout history in order to avoid making the same mistakes as in the past. Thus, in his letter bin Laden focuses initially on the importance of gaining popular support. He then outlines how the importance of popular support affects al-Qaida's "work" on the military and media axis, respectively.

Regarding the military axis, he argues that al-Qaida's general line per now is to avoid confrontation with the local rulers, but that it is okay to fight the rulers in self-defense. In what seems like a new proposal, thought of after receiving the consultations from al-Qaida's other senior leaders about Yemen, he now suggests that we should "avoid operations [against Americans] in Islamic countries, with the exception of countries that have fallen under direct invasion and occupation." This might rule out attacking Americans inside Yemen, depending on one's definition of the nature of the conflict there. In later communications, bin Laden mentions Pakistan and Saudi Arabia as places where al-Qaida should avoid attacking Americans.[42] He says that this new policy would fulfill two purposes—to avoid Muslim civilian casualties, and to avoid massive crackdowns on the Islamists by the local regime. Bin Laden mentions specifically that this is what happened to jihadists in Egypt and later, in Saudi Arabia, confirming that he is well aware of the failed campaign of al-Qaida in Saudi Arabia in 2003–7, and does not want to repeat it.

Wrapping up the discussion of the military axis, bin Laden indicates that the most important priority for al-Qaida at this stage is "to continue draining the head of disbelief and the lifeblood of the apostate regime on the open fronts," in what seems to be a nod to Ayman al-Zawahiri, who argued to bin Laden in May 2010 that the most important priority for al-Qaida at this stage is to drain the Americans by fighting them in Iraq and Afghanistan (as opposed to through international terrorist attacks). But bin Laden maintains his previous conviction that in addition to draining the Americans on the "open fronts," we must strive to carry out devastating terrorist attacks on the United States, preferably inside America, but if not, on American interests in a "non-Muslim country."

Regarding the "media axis," bin Laden's main suggestion is to form a central media committee to advise and guide all of al-Qaida's propaganda products, "speeches, film and writing," from the center and from the regions. As with the military work, the aim of forming this committee is to avoid mistakes, improve the public image of al-Qaida, and win popular support. Bin Laden's suggestions go further than previous al-Qaida policies in this era. He suggests that if any group makes a mistake, such as shedding innocent Muslim blood, "the brothers … must apologize and bear responsibility for what happened, … If some brothers in the regions fall short in this area, we must bear responsibility and apologize [on their behalf]." Bin Laden gives examples of how the messaging of the regions is sometimes narrowly focused on local issues rather than "our brothers in Palestine," which contradicts al-Qaida's general policy. All messages, says bin Laden, should portray al-Qaida as "a global organization striving to liberate Palestine and all Muslim countries and to establish the Islamic caliphate that governs by the law of God."

Bin Laden sums up the discussion by saying that he wants al-Qaida to prepare two memorandums, one for military work and the other for media work and send them to the regions. He sums up the most important priorities: "winning over the masses of the nation and correcting some of the wrong perceptions that have occurred in their minds about the mujahidin, in addition to increasing the exhaustion of the head of disbelief."

He adds that he also wants to send a set of administrative guidelines to the regions, including rules regulating succession, appointment of Emirs, and annual reporting to *al-qaʿida fil-markaz* ("al-Qaida Central"), adding that "I see no problem with using [this term]."[43] The term "al-Qaida Central" was in fact coined by the CIA and used in public from at least 2004.[44] These paragraphs further confirm that bin Laden's intention at this stage is to transform al-Qaida from a dispersed network of regional affiliates and back to a centralized organization. There is nothing unusual about this strategy—it can be seen as the natural consequence of al-Qaida's regional expansion and the political opportunities opening up in Yemen and Somalia, coupled with the recent bitter experiences from Iraq and Saudi Arabia.

Outlining the new general policies for al-Qaida takes up about half of bin Laden's fifty-seven-page letter. The other half is dedicated to continuing the discussion on Yemen, and other topics. Bin Laden has read the inputs from the rest of al-Qaida, suggesting that escalation between AQAP and the Yemeni government is unavoidable, and the suggestion that AQAP should declare an Islamic State in order to position itself for a future political takeover in Yemen. Bin Laden, somewhat stubbornly, maintains his previous view that AQAP should "halt the escalation" against the regime and research options for a truce. He thinks that Yemen should be a "supply and reserve force for the mujahidin" rather than an "open front." As for declaring an Islamic State, he is strongly against it, because he is convinced that the project would fail and that it would not benefit the jihad. He says that the only countries that are currently ripe for establishing Islamic states are Iraq, Afghanistan, and Somalia.

At the end of the letter, bin Laden returns to the topic of external operations, stressing their importance, and adding that al-Qaida central needs to coordinate all external operations conducted from the regions, and that there should be an official dedicated to this task, if possible. The instruction is in line with the general policy of centralizing and standardizing al-Qaida's military operations and messaging strategy, but it is removed from the practical realities of al-Qaida, in particular the lack of competent personnel to lead external operations, as detailed in Chapter 6. All of the above suggests that bin Laden had accepted that al-Qaida had now changed fundamentally, or as he put it: "After more than two decades, [al-Qaida] is beginning an important and critical new phase."[45]

Reactions to Bin Laden's "New Phase" Strategy

Atiyah's initial reaction to bin Laden's fifty-seven-page letter came two weeks later.[46] He disagreed with bin Laden's opinions on Yemen, saying it would be a "fundamental mistake" to ask AQAP to stop escalating. But he says he will convey some of the ideas to al-Wuhayshi to get his feedback. A few days afterward on July 18, 2010, Atiyah wrote a letter to al-Wuhayshi, presenting bin Laden's idea of "halting the escalation" and "researching options for a truce," with the caveat that these ideas are still being discussed among al-Qaida's senior leadership and that al-Qaida urgently needs to hear from al-Wuhayshi his assessment of the situation on the ground.[47]

Between August and October 2010, bin Laden drafted letters to the Emirs of al-Qaida's regions in Somalia, Yemen, and Algeria, respectively. The letters give a good indication of how bin Laden planned to operationalize his new vision for al-Qaida. As for Somalia, his suggestions were in line with Atiyah's previous letter: Al-Shabaab should not announce an Islamic State, but implement it in practice on the ground—and they should not join al-Qaida in public, but carry out the unity in secret. Around the same time as he wrote to al-Shabaab, bin Laden made an important policy decision internally in al-Qaida which was in line with al-Qaida's new state-making ambitions: He wrote to Abu Yahya and asked him to pay special attention to the case of Somalia, and to dedicate himself to provide Sharia guidance to al-Shabaab:

> For in reality, there has been an Emirate established on the ground in Somalia with millions of followers. Taking concern in this is a duty upon us, especially in the terms of Sharia [guidance]. We have been working day and night to [achieve] what we desire in the establishment of a Muslim Nation. Therefore, we must guide them … and a large part of this is tied with you.[48]

On August 28, 2010, Atiyah writes to bin Laden some more of his thoughts about the issue of "announcing the state," both in Somalia and Yemen, which gives more nuance to the discussion.

> What is meant by "establishing the state"? If what is meant is to announce it (as the brothers in Iraq did), then that is one thing, and we have known our opinion

about it, which is that we reject it, to the point that we advise the brothers in Somalia now—even though their situation is much better than the situation of the Iraqis—not to announce it, because these "announcements," manifestations, formations, political molds, and framed entities that imitate contemporary situations are unnecessary and their evil is more likely than their good for us, at least in our current stages, because they place us under the burden of the masses' demands to fulfill their rights (services, security, including food security, which is the most critical; the judiciary, education, health, etc.), so the poor struggling Islamic movement becomes involved in the cycle of "serving the people" and providing for their needs before it matures and completes its real ability and influence, and this is fatal![49]

In other words, Atiyah has modified the earlier argument of the al-Qaida Shura where they supported the establishment of an Islamic State in Yemen. Atiyah agrees with bin Laden that merely *announcing* a state does not carry a significant propaganda value in itself. In his letter, Atiyah specifically rejects groups who think that establishing the state is equal to implementing Hudud punishments (he mentions Taliban as an example). But as far as Atiyah is concerned, AQAP could do like al-Shabaab and "establish the pillars for the state" on the ground, so they could position themselves to fill a future power vacuum in Yemen. To reach a compromise with bin Laden, he suggests that AQAP could "seek to achieve actual, realistic and real influence on the ground quietly and without any announcements or claims whatsoever," and to work through the tribes in providing services to the people such as Islamic courts, trade opportunities, and the like.[50]

In the same letter, Atiyah reacts to bin Laden's suggestion to avoid targeting Americans in Muslim countries. Atiyah calls for nuance and consideration of local conditions.

> I do not prefer to put a regulation that stipulates this, but we can make it a recommendation … And we can stipulate that some countries are forbidden to work in (for example: the State of Qatar, and the Kingdom of Bahrain) … We can also stipulate: the permissibility of striking military and intelligence targets and the headquarters of major companies, for example, without others, meaning without striking tourists, for example. The point is to differentiate between targets.[51]

As for Yemen, bin Laden drafted a letter to al-Wuhayshi on August 27, 2010, which he sent to Atiyah for consultation. He repeated his previous arguments that AQAP should not escalate and should be a reserve force and logistics area for the mujahidin on the open fronts. Atiyah did not immediately forward the letter because he wanted to wait for al-Wuhayshi's reactions to his previous letter, which contained many of the same points.[52]

Bin Laden also wrote a letter to Abu Musab Abdul Wudud, the leader of AQIM, with his detailed recommendations for the "new stage."[53] In short, he wants AQIM in this stage to focus on propaganda and on kidnapping Western diplomats from countries with troops in Afghanistan. The order for AQIM to focus on propaganda activities was probably inspired by an idea from Sheikh Yunus, who wrote to bin Laden about the importance of issuing jihadist propaganda in French. As for kidnapping Westerners to put pressure on Europe, this effort actually succeeded in early 2011, when two French hostages were released by AQIM in exchange for a promise from the French president that France would pull out all its troops from Afghanistan.[54]

In November 2010, Ayman al-Zawahiri was finally able to write his opinions about the "new stage" and al-Qaida's instructions to the regions. He is mostly concerned with al-Qaida's strategy toward Afghanistan and Iraq, which he has mentioned previously as the two most important "fronts" al-Qaida are currently engaged in. His thoughts on Afghanistan were discussed in Chapter 5, and include a strategy to lay low for now, while gradually trying to convert Taliban to a global jihadist agenda. As for Iraq, he urges bin Laden to praise the new Emir for the Islamic State of Iraq, Abu Bakr al-Baghdadi, and he repeats his previous suggestion that bin Laden should increase his incitement of the Yemeni population. About Somalia, he said that he thinks they should announce the pledge of allegiance to al-Qaida, to achieve "clarity in the identity and banner," as al-Shabaab themselves had suggested in a previous letter, and also because he fears that in the future, if the pledge is kept secret, the Taliban might pressure al-Qaida to announce they have no affiliation with al-Shabaab.

The reaction from Al-Wuhayshi in Yemen arrives in February 2011, at the start of the Arab Spring uprisings. As predicted by Atiyah and the other senior al-Qaida members, al-Wuhayshi is against bin Laden's suggestion to establish a truce, because AQAP is currently in the middle of an escalation. His answer is long and detailed, but it can be summarized with the following quote:

> Our situation is progressing and increasing and most of the war is in self-defense … by God the hope is very great beyond what you imagine, as we are destroying the enemy and building ourselves and all our reliance is on spoils, so the truce or stopping work during this period we see as inappropriate …[55]

He also talks about the incompatibility of launching external operations without also having to engage in acts of self-defense.

> Our external work is ongoing and will not stop with the help of God, and we
> are dedicating energy and effort to it, and its establishment depends on the
> formation of a group that protects it, as it cannot be established without a base
> from which it launches, and this group cannot be left to work without agents
> conspiring against it, and so on.[56]

In other words, the advice of al-Qaida's senior leaders to bin Laden in 2010 was prescient, as they accurately predicted that al-Wuhayshi would not be willing to de-escalate in Yemen. After the onset of the Arab Spring revolutions, in 2011–12, AQAP and its front organization Ansar al-Sharia declared and ran several self-declared Islamic Emirates in Yemen's Abyan Province, and in 2015, repeated the state experiment in the Hadramawt.[57] In the end, the Yemeni regime led by Ali Abdullah Saleh was deposed by the Houthi movement, while AQAP in the end lost all of its senior leaders to a US-led drone campaign, including Anwar al-Awlaki (2011), Nasir al-Wuhayshi (2015), Qasim al-Raymi (2020), and Khalid Batarfi (2024), and was in the end marginalized.

Summary

To sum up this section, al-Qaida in 2009–10 developed a "new vision" which in practice meant that al-Qaida started seeing itself a "center with regions," and a template for a future Caliphate. This type of terminology was previously not part of al-Qaida's internal discussions, suggesting that al-Qaida had transitioned from being an organization focused on global jihad to an organization focused on "jihadist" state-building and governance in the Middle East.

The main reason for this development appears to have been two things: The failure of al-Qaida in Iraq, and the rise of new and potentially powerful al-Qaida branches in Yemen and Somalia. The escalating situation in Yemen motivated bin Laden to formulate a comprehensive strategy for al-Qaida, which initially included adopting a more population-centric approach, to avoid battles with apostate regimes, and to focus all their energies on fighting the United States. He wanted AQAP to stop its escalation with the Yemeni government and for Yemen to be a reserve area and logistics hub for the jihad movement, whose activities should concentrate on supporting the active frontlines in Iraq and Afghanistan, and of consolidating the territorial control of al-Shabaab in Somalia.

Bin Laden's main advice to AQAP was to stop the escalation against Ali Abdullah Saleh's regime. He also called for concentrating all of al-Qaida's energies on attacking the United States. The other al-Qaida leaders criticized this approach, pointing out the incompatibility of the two agendas: If AQAP attacked the United States from Yemen, they would inevitably also have to confront the Yemeni regime, which would be pressured by the United States to crack down on al-Qaida in Yemen. It seems that bin Laden in the end moderated his advice, recommending that AQAP should also carry out attacks on Yemeni security forces, but only in self-defense. However, he maintained his original advice of seeking a truce or de-escalation with the Yemeni regime. As we have heard, this advice fell on deaf ears when it reached the AQAP leader Nasir al-Wuhayshi, because AQAP was already in the middle of a confrontation with the Yemeni regime, and were building up popular support in Yemen for this very reason.

Another major event that changed al-Qaida's thinking in this period was that al-Shabaab, which was on the brink of establishing an Islamic State in Somalia, wanted to join al-Qaida. The irony was that al-Shabaab was inspired by al-Qaida's unruly affiliate in Iraq, which had established the Islamic state in Iraq (ISI) in 2006. Al-Shabaab did not know that ISI had been established without consulting the al-Qaida leadership, and that bin Laden had endorsed it only reluctantly. The expansion and fame of ISI in Iraq gave al-Qaida an image of being a supporter of Islamic state projects, which in turn encouraged other groups with state-building ambitions, such as al-Shabaab, to join it. Al-Qaida had no choice but to adapt to this new reality, which in practice required al-Qaida's central organization in Pakistan to take on a new set of tasks, including the drafting of a set of "general policies" for al-Qaida's regions. In this context, al-Qaida's senior leaders started talking about the re-establishment of the Caliphate as a real, rather than a hypothetical goal for al-Qaida.

Concluding Remarks

None of the enemies scare me, I swear. No matter who they are, or how intimidating they may be … But I do worry about ours and our brothers' mistakes, bad behavior, and lack of wisdom.[1]
　　　　　—Atiyah, in a letter to senior al-Qaida leaders (March 2007)

In the introduction chapter, I asked two overarching questions about al-Qaida after 9/11: How did al-Qaida react to the opportunities and challenges brought about by the War on Terror? And how did al-Qaida's organization and ideology change in the process? The theoretical starting point for my analysis was the observation that groups are shaped by the local environments in which they operate. The main argument presented in this book is that al-Qaida in the decade after 9/11 changed from being a group focused on global jihad to a group focused on "jihadist" state-building. The most surprising finding in the research was that by mid-2010, al-Qaida had come to view its own organization as a template for the future caliphate—a change of self-image so profound that Osama bin Laden considered changing the name of al-Qaida altogether. However, al-Qaida's Iraqi affiliate was already several steps ahead of al-Qaida in this process. Al-Qaida in Iraq had changed its name to the Islamic State in Iraq already back in 2006, and in 2014, ISIS hijacked al-Qaida's plan to declare a Caliphate while al-Qaida drifted into irrelevance. In this context, it is pertinent to ask what became of al-Qaida's worldview of global jihadism, but first, I will provide a brief summary of the book's main findings.

After 9/11, al-Qaida's main goal was to continue the "global jihad" against the United States, and this war manifested in two ways: first, through a top-down organized international terrorist campaign, and second, by supporting insurgencies fighting the US-led invasions of Iraq and Afghanistan. Chapters 3 and 6 told the story of al-Qaida's External Operations office in Pakistan, which was responsible for the international terrorist campaign. The office's activities were severely constrained by the War on Terror, first by Pakistani police and security forces, and later by US drone strikes. These challenges forced al-Qaida to scale down its international terrorist ambitions and to explore other and simpler ways of terrorizing the West. The Abbottabad documents indicate that most of al-Qaida's senior leadership accepted these realities. They believed the wars in Iraq and Afghanistan were sufficient to weaken the United States and deplete its economy, and that al-Qaida should lie low and wait for the inevitable US withdrawal from both countries. Only bin Laden disagreed and thought al-Qaida needed to stage another spectacular attack on the United States. As a compromise, al-Qaida in the end agreed to appoint the young and talented Yunus al-Mauritani to lead al-Qaida's external operations in 2010, and bin Laden became his direct supervisor. However, al-Mauritani's project was vulnerable because it rested solely on one person who had to build up a new team from scratch. When al-Mauritani was arrested in Pakistan in the fall 2011, the project fell apart.

Due to constraints on al-Qaida's external operations, al-Qaida changed in two ways. The first was that al-Qaida adopted a method where they inspire attacks through propaganda, rather than top-down organized attacks. This shift was announced by Ayman al-Zawahiri in a speech he published shortly after he became leader of al-Qaida in 2011. The other change was that al-Qaida sought to assign more responsibility for external operations to the regions. This change had started already back in 2004, when al-Qaida established their first regional branch, al-Qaida in Iraq. The main motivator initially was the pressure put on al-Qaida by Pakistani Army and police operations. To some extent, al-Qaida's mid-level leaders brought this campaign upon themselves because they had started cooperating with Pakistani militants who wanted to bring down the Musharraf regime. Al-Qaida's Pakistan policy did not really become clear until 2009, when al-Qaida followed signals from Afghan Taliban (and their foreign advisors) to concentrate on jihad in Afghanistan rather than Pakistan. Only in 2010 did bin Laden initiate a policy for all of al-Qaida's regions to focus on only a few enemies at once. This suggests that throughout the whole first decade of the War on Terror, al-Qaida suffered from organizational weakness, which is unsurprising given how depleted the organization already was in 2002.

The US-led invasions of Afghanistan and Iraq gave al-Qaida a welcome opportunity to fight US forces directly on the battlefield. In Chapters 2 and 5, I described al-Qaida's participation in the war in Afghanistan, while Chapter 4 described al-Qaida's participation in Iraq. These wars became al-Qaida's core activity after 2001. They represented an opportunity to weaken the US economy, but more importantly, they represented opportunities to rally the Muslim world behind al-Qaida's banner of "global jihadism." However, both frontlines posed challenges to al-Qaida, which in turn caused al-Qaida to change its aims and methods.

In Afghanistan, the main challenge was that the Taliban treated al-Qaida as guests and did not want to adopt their 'global jihad' agenda. Over time, al-Qaida came to suspect that the Quetta Shura and Mullah Omar were under the influence of Pakistani intelligence. Nevertheless, in 2010 bin Laden sent a few letters of courtesy to Mullah Omar, suggesting that the al-Qaida leaders had agreed on taking a pragmatic approach toward the Taliban. But in the long term, bin Laden was eager for all of al-Qaida's senior leaders to move far away from the influence of the "hypocritical" Taliban. Whether bin Laden's hunch was right or not, this was one among several factors that in mid-2010 encouraged al-Qaida to strengthen the role of its regions.

In Iraq, the main challenge for al-Qaida was the polarization of the Sunni insurgent movement into a Salafi and a non-Salafi faction. In this context, al-Qaida decided to support the Salafi faction, and bin Laden's general policy was to work for unity between the two major Salafi-jihadi groups, al-Qaida in Iraq and Ansar al-Sunnah. However, the two groups failed to unite and over time, al-Qaida in Iraq was marginalized by the rest of the Sunni Iraqi resistance movement and accused of descending into *takfirism*, which in some ways resembled the fate of the GIA in the Algerian Civil War in the 1990s. This exclusivist behavior was anathema to al-Qaida, but because al-Qaida's leaders were isolated in Pakistan, they had no way of correcting ISI's behavior. In 2006 and 2007, al-Qaida attempted to send several representatives to Iraq on fact-finding missions, but none succeeded. From 2008, al-Qaida downgraded its efforts towards Iraq, suggesting that al-Qaida's senior leaders were starting to give up on their Iraqi affiliate.

Parallel to the decline of al-Qaida's relationship to ISI, al-Qaida in 2007–9 gained three new affiliates in Algeria, Yemen, and Somalia. Chapter 7 explained how these new regional affiliates pushed al-Qaida central toward formulating policies related to governance and state-building. It was in this process that al-Qaida for the first time started thinking of itself as a "center with regions" modeled after the historical Caliphate. This shift was probably not the result of a conscious strategy, but more like an afterthought caused by al-Qaida's need in the late 2000s to find new ways of implementing its global jihadist agenda. The shift from a "far enemy" to a "caliphate" doctrine can be seen as the result of a process started by al-Qaida in Iraq, which declared an "Islamic State" already back in 2006. The initial battlefield successes of AQI, and in particular its highly innovative and effective propaganda campaign, created a powerful symbol of Salafi-jihadi resistance that the senior al-Qaida leadership in Pakistan also adopted, even if Osama bin Laden was reluctant at first to directly endorse the Islamic State in Iraq.

The shift to a "caliphate doctrine" can also be seen as the consequence of al-Qaida's failure to apply bin Laden's global jihadism to the insurgencies in Afghanistan and Iraq. In Afghanistan, al-Qaida had failed to create an insurgency dedicated to global jihad, while in Iraq, al-Qaida had likewise failed to create a local affiliate loyal to al-Qaida's senior leadership in Pakistan. In the end, al-Qaida in 2010 replaced bin Laden's "far enemy doctrine" with a new vision for how to implement global jihad, which relied on seeing al-Qaida as a center with regions and a template for a future caliphate. However, by now al-Qaida was so weakened by the War on Terror that the group was unable to implement the new vision, and when the Arab Spring in 2011 opened up new opportunities for territorial control by Islamist rebels, al-Qaida was soon overrun by the larger and far more competent Islamic State in Iraq and Syria (ISIS).

In conclusion, it is pertinent to ask what became of al-Qaida's worldview of "global jihadism." One could say that ISIS continued al-Qaida's global jihadist project in the 2010s, but it was a very different project than the one bin Laden had constructed in the 1990s. Bin Laden's global jihadism was anti-American by nature and rooted in anti-imperialist movements of the twentieth century. Zawahiri's (and later ISIS') global jihadism was territorial in nature and rooted in the discursive tradition of Salafi-jihadism, with its emphasis on criticizing the "secular" nature of modern Muslim regimes, and calling for their replacement by regimes governed by Sharia law. When translated to a global setting, this type of jihadism was inherently flawed because it was designed to contest the legitimacy of autocratic regimes, not to fight modern empires. Zawahiri understood this weakness, because he himself had been part of the Salafi-jihadi trend that had fought the Egyptian regime in the 1980s and 1990s. In 2013, he therefore tried to stop ISIS from expanding into Syria, and this brought him into a direct conflict with the ISIS leader, Abu Bakr al-Baghdadi. ISIS thus separated from al-Qaida, and started propagating a particular and extremist version of global jihadism which was shaped by the violent and sectarian context of the Iraq war.

Al-Zawahiri stayed true to his Salafi-jihadi background, but his version of Salafi-jihadism was no longer a relevant mobilization frame in the polarized environment of the Middle East in the 2010s. Violent activists were now mainly divided along the old fault line of the Muslim Brotherhood versus the Salafis (the *ikhwani-salafi* divide), and with ISIS dominating the space of the Salafi-jihadists, al-Qaida had no choice but to move closer to non-Salaf-jihadi groups such as the traditionalist Taliban or the Brotherhood-inspired Hamas. Over time, this led to a dilution of al-Qaida's Salafi-jihadi *manhaj* and ultimately a split between doctrinal ideologues (like Zawahiri) on one side and pragmatic activists (like Sayf al-Adl) on the other. On the membership level, al-Qaida's followers were absorbed into the support networks of other, and larger Islamist movements such as the Taliban and Hamas, or they continued as local insurgent groups.

Appendix 1
List of propaganda statements by Osama bin Laden and Ayman al-Zawahiri, 2002–4[1]

Table 1 Osama bin Laden statements in 2002–4

Date	Title or topic	Type	Published by
25.08.2002	Handwritten letter from bin Laden to the Afghan people	Letter	*Islam Online*
06.10.2002	Bin Laden calls on Americans to convert	Audio	*Al-Jazeera*
27.10.2002	Handwritten "testament" signed bin Laden and dated December 14, 2001	Letter	*Al-Majalla*
12.11.2002	Bin Laden comments on recent terrorist attacks around the world, including the Bali bombings in October 2002	Audio	*Al-Jazeera*
11.02.2003	Message to our Muslim Brothers in Iraq	Audio	*Al-Jazeera*
16.02 2003	Sermon on the first day of Id al-Adha	Audio	Islamist web sites
08.04.2003	Calling for suicide attacks in Afghanistan	Audio	*Associated Press*
07.07.2003	Attacking Muslim scholars	Audio	Islamist web sites
10.09.2003	Video with bin Laden and Zawahiri [note: The footage was taped in late 2001]	Audio	*Al-Jazeera*
18.10.2003	Message to the American people	Audio	*Al-Jazeera*
18.10.2003	Message to the Iraqi people	Audio	*Al-Jazeera*
04.01.2004	Message to brothers and sisters in the whole Islamic Nation	Audio	*Al-Jazeera*
14.04.2004	Message to the people of Europe [offering armistice]	Audio	*Al-Jazeera / Al-Arabiyya*
06.05.2004	"O Iraqi People," offering bounty for Kofi Annan et al	Audio	Islamist websites
29.10.2004	Bin Laden addressing the American people before the US elections	Video	*Al-Jazeera*
16.12.1004	Message to the Muslims in the land of the two holy places especially and to Muslims elsewhere more generally	Audio	Islamist web sites
27.12.2004	Message to the sons of the two rivers [announcing Zarqawi as leader of AQI]	Audio	*Al-Jazeera/* Islamist web

Table 2 Ayman al-Zawahiri statements 2002–4

Date	Title or topic	Type	Published by
09.10.2002	Zawahiri threatens US allies	Audio	*Al-Sahab /AP*
21.05.2003	About collaborating Arab countries	Audio	*Al-Jazeera*
03.08.2003	About Guantanamo Bay prisoners	Audio	*Al-Arabiyya*
10.09.2003	Video with bin Laden and Zawahiri	Audio	*Al-Jazeera*
28.09.2003	Message to Muslims in Pakistan and Afghanistan	Audio	*Al-Jazeera / Al-Arabiyya*
19.12.2003	The second anniversary of the Tora Bora battle	Audio	*Al-Jazeera*
24.02.2004	On the State of the Union Speech	Audio	*Al-Jazeera / Al-Arabiyya*
24.02.2004	On the French headscarf ban	Audio	*Al-Jazeera / Al-Arabiyya*
25.03.2004	Calling for Musharraf overthrow	Audio	*Al-Jazeera*
11.06.2004	Denouncing the Greater Middle East initiative	Audio	*Al-Arabiyya*
09.09.2004	Zawahiri saying US defeat a question of time	Video	*Al-Jazeera*
01.10.2004	Zawahiri calling for united Muslim resistance	Audio	*Al-Jazeera*
29.11.2004	Denouncing US elections	Video	*Al-Jazeera*

Notes

Preface

1 "Bin Laden's Bookshelf," *Office of the Director of National Intelligence* (ODNI), https://www.dni.gov/index.php/features/bin-laden-s-bookshelf; and "November 2017 Release of Abbottabad Compound Material," *Central Intelligence Agency*, November 1, 2017. https://www.cia.gov/library/abbottabad-compound/index.html.

2 "Hijri-Gregorian Converter," *IslamiCity*, https://www.islamicity.org/hijri-gregorian-converter/.

3 "Harmony Program," *CTC West Point*, https://ctc.westpoint.edu/harmony-program/.

4 As of June 2025, hosted at www.mafa.world.

Introduction

1 For a recent example, see, e.g., *"al-ustadh al-duktur Abu Khalid rahimahu Allah,"* *al-Sahab*, October 2024, released via *Chirpwire.net*, author's collection.

2 There are notable exceptions, including, but not limited to: Nelly Lahoud, *The Bin Laden Papers: How the Abbottabad Raid Revealed the Truth about al-Qaeda, Its Leader and His Family* (New Haven, CT: Yale University Press, 2023); Peter L. Bergen, *The Rise and Fall of Osama bin Laden* (New York: Simon & Schuster, 2021); Adrian Levy and Kathy Scott-Clark, *The Exile: The Flight of Osama bin Laden* (New York and London: Bloomsbury, 2017); Barak Mendelsohn, *The al-Qaeda Franchise: The Expansion of al-Qaeda and Its Consequences* (Oxford: Oxford University Press, 2016).

3 See, e.g., Michael Elliott, "Al-Qaeda: Reeling Them In," *TIME*, September 23, 2002, https://time.com/archive/6667248/al-qaeda-reeling-them-in/; "Wolfowitz: 'We Are Moving to Victory,'" *CNN*, September 11, 2003, https://edition.cnn.com/2003/ALLPOLITICS/09/09/sprj.irq.wolfowitz.cia/index.html.

4 The term "al-Qaida Central" was probably introduced by the CIA. See, e.g., CIA Director George Tenet's use of the term in a Senate Hearing in February 2004. "Statement of the honorable George J. Tenet, Director of Central Intelligence," in "Hearing before the Select Committee on Intelligence of the United States Senate, 108th Congress, Second Session: Current and projected national security threats to

the United States," Transcript, Senate Hearing 108–588, U.S. Government Printing Office, February 24, 2004, https://www.intelligence.senate.gov/hearings/current-and-projected-national-security-threats-united-states-february-24-2004.

5   See Chapter 7 for details.

6   See, e.g., the voluntary testimony of Khalid Sheikh Mohammed, given in 2014 in *USA v. Sulaiman Abu Ghayth*, United States District Court, Southern District of New York, Case 1:98-cr-01023-LAK, Document 1597–1, Page 14.

7   An example of such an advisor, with direct access to bin Laden in the 1990s, was the Egyptian journalist and Afghan-Arab veteran, Mustafa Hamid, whose writings are quoted throughout this book.

8   See Chapter 3 for details.

9   A key primary source to understanding the activities of the Military Committee in 1998–2001 is the autobiography written by Abu Hafs al-Masri's secretary, Fadil Harun. See Fadil Harun, *al-harb 'ala al-islam*, published online, n.d. [ca. 2009], author's collection.

10   Ahmed Abou El Zalaf, "The Special Apparatus (al-Niẓām al-Khāṣṣ): The Rise of Nationalist Militancy in the Ranks of the Egyptian Muslim Brotherhood," *Religions* 13, no. 1 (2022): 77.

11   For a history of Abdullah Azzam's Services Office, see Thomas Hegghammer, *The Caravan: Abdallah Azzam and the Rise of Global Jihad* (Cambridge: Cambridge University Press, 2020).

12   See, e.g., Mendelsohn, *The al-Qaeda Franchise*.

13   For background on the Afghan-Arabs, see 'Abd Allāh Anas and Tam Hussein, *To the Mountains: My Life in Jihad, from Algeria to Afghanistan* (London: Hurst, 2019); and Hegghammer, *The Caravan*.

14   James Paterson came to a similar conclusion in his study of al-Qaida propaganda. James Paterson, "Al-Qaeda as a Spatial Orientated Movement: Interactions between Transnational and Local Jihadism," *Small Wars & Insurgencies*, DOI: 10.1080/09592318.2024.2314653 (February 15, 2024).

15   Anne Stenersen, *Al-Qaida in Afghanistan* (Cambridge: Cambridge University Press, 2017).

16   Raphaël Lefèvre, *Jihad in the City: Militant Islam and Contentious Politics in Tripoli* (Cambridge: Cambridge University Press, 2021) and Donatella Della Porta, *Clandestine Political Violence: A Social Movements Perspective* (Cambridge: Cambridge University Press, 2013).

17   See, e.g., Daniel Byman and Asfandyar Mir, "How Strong Is al-Qaeda? A Debate," *War on the Rocks*, May 20, 2022, https://warontherocks.com/2022/05/how-strong-is-al-qaeda-a-debate/.; and Bruce Hoffman, "Al-Qaeda's Resurrection," *Council on Foreign Relations*, March 6, 2018, https://www.cfr.org/expert-brief/al-qaedas-resurrection.

18   My definitions of the macro-, meso- and micro-levels are inspired by Raphaël Lefèvre, *Jihad in the City: Militant Islam and Contentious Politics in Tripoli* (Cambridge: Cambridge University Press, 2021), 29–30.

Chapter 1

1   *"Kayfa ta'amala ikhwanina al-mujahidin ma'a al-nidham al-rafidi,"* Muharram 1428 H / January/February 2007, Abbottabad documents.

2   "Presidential Address to the Nation," *The White House*, October 7, 2001, https://georgewbush-whitehouse.archives.gov/news/releases/2001/10/20011007-8.html.

3   Doug Stanton, *Horse Soldiers: The Extraordinary Story of a Band of US Soldiers Who Rode to Victory in Afghanistan* (New York: Simon & Schuster, 2009), 118.

4   Stanton, *Horse Soldiers*, 51.

5   There are several Taliban members with the name Abdul Baqi. This is possibly a reference to the Mullah Abdul Baqi born in Nangarhar.

6   *"Akhbar yawm al-ahad—Afghanistan,"* Markaz al-Dirasat, November 11, 2001, author's collection.

7   Hamid Mir, "How Osama bin Laden Escaped Death 4 Times after 9/11," *Canada Free Press*, September 8, 2007, https://canadafreepress.com/2007/mir090907.htm.

8   Abd al-Hadi al-Iraqi, *"malhamat qal'a janki,"* March 14, 2002, Abbottabad documents.

9   David Hicks, *Guantanamo: My Journey* (Sydney: Random House Australia, 2010).

10 The historical account in this section was based on jihadist and US sources, including Mullah Abdul Baqi, "The Battle of Qila-e-Jangi," author's collection; Abd al-Hadi al-Iraqi, *"malhamat qal'a janki,"* March 14, 2002, Abbottabad documents; and US accounts including Gary Schroen, *First In: An Insider's Account of How the CIA Spearheaded the War on Terror in Afghanistan* (New York: Presidio Press, 2005), and Stanton, *Horse Soldiers*.

11 Qotoz, *"kunt jaran li-abi mus'ab al-zarqawi,"* June 27, 2006, author's collection.

12 See, for instance, "Abu Abd al-Rahman al-Kanadi," in Abu Ubayda al-Maqdisi, *"shuhada' fi zaman al-ghurba,"* *Al-Fajr Media Center*, n.d. [c. 2008], author's collection.

13 Qotoz, *"kunt jaran li-abi mus'ab al-zarqawi,"* June 27, 2006, author's collection.

14 The Taliban finally conquered Panjshir after they took power in Kabul in 2021. "Taliban Claim Control of Panjshir, Opposition Says Resistance Will Continue," *Reuters*, September 7, 2021. https://www.reuters.com/world/india/taliban-claim-control-panjshir-evacuation-flights-await-clearance-2021-09-06/.

15 The CIA's early support to the Northern Alliance in 2001 is described in Schroen, *First In;* and Gary Bernsten, *Jawbreaker: The Attack on Bin Laden and Al-Qaeda: A Personal Account by the CIA's Key Field Commander* (New York: Random House, 2005).

16 Bernsten, *Jawbreaker*.

17 Abd al-Hadi al-Iraqi, *"malhamat qal'a janki,"* March 14, 2002, Abbottabad documents.

18 The interview was later posted on the website *Markaz al-Dirasat*. See Tayseer Allouni, "Document—The Unreleased Interview with Usamah bin Laden,"

Religioscope, July 20, 2002, https://english.religion.info/2002/07/20/document-the-unreleased-interview-with-usamah-bin-laden/.

19 New arrivals to Kandahar were sent to this rear base to train, because al-Qaida's al-Farouq camp was closed.

20 Mustafa Hamid, *salib fi sama kandahar*, n.d. [*c.* 2006], author's collection.

21 Author's conversation with a US journalist who covered the US war in Afghanistan in 2001.

22 Abd al-Hadi al-Iraqi, "*malhamat qal'a janki*," March 14, 2002, Abbottabad documents.

23 Abu Sulayman al-Farsi, "*qissat al-mujahidin al-asra wa al-shuhada' kamila fi qal'a janja bi-mazar al-sharif kama yarwiha ahad al-najin minha*," re-posted on defense-arab.com on December 20, 2009, author's collection.

24 Mullah Abdul Baqi, "The Battle of Qila-e-Jangi," author's collection.

25 Mullah Abdul Baqi, "The Battle of Qila-e-Jangi," author's collection; the story is supported by Abdul Hai Mutma'in, *Taliban: A Critical History from Within* (Berlin: First Draft Publishing, 2019), 208.

26 Mullah Abdul Baqi, "The Battle of Qila-e-Jangi," author's collection.

27 Muta'min, *Taliban: A Critical History from Within*, 208.

28 Stanton, *Horse Soldiers*, 283–4.

29 Mullah Abdul Baqi, "The Battle of Qila-e-Jangi," author's collection; Abd al-Hadi al-Iraqi, "*malhamat qal'a janki*," March 14, 2002, Abbottabad documents; and Abu Sulayman al-Farsi, "*qissat al-mujahidin al-asra.*"

30 Number estimates vary from 350 to 600 fighters. Abd al-Hadi al-Iraqi, "*malhamat qal'a janki*," March 14, 2002, Abbottabad documents; and Mullah Abdul Baqi, "The Battle of Qila-e-Jangi," author's collection.

31 Abu Sulayman al-Farsi, "*qissat al-mujahidin al-asra.*"

32 This section is based on several jihadist accounts, including Mullah Abdul Baqi, "The Battle of Qila-e-Jangi," and Abu Sulayman al-Farsi, "*qissat al-mujahidin al-asra*," and US accounts, including Stanton, *Horse Soldiers*, and Toby Harnden, *First Casualty: The Untold Story of the CIA Mission to Avenge 9/11* (New York: Little, Brown and Company, 2021).

33 Mullah Abdul Baqi, "The Battle of Qila-e-Jangi," author's collection.

34 See Richard A. Serrano, "Driven by a Son's Sacrifice," *Los Angeles Times*, April 7, 2005, https://www.latimes.com/archives/la-xpm-2005-apr-07-na-spann7-story.html.

35 Sayf al-Adl, "*taht zilal al-rammah*," Part 5, n.d. [*c.* 2003], author's collection.

36 Sayf al-Adl, "*taht zilal al-rammah*," Part 5.

37 Ibid.

38 Vernie Liebl, "Al Qaida on the US Invasion of Afghanistan in Their Own Words," *Small Wars & Insurgencies* 23, no. 3 (2012): 542–68; Hamid, *salib fi sama kandahar*.

39 The two others were Osama bin Laden and the Egyptian Abu 'Ubaydah al-Banshiri. The latter drowned in an accident in Lake Victoria, Kanya in 1996.

40 Osama bin Laden, "*al-qarar*," private notebook, November 11, 2002, Abbottabad documents.

41 "Bin Laden at Son's Afghan Wedding," *BBC*, January 10, 2001, http://news.bbc. co.uk/2/hi/world/monitoring/media_reports/1110108.stm.

42 Hamid, *salib fi sama kandahar*, 261; Liebl, "Al Qaida on the US Invasion of Afghanistan in Their Own Words."

43 Fadil Harun, "*al-harb 'ala al-islam*," Part 2, 431.

44 Sayf al-Adl, "*taht zilal al-rammah*," Part 5.

45 "Stipulation of Fact," *United States v. David Matthew Hicks*, March 29, 2007.

46 Sayf al-Adl lists "Abu Mus'ab al-Urdunni" as a commander-in-charge of one of the groups in the "city sector" and states he came from Herat. Sayf al-Adl, "*taht zilal al-rammah*," Part 5.

47 According to the memoirs of a CIA officer who was present at the Battle for Kandahar, US intelligence initially thought there was a security perimeter around Kandahar city, referred to as the "ring of fire." In reality, the "ring of fire" was comprised of defunct military equipment which was misinterpreted on satellite imagery to represent real military positions. Duane Evans, *Foxtrot in Kandahar: A Memoir of a CIA Officer in Afghanistan at the Inception of America's Longest War* (El Dorado, CA: Savas Beatie, 2017), 171–82.

48 See, e.g., Evans, *Foxtrot in Kandahar;* Robert L. Grenier, *88 Days to Kandahar: A CIA Diary* (New York: Simon & Schuster, 2015), and Pete Blaber, *The Mission, the Men, and Me: Lessons from a Former Delta Force Commander* (New York: Berkley Caliber, 2008).

49 al-Maqdisi, "*shuhada' fi zaman al-ghurba*"; Hamid, *salib fi sama kandahar*.

50 Sayf al-Adl, "*taht zilal al-rammah*," Part 5.

51 Evans, *Foxtrot in Kandahar*.

52 Grenier, *88 Days to Kandahar*.

53 Sayf al-Adl, "*taht zilal al-rammah*," Part 5.

54 Evans, *Foxtrot in Kandahar*, 177; Grenier, *88 Days to Kandahar*.

55 Mutma'in, *Taliban: A Critical History from Within*, 216.

56 Hamid, *salib fi sama kandahar*; Sayf al-Adl, "*taht zilal al-rammah*," Part 5; Erik Eckholm, "Kandahar Hospital Was Unhappy Host to 18, Not 11, Armed Unholy Warriors," *New York Times*, December 18, 2001.

57 Sayf al-Adl, "*taht zilal al-rammah*," Part 5.

58 Grenier, *88 Days to Kandahar*.

59 Peter Bergen, "The Account of How We Nearly Caught Osama bin Laden in 2001," *The New Republic*, 2009, https://newrepublic.com/article/72086/the-battle-tora-bora.

60   Author's conversation with former US military official. US military accounts confirm that only cars moving at night could be bombed, see, e.g., Evans, *Foxtrot in Kandahar,* 177.

61   Qotoz, "*kunt jaran li-abi mus'ab al-zarqawi.*"

62   "Zawahiri's Letter to Zarqawi," July 9, 2005, Harmony Program, CTC West Point, https://ctc.westpoint.edu/harmony-program/zawahiris-letter-to-zarqawi-original-language-2/.

63   Qotoz, "*kunt jaran li-abi mus'ab al-zarqawi.*"

64   Obaid Ali, Sayed Asadullah Sadat, and Christian Bleuer, "One Land, Two Rules (8): Delivering Public Services in Insurgency-Affected Insurgent-Controlled Zurmat District," *Afghanistan Analysts Network,* September 4, 2019.

65   For background on Barmal, South Waziristan and the Wazir tribe, see, e.g., Mansur Khan Mahsud, "The Taliban in South Waziristan," in Peter Bergen (ed.), Katherine Tiedemann (contributor), *Talibanistan: Negotiating the Borders between Terror, Politics, and Religion* (Oxford: Oxford University Press, 2013), 164–201; Chris Harnisch, "Question Mark of South Waziristan: Biography and Analysis of Maulvi Nazir Ahmad," *AEI,* July 17, 2009; and "Meeting with Mullah Nazir," *al-Sahab,* 2009, author's collection.

66   Mutma'in, *Taliban: A Critical History from Within,* 224. "Nek Mohammed," *Frontline,* October 3, 2006, https://www.pbs.org/wgbh/pages/frontline/taliban/militants/mohammed.html.

67   Detailed accounts of bin Laden's whereabouts after Tora Bora can be found in Wesley Morgan, *The Hardest Place: The American Military Adrift in Afghanistan's Pech Valley* (New York: Random House, 2021); in addition to Bergen, *The Rise and Fall.* For an alternative account, purportedly from bin Laden's own son, see Mustafa Hamid, "*najl bin ladin yarwa qissat walidu min Tora Bora ila Abbottabad* [Bin Laden's son narrates the story of his father, from Tora Bora to Abbottabad]," Parts 1–3, June 28—July 3, 2017, *Mafa al-Siyasi* (www.mafa.world).

68   Osama bin Laden, "*dhikr Tora Bora, Ramadhan 1424,*" audiotape, n.d. [*c.* 2003], Abbottabad documents.

69   Hamid, *salib fi sama kandahar.*

70   Fadil Harun, *al-harb 'ala al-islam.*

71   Mutma'in, *Taliban: A Critical History from Within,* 210.

72   Hamid, *salib fi sama kandahar.*

73   For eyewitness accounts of the situation in Jalalabad in late 2001, see, e.g., Philip Smucker, *Al Qaeda's Great Escape: The Military and the Media on Terror's Trail* (Washington, DC: Potomac Books, 2004); Lucy Morgan Edwards, *The Afghan Solution: The Inside Story of Abdul Haq, the CIA and How Western Hubris Lost Afghanistan* (London: Pluto Press, 2011).

74   Morgan, *The Hardest Place,* 6; Levy and Scott-Clark, *The Exile,* 73–4.

75 Bergen, *The Rise and Fall*, 76.

76 See, e.g., *"min qisas shuhada' al-'arab: Abu Hafs al-Kuwaiti,"* *Sayd al-Fawa'id forums*, http://www.saaid.net/Doat/hamad/33.htm.

77 115 Yemenis were held at Guantánamo since 2002. As of 2025, three are still held there, and three died in custody. The rest were transferred to other countries. The Guantánamo Docket, *New York Times*, updated May 14, 2025, https://www. nytimes.com/interactive/2021/us/guantanamo-bay-detainees.html.

78 Memoirs written by former bin Laden bodyguards include Nassar al- Bahri, *Guarding Bin Laden: My Life in al-Qaeda* (Great Britain: TMP, 2013); Abu al-Shukara al-Hindukushi, *mudhakkarati min kabul ila baghdad, al-juz 1–9,"* n.d. [*c.* 2007], author's collection.

79 Bergen, *The Rise and Fall*, 172.

80 Mustafa Hamid claims bin Laden left around December 6th; while other accounts say December 12–13. See Hamid, *salib fi sama kandahar*; Levy and Scott-Clark, *The Exile*, 77. A summary of the various US accounts of bin Laden's escape can be found in Morgan, *The Hardest Place*, 6.

81 For a detailed account of bin Laden's escape, see Bergen, *The Rise and Fall*, 175–7.

82 Levy and Scott-Clark, *The Exile*, 77–9.

83 The number is based on Harmony Document no. AFGP-2002-003790, presented in a redacted version in *Hadi v. Bush*, Case 1:08-cv-01228-RMC, Document 118–9, filed on September 19, 2011, 26–7.

84 If any senior al-Qaida leaders were killed in Tora Bora, they would probably have been eulogized in later al-Qaida propaganda. In 2004, al-Qaida's media official suggested making a documentary about the Arabs [meaning al-Qaida members] killed during the US invasion of Afghanistan, and he only mentioned four individuals: two were killed in Kandahar, and one was killed in Shah-i-Kot. The last one, Abu Turab al-Urdunni (real name Faysal al-Hilalat), was probably also killed in Kandahar, see, e.g., *"bin ladin yarhal fi al-waqt al-munasib,"* *Al-Ghad*, July 25, 2011.

85 See, e.g., Asad [Asadullah Abd al-Rahman?], letter to *"mashayikhna al-afadil,"* September 5, 2002, Abbottabad documents.

86 Hamid, *salib fi sama kandahar*, 245.

87 Bergen, *The Rise and Fall*, 176; Levy and Scott-Clark, *The Exile*, 78.

88 The sentence was found in a note believed to be written by bin Laden, and has been referred to as "bin Laden's testament" dated December 14, 2001. It was printed in the London-based Arabic magazine *al-Majalla* in October 2002. See *al-Majalla*, October 27–November 2, 2002.

89 Levy and Scott-Clark, *The Exile*, 82.

90 Ibid., 86.

91 The description of the Shura is based on *"Kayfa ta'amala ikhwanuna al-mujahudin ma'a al-nidham al-rafidi,"* Muharram 1428 H / January/February 2007, Abbottabad documents.

92 "*Kayfa ta'amala ikhwanuna al-mujahudin ma'a al-nidham al-rafidi*," Muharram
    1428 H / January/February 2007, Abbottabad documents.
93 Ibid.
94 al-Maqdisi, "*shuhada' fi zaman al-ghurba*."

Chapter 2

1   Khalid Habib, handwritten letter to bin Laden, n.d. [fall 2004], Abbottabad documents.
2   Abbottabad documents show that al-Qaida tried to find ways of contacting Mullah
    Omar around 2007–8, but were unable to do so. These sources are further discussed
    in Chapter 5.
3   The Taliban's senior leadership committee is formally known as the "Rahbari
    Shura," but since it was based in the city of Quetta, Pakistan, it is commonly known
    as the "Quetta Shura." It was formed around 2003. Antonio Giustozzi, *The Taliban
    at War, 2001–2021* (New York: Oxford University Press, 2022), 28; 32.
4   Roel Meijer, "Yusuf al-Uyairi and the Making of a Revolutionary Salafi Praxis,"
    Die Welt des Islams 47, no. 3–4 (2007): 429; Jarret Brachman, "The Next Osama,"
    Newsweek, September 10, 2009.
5   "Interview with Al-Qaeda's Field Commander Abu Laith Al-Libi," originally
    posted on www.jehad.net, July 9, 2002, translated and posted on *Mario's Cyberspace
    Station*, mprofaca.cro.net, July 19, 2002, author's collection.
6   "Interview with Al-Qaeda's Field Commander Abu Laith Al-Libi," July 9, 2002.
7   Thomas Hegghammer, *Jihad in Saudi Arabia: Violence and Pan-Islamism since 1979*
    (Cambridge: Cambridge University Press, 2010), 170–1.
8   "Domain Report—AlemArh.com" and "Domain Report—AlMuQatIla.com,"
    DomainTools, April 4, 2023, author's collection.
9   Brachmann, "The Next Osama"; "Sheikh Abu Yahya al-Libi, An Interview with as-
    Sahab," June 17, 2006.
10 LIFG had rejected bin Laden's offer to join his "Global Islamic Front against the
    Jews and Crusaders" in 1998, and LIFG was generally opposed to bin Laden's plans
    of carrying out terrorist attacks on the US from the soil of Afghanistan. Many
    years later however, in late 2007 a breakaway faction of the LIFG comprised of Abu
    al-Layth al-Libi and Abu Yahya al-Libi eventually joined al-Qaida. When I refer to
    "LIFG" in this book, I generally refer to this LIFG breakaway faction, rather than
    the remnants of the LIFG in Libya, many of whom later renounced armed jihad.
    Camille Tawil, *Brothers in Arms: The Story of al-Qa'ida and the Arab Jihadists*, trans.
    Robin Bray (London: Saqi Books, 2011), 168.
11 Meijer, "Yusuf al-Uyairi and the Making of a Revolutionary Salafi Praxis," 429.
12 See, for instance, "Interview with Al-Qaeda's Field Commander Abu Laith Al-Libi,"
    July 9, 2002.

13 Giustozzi, *The Taliban at War*, 31–3.

14 Ibid., 18.

15 Richard W. Stewart, "The US Army in Afghanistan: Operation Enduring Freedom, October 2001–March 2002," *Center of Military History*, CMH Pub 70-83-1, 44; for a popular account of Operation Anaconda, see Sean Naylor, *Not a Good Day to Die: The Untold Story of Operation Anaconda* (New York: Berkley Books, 2005).

16 See, for instance, Paul L. Hastert, "Operation Anaconda: Perception Meets Reality in the Hills of Afghanistan," *Studies in Conflict & Terrorism* 28, no. 1 (2005): 11–20.

17 Hastert, "Operation Anaconda: Perception Meets Reality in the Hills of Afghanistan," 11–20.

18 See, for example, "*ahdath Shai Kot, rawayatan wa-tahlilan bi-qalam al-shaykh 'Abd al-'Adhim*," Al-Emarah, n.d. [ca 2002], author's collection.

19 Abdul Hai Mutma'in, *Taliban: A Critical History from Within* (Berlin: First Draft Publishing, 2019), 219–22.

20 "*Ahdath Shai Kot, rawayatan wa-tahlilan bi-qalam al-shaykh 'Abd al-'Adhim*," Al-Emarah, n.d. [*c.* 2002], author's collection; and Mutma'in, *Taliban: A Critical History from Within*, 128, 224.

21 "*ahdath Shai Kot, rawayatan wa-tahlilan bi-qalam al-shaykh 'Abd al-'Adhim*," Al-Emarah, n.d. [*c.* 2002], alemarh.com, author's collection.

22 Ibid.; see also Abu 'Ubayda al-Maqdisi, "*shuhada' fi zaman al-ghurba*," al-Fajr Media Center, n.d. [*c.* 2008], author's collection.

23 "*Ahdath Shai Kot, rawayatan wa-tahlilan bi-qalam al-shaykh 'Abd al-'Adhim*," Al-Emarah, n.d. [*c.* 2002], author's collection.

24 "*Kayfa ta'amala ikhwanina al-mujahidin ma'a al-nidham al-rafidi*," Muharram 1428 H / January/February 2007, Abbottabad documents.

25 "*Ahdath Shai Kot, rawayatan wa-tahlilan bi-qalam al-shaykh 'Abd al-'Adhim*," Al-Emarah, n.d. [*c.* 2002], author's collection; al-Maqdisi, "*shuhada' fi zaman al-ghurba*."

26 *USA v. Usama bin Laden, et al.*, United States District Court, Southern District of New York, Indictment, S(9) 98 Cr. 1023 (LBS).

27 "Abd al-Wakil al-Masri," in al-Maqdisi, "*shuhada' fi zaman al-ghurba*"; *USA v. Usama bin Laden, et al.*, 33.

28 *USA v. Usama bin Laden, et al.*, 38.

29 Anne Stenersen, *Al-Qaida in Afghanistan* (Cambridge: Cambridge University Press, 2017), 143–4.

30 "*Katibat al-ansar*," undated, AFGP-2002-000047.

31 Abu 'Ubayda al-Maqdisi, "*shuhada' fi zaman al-ghurba*."

32 They include Abu Bakr 'Azzam al-Urdunni (Kandahar), Abu Ahmad al-Suri (Kabul), Abu al-Hassan al-Sumali (Kabul), Abu 'Amir al-Ashqar al-Filistini (Kandahar), Abu Bakr al-Maghribi (Kabul). Also, Abu al-Haytham al-Yemeni, "led one of the groups" at Shah-i-Kot, according to a biography published by al-Sahab. Al-Maqdisi, "*shuhada' fi zaman al-ghurba*"; "*rihat al-janna*," al-Sahab, n.d., author's collection.

33 Except for Abd al-Wakil al-Masri, there is no overlap between lists of "martyrs" at Shah-i-Kot, and al-Qaida membership lists from *c.* 1998 to 2001, see in particular "*asma' afrad al-Qa'ida,*" n.d., AFGP-2002-600046; and "*asma' tamam al-qa'ida,*" n.d., AFGP-2002-600177.

34 An eyewitness account written by Abu al-Layth al-Libi indicates that al-Libi himself was the most high-ranking Arab commander present, which makes sense given that Abu al-Layth probably had his fighting group intact at that time, while Abd al-Hadi had not. See "*ahdath Shai Kot, rawayatan wa-tahlilan bi-qalam al-shaykh 'Abd al-'Adhim,*" Al-Emarah, n.d. [*c.* 2002], author's collection; see also "Stipulation of Fact," PE 39, *United States v. Abd al Hadi al Iraqi*, June 9, 2022.

35 See, e.g., Naylor, *Not a Good Day to Die*.

36 Richard W. Stewart, "The US Army in Afghanistan: Operation Enduring Freedom, October 2001–March 2002," Center of Military History, CMH Pub 70-83-1, 42.

37 "*Ahdath Shai Kot, rawayatan wa-tahlilan bi-qalam al-shaykh 'Abd al-'Adhim,*" Al-Emarah, n.d. [*c.* 2002], author's collection.

38 Ibid. Some accounts state that Sayf al-Rahman Mansour was killed alongside Maulavi Jawad, but that his death was hidden from the public. Mutma'in, *Taliban: A Critical History from Within*, 226.

39 "Interview with Al-Qaeda's Field Commander Abu Laith Al-Libi," July 9, 2002; see also "Good news … an ambush like no other, and the result was the death of eight Americans [in Arabic]," alemarh.com, reposted on *Muntada al-thaqafa al-islamiyya*, March 20, 2002, author's collection.

40 Peter L. Bergen, *The Rise and Fall of Osama bin Laden* (New York: Simon & Schuster, 2021), 180–3; 209.

41 Yosri Fouda and Nick Fielding, *Masterminds of Terror: The Truth behind the Most Devastating Terrorist Attack the World Has Ever Seen* (London: Penguin, 2003); Adrian Levy and Kathy Scott-Clark, *The Exile: The Flight of Osama bin Laden* (New York and London: Bloomsbury, 2017).

42 "Al Adl letter," June 13, 2002, Harmony Program.

43 Ibid.

44 "Stipulation of Fact," PE 39, *United States v. Abd al Hadi al Iraqi*, June 9, 2022.

45 Senate Select Committee on Intelligence, "Committee Study of the Central Intelligence Agency's Detention and Interrogation Program," *United States Senate*, April 3, 2014, vii.

46 "Al-'Adl Letter," June 13, 2002, Harmony Program; Asad [Asadullah Abd al-Rahman?], letter to "*mashayikhna al-afadil,*" September 5, 2002, Abbottabad documents; Abu Sa'd [Osama bin Laden], letter to Abu al-Faraj and Abd al-Hadi, November 19, 2002, Abbottabad documents.

47 The dynamic of the "yes-men" around bin Laden was described in Asad [Asadullah Abd al-Rahman?], letter to "*mashayikhna al-afadil,*" September 5, 2002, Abbottabad documents.

48   For further details on the tension between KSM and Sayf al-Adl in Pakistan in 2002, see Levy and Scott-Clark, *The Exile,* 112; and Senate Select Committee on Intelligence, "Committee Study of the Central Intelligence Agency's Detention and Interrogation Program." These two accounts both indicate that KSM and Sayf al-Adl disagreed on the fate of US citizen and *Wall Street Journal* journalist Daniel Pearl, who was kidnapped and later murdered by KSM's group.

49   Levy and Scott-Clark, *The Exile,* 203.

50   "Al Adl letter," June 13, 2002, Harmony Program.

51   Bergen, *The Rise and Fall,* 182.

52   "Al-Nida webpage 2001–2002." FFI Archive.

53   A detailed account of al-Qaida's various international terrorist attacks in the 1990s and early 2000s can be found in Ali H. Soufan, *The Black Banners: Inside the Hunt for Al Qaeda* (London: Penguin, 2011).

54   Abu Sa'd [Osama bin Laden], letter to Abu al-Faraj and Abd al-Hadi, November 19, 2002, Abbottabad documents.

55   See, e.g., Osama bin Laden, "*al-shura,*" n.d. [mid-2004], Abbottabad documents.

56   Abu Sa'd [Osama bin Laden], letter to Abu al-Faraj and Abd al-Hadi, November 19, 2002, Abbottabad documents.

57   Ibid.

58   Ibid.

59   Mustafa Hamid, *salib fi sama kandahar,* n.d. [*c.* 2006], 88.

60   Mustafa Hamid and Leah Farrall, *The Arabs at War in Afghanistan* (London: Hurst, 2015), 277.

61   Nadeem Shaker, "Osama bin Laden Sends His Greetings to Afghans," *IslamOnline,* August 25, 2002, author's collection.

62   Osama bin Laden, letter to Abu Fatima and Tawfiq, December 9, 2004, Abbottabad documents.

63   Uthman, handwritten letter to Tawfiq, August 14, 2004, Abbottabad documents.

64   Thomas Hegghammer, *The Caravan: Abdallah Azzam and the Rise of Global Jihad* (Cambridge: Cambridge University Press, 2020).

65   Abu Sa'd [Osama bin Laden], letter to Abu al-Faraj and Abd al-Hadi, November 19, 2002, Abbottabad documents.

66   See, for instance, Mutma'in, *Taliban: A Critical History from Within,* 215.

67   Abu al-Layth's independent sources of income are referenced indirectly in Abbottabad letters, such as in Osama bin Laden, letter to Abu Fatima and Tawfiq, December 9, 2004, Abbottabad documents. It is not clear where Abu al-Layth got his income from, but the Libyan Islamic Fighting Group (LIFG) had a historical network of militant activists spread across Pakistan and the MENA region.

68   Wakil Khan [Tawfiq], letter to bin Laden, October 18, 2004, Abbottabad documents.

69   Khalid Habib, handwritten letter to bin Laden, n.d. [fall 2004], Abbottabad documents; and Abu Hassan al-Sa'idi, handwritten letter to "*al-ikhwa al-kuram al-afadil*," September 8, 2004, Abbottabad documents.

70   al-Maqdisi, "*shuhada' fi zaman al-ghurba*," 128–30.

71   "Pakistan: Top Terror Suspect Arrested," *Voice of America News*, July 29, 2004, https://www.voanews.com/a/a-13-a-2004-07-29-11-pakistan-66890537/261768.html.

72   There are some indications that Abu Faraj delivered handwritten notes from bin Laden to Abd al-Hadi in the Shakai valley in 2003. See Senate Select Committee on Intelligence, "Committee Study of the Central Intelligence Agency's Detention and Interrogation Program," 373.

73   See appendix: "List of Propaganda Statements by Osama bin Laden and Ayman al-Zawahiri, 2002–2004."

74   For a biography of Abu al-Layth in English, see Kévin Jackson, "Abu al-Layth al-Libi," West Point, NY: Combating Terrorism Center, 2015, https://ctc.westpoint.edu/wp-content/uploads/2015/03/CTC_Abu-al-Layth-al-Libi-Jihadi-Bio-February2015-1.pdf.

75   al-Maqdisi, "*shuhada' fi zaman al-ghurba*."

76   *USA v. Abdullah Ahmed Khadr*, indictment, United States District Court, District of Massachusetts, Case 1:06-CR-10028-GAO, February 8, 2006.

77   "*Harb al-mustad'afin*," *al-Sahab*, April 2005, author's collection.

78   "Stipulation of Fact," PE 39, United States v. Abd al Hadi al Iraqi, June 9, 2022.

79   Ibid.; Ann Scott Tyson, "Going in Small in Afghanistan," *Christian Science Monitor*, January 14, 2004, https://www.csmonitor.com/2004/0114/p01s04-wosc.html; and Khalid Habib, handwritten letter to bin Laden, n.d. [fall 2004], Abbottabad documents.

80   Khalid Habib, handwritten letter to bin Laden, n.d. [fall 2004], Abbottabad documents; and Senate Select Committee on Intelligence report, 2014.

81   Khalid Habib, handwritten letter to bin Laden, n.d. [fall 2004], Abbottabad documents.

82   *USA v. Abdullah Ahmed Khadr*, indictment, United States District Court, District of Massachusetts, Case 1:06-CR-10028-GAO, February 8, 2006.

83   Abu Sa'ad [Osama bin Laden], letter to Abu al-Faraj and Abd al-Hadi, November 19, 2002, Abbottabad documents.

84   "*Rihat al-janna 5*," *al-Sahab*, n.d.; "*amaliyyat al-jabal—Afghanistan*," n.d., author's collection.

85   Jaragh al-Din, letter to Abd al-Rahman, n.d. [*c*. 2004], Abbottabad documents.

86   Carlotta Gall, "Kabul Bombing Kills 4 German Soldiers and Wounds 29," *New York Times*, June 8, 2003; UNAMA, "Suicide Attacks in Afghanistan (2001–2007)," United Nations Assistance Mission to Afghanistan, September 1, 2007.

87　"Stipulation of Fact," PE 39, *United States v. Abd al Hadi al Iraqi*, June 9, 2022.

88　"JTF GTMO Detainee Assessment for FNU Chaman," ISN US9AF-001021DP, Joint Task Force Guantanamo, August 17, 2005.

89　Uthman al-Shihri, letter to Tawfiq, August 14, 2004, Abbottabad documents.

90　For an overview of ISI's involvement in the war in Afghanistan after 2001, see Steve Coll, *Directorate S: The C.I.A. and America's Secret Wars in Afghanistan and Pakistan, 2001–2016* (London: Allen Lane, 2018).

91　Uthman al-Shihri, letter to bin Laden, n.d. [c. 2007], Abbottabad documents.

92　The description of the suicide bomber is based on "Abd al-Rahman al-Najdi," in al-Maqdisi, *"shuhada' fi zaman al-ghurba,"* 135–6.

93　UNAMA, "Suicide attacks in Afghanistan (2001–2007)," United Nations Assistance Mission to Afghanistan, September 1, 2007.

94　"Abu Abd al-Rahman al-Masri," in al-Maqdisi, *"shuhada' fi zaman al-ghurba,"* 128–30; see also *Rihat al-Janna*, author's collection.

95　"Excerpts from Purported bin Laden Tape," *Associated Press*, April 8, 2003; Kathy Gannon, "Purported bin Laden Tape Urges Attacks," *Associated Press*, April 8, 2003.

96　Al-Maqdisi, *"shuhada' fi zaman al-ghurba,"* 88–90.

97　The first complex attack in Kabul was the attack on the Serena Hotel in Kabul on January 14, 2008. This attack actually preceded the spectacular Mumbai attacks in India, which took place on November 26, 2008. For a detailed account of the Mumbai attacks, see Cathy Scott-Clark and Adrian Levy, *The Siege: 68 Hours inside the Taj Hotel* (New York: Penguin, 2013).

98　M. Ilyas Khan, "Profile of Nek Muhammad," *Dawn*, June 19, 2004.

99　Abu Hassan al-Sa'idi, handwritten letter to *"al-ikhwa al-kuram al-afadil,"* September 8, 2004, Abbottabad documents; Khalid Habib, handwritten letter to bin Laden, n.d. [fall 2004], Abbottabad documents.

100　Khalid Habib, handwritten letter to bin Laden, n.d. [fall 2004], Abbottabad documents; Wakil Khan [Tawfiq], letter to bin Laden, October 18, 2004, Abbottabad documents.

101　Osama bin Laden, *"nurid tatmin an awlad azmarai,"* n.d. [mid-2004], Abbottabad documents.

102　Abu Hassan al-Sa'idi, handwritten letter to *"al-ikhwa al-kuram al-afadil,"* September 8, 2004, Abbottabad documents.

103　Osama bin Laden, letter to Abu Fatima and Tawfiq, December 9, 2004, Abbottabad documents.

104　Khalid Habib, handwritten letter to bin Laden, n.d. [fall 2004], Abbottabad documents.

105　Wakil Khan [Tawfiq], letter to bin Laden, October 18, 2004, Abbottabad documents.

106　Abu Hassan al-Sa'idi, handwritten letter to *"al-ikhwa al-kuram al-afadil,"* September 8, 2004, Abbottabad documents.

Chapter 3

1   Quoted in Marc Sageman, *The London Bombings* (Philadelphia, PA: University of Pennsylvania Press, 2019), Kindle edition, Loc. 2410.

2   Ibid.

3   Some standard works include Sageman, *The London Bombings*; Fernando Reinares, *Al-Qaeda's Revenge: The 2004 Madrid Train Bombings* (Washington, DC: Woodrow Wilsom Center Press, 2016); Petter Nesser, *Islamist Terrorism in Europe* (Oxford: Oxford University Press, 2015).

4   Marc Sageman, *Misunderstanding Terrorism* (Philadelphia, PA: University of Pennsylvania Press, 2017), 48; see also Reinares, *Al-Qaeda's Revenge.*

5   See, e.g., Brynjar Lia and Thomas Hegghammer, "Jihadi Strategic Studies: The Alleged Al Qaida Policy Study Preceding the Madrid Bombings," *Studies in Conflict & Terrorism* 27, no. 5 (2004): 355–75.

6   Yassin Musharbash, "Al-Kaida: In ihren eigenen Worten," *Die Zeit*, March 15, 2012.

7   Osama bin Laden, letter to Abu Fatima and Tawfiq, December 9, 2004, Abbottabad documents.

8   As detailed in Bergen, *The Rise and Fall*, 181–3; 209.

9   There is another Abbottabad document not included here, referred to by Nelly Lahoud as a "strategy document of al-Qaida" from 2002. In my assessment, this document is not a piece of personal correspondence between al-Qaida leaders in Pakistan, but part of an online discussion between two individuals using the aliases "Hazim al-Madani" and "'Isam al-Qamari." Hazim al-Madani is an online persona associated with Sayf al-Adl. Nelly Lahoud, *The Bin Laden Papers: How the Abbottabad Raid Revealed the Truth about al-Qaeda, Its Leader and His Family* (New Haven, CT: Yale University Press, 2023); Senate Select Committee on Intelligence, "Committee Study of the Central Intelligence Agency's Detention and Interrogation Program," *United States Senate*, April 3, 2014; Osama bin Laden, letter to Hamza Rabia, n.d. [*c.* mid-2004], Abbottabad documents.

10   Thomas Hegghammer, "Al-Qaida Statements 2003–2004—A Compilation of Translated Texts by Usama bin Ladin and Ayman al-Zawahiri," FFI Report-2005/01428, 44.

11   Bin Laden refers to previous correspondence from Rabia in Osama bin Laden, letter to Hamza Rabia, n.d. [*c.* mid-2004], Abbottabad documents.

12   Osama bin Laden, "*qabl 'an tiqra' al-risala* [Before you read the letter]," December 9, 2004, Abbottabad documents.

13   There are indications of this in the letter. For example, in three bullet points at the end of the letter (which differ in style from the rest of the letter) he refers to the arrest of Ahmed Khalfan Ghailani in July 2004. There is another version of the Hamza Rabia letter on bin Laden's computer which is missing the introduction and end section.

14 Al-Maqdisi, *"shuhada' fi zaman al-ghurba,"* 95–6.

15 Ibid.

16 Wakil Khan [Tawfiq], letter to bin Laden, October 18, 2004, Abbottabad documents.

17 Senate Select Committee on Intelligence, "Committee Study of the Central Intelligence Agency's Detention and Interrogation Program," United States Senate, April 3, 2014.

18 "FACTBOX-Assassination Attempts against Pakistan's Musharraf," *Reuters,* August 9, 2007; Syed Saleem Shahzad, "Pakistan Gets Its Man … Sort Of," *Asia Times,* September 29, 2004; Senate Select Committee on Intelligence, "Committee Study of the Central Intelligence Agency's Detention and Interrogation Program," 373.

19 Senate Select Committee on Intelligence, "Committee Study of the Central Intelligence Agency's Detention and Interrogation Program," 259–60.

20 Reinares, *Al-Qaeda's Revenge,* 52–3.

21 *"'iraq al-jihad amal wa-akhtar,"* al-hay'a al-I'lamiyya li-nusrat al-sha'b al-'iraqi, n.d. [December 2003], author's collection; for an analysis, see Lia, "Jihadi Strategic Studies: The Alleged Al Qaida Policy Study Preceding the Madrid Bombings," 355–75.

22 Hegghammer, "Al-Qaida statements 2003–2004—A compilation of translated texts by Usama bin Ladin and Ayman al-Zawahiri," 56–9.

23 Osama bin Laden, letter to Hamza Rabia, n.d. [*c.* mid-2004], Abbottabad documents.

24 Bin Laden lists Poland as a country that should be attacked. The "Iraqi jihad" document also mentions Poland, but argues that a terrorist attack here or in other former Eastern Bloc countries would not make a difference.

25 Osama bin Laden, letter to Hamza Rabia, n.d. [*c.* mid-2004], Abbottabad documents.

26 This is based on references in bin Laden's letter to political events in June 2004.

27 Osama bin Laden, letter to Hamza Rabia, n.d. [*c.* mid-2004], Abbottabad documents.

28 Hazim al-Madani, letter to 'Isam al-Qamari, n.d. [*c.* mid-2002], Abbottabad documents.

29 "Hazim al-Madani" described himself as someone who is from the "sons of al-Qaida" and who is a member of the online jihadist community, suggesting a lack of militant experience. This contradicts the hypothesis that he is Sayf al-Adl, unless he chose to be deliberately deceptive about his own background in his writings. In 2002, Hazim al-Madani was a contributor on the *al-Mahrousa* forum run by the al-Gama'a al-Islamiyya member Osama Rushdie, in the Netherlands, perhaps suggesting a link to that group. Hazim al-Madani, letter to 'Isam al-Qamari, n.d. [*c.* mid-2002], Abbottabad documents.

30 *"'iraq al-jihad amal wa-akhtar,"* al-hay'a al-I'lamiyya li-nusrat al-sha'b al-'iraqi, n.d. [December 2003], author's collection.

31 Lia, "Jihadi Strategic Studies: The Alleged Al Qaida Policy Study Preceding the Madrid Bombings," 355–75.

32 One of the suspects is the Egyptian al-Jama'a al-Islamiyya network, based in part in Iran and across Europe. In their statements, the Abu Hafs al-Masri Brigades often demanded the release of JI's spiritual leader, the "Blind Sheikh" 'Umar Abd al-Rahman, from jail.

33 "Hazim al-Madani" collection of statements, Abbottabad documents.

34 Kata'ib Abu Hafs al-Masri, *"Kharitat tariq al-mujahidin,"* July 1, 2004, Abbottabad collection.

35 There is only one other example that I am aware of: The Abu Hafs al-Masri Brigades suggested to carry out revenge attacks for the Prophet Mohammed Cartoons in February 2006, and bin Laden issued a statement about the same in April the same year.

36 Shahzad, "Pakistan Gets Its Man … Sort Of."

37 Senate Select Committee on Intelligence, "Committee Study of the Central Intelligence Agency's Detention and Interrogation Program," 260.

38 "Doubts Cloud Pakistani Cleric's Death," *Al-Jazeera*, August 21, 2004.

39 Wakil Khan [Tawfiq], letter to bin Laden, October 18, 2004, Abbottabad documents.

40 Osama bin Laden, letter to Abu Fatima and Tawfiq, December 9, 2004, Abbottabad documents.

41 Osama bin Laden, letter to Hamza Rabia, n.d. [*c.* mid-2004], Abbottabad documents.

42 Musharbash, "Al-Kaida: In ihren eigenen Worten."

43 Musharbash, "Al-Kaida: In ihren eigenen Worten"; and author's conversation with researcher at the Norwegian Defense Research Establishment (FFI), who wrote a report (exempt from public disclosure) comparing bomb-making techniques in European terrorist plots from 2005 to 2010.

44 Atiyah Abd al-Rahman, letter to bin Laden, August 22, 2009, Abbottabad documents; Nic Robertson, Paul Cruickshank, and Tim Lister, "Documents Give New Details on al Qaeda's London Bombings," *CNN*, April 30, 2012.

45 Robertson, Cruickshank, and Lister, "Documents Give New Details on al Qaeda's London Bombings."

46 Atiyah Abd al-Rahman, letter to Hajji Uthman, n.d. [*c.* January 26, 2006], Abbottabad documents.

47 "'Atiyah's Letter to Zarqawi," December 11, 2005, Harmony Program, CTC West Point, https://ctc.westpoint.edu/harmony-program/atiyahs-letter-to-zarqawi-original-language-2/.

48 Atiyah Abd al-Rahman, letter to Hajji Uthman, n.d. [*c.* January 26, 2006], Abbottabad documents.

49 Sageman, *The London Bombings*, Loc. 4067–73.

50	Ibid., 4145–62.

51	Atiyah Abd al-Rahman, letter to 'Abd al-Hamid, n.d. [*c.* July 2007], Abbottabad documents.

Chapter 4

1	Ayman al-Zawahiri, "*fursan that rayat al-nabi*," July 2, 2001, 167–8.

2	Ibid., 168.

3	Ibid., 164.

4	Osama bin Laden, letter to Atiyah, July 6, 2010, Abbottabad documents.

5	For a good overview of the Iran-Saudi Arabia rivalry in Iraq, see Simon Mabon, *The Struggle for Supremacy in the Middle East: Saudi Arabia and Iran* (Cambridge: Cambridge University Press, 2023), 77–101.

6	Al-Qaida in Saudi Arabia (QAP) is often regarded as al-Qaida's first official "branch," but QAP's founding history was different than for al-Qaida in Iraq. The formation of QAP can arguably be traced back to the pre-9/11 period and was directly tied to bin Laden's 1996 and 1998 Declarations of Jihad. The QAP founder, Yusuf al-Ayeri, met with bin Laden in Kandahar in 2000 and agreed to work for al-Qaida, and bin Laden subsequently appointed him to lead al-Qaida's activities on the Arabian Peninsula. For a history of QAP, see Hegghammer, *Jihadi in Saudi Arabia.*

7	See, e.g., Brian H. Fishman, *The Master Plan: ISIS, Al-Qaeda, and the Jihadi Strategy for Final Victory* (New Haven, CT: Yale University Press, 2016); and Truls Tønnessen, *Al-Qaida in Iraq: The Rise, the Fall and the Comeback*, PhD Thesis, Faculty of Humanities, University of Oslo, 2015. The most well-known jihadist source about Abu Musab al-Zarqawi is a handwritten letter purportedly written by Sayf al-Adl in 2005, and smuggled out of Iran and to the Jordanian journalist Fu'ad Hussayn. Sayf al-Adl, "*al-sira al-jihadiyya lil-qa'id al-dhabbau Abi Mus'ab al-Zarqawi,*" author's collection. There have been doubts about the document's authenticity; for a discussion, see, e.g., Brian Fishman, "Revising the History of al-Qa`ida's Original Meeting with Abu Musab al-Zarqawi," *CTC Sentinel* 9, no. 6 (October 2016): 28–33.

8	For a backgrounder on Ansar al-Islam, see Brynjar Lia, "A Kurdish al-Qaida? Making Sense of the Ansar al-Islam Movement in Iraqi Kurdistan in the Early 2000s," *Religions* 13, no. 3 (2022): 203.

9	Senate Select Committee on Intelligence, "Committee Study of the Central Intelligence Agency's Detention and Interrogation Program," *United States Senate*, April 3, 2014, 374–5.

10	"Zarqawi Letter: February 2004 Coalition Provisional Authority English Translation of Terrorist Musab al Zarqawi Letter Obtained by United States

Government in Iraq," n.d. [January 2004], *US Department of State Archive*, https://2001-2009.state.gov/p/nea/rls/31694.htm.

11 Ibid.

12 Zarqawi later claimed he was behind the attack on the Imam Ali Mosque. See Wakil Khan [Tawfiq], letter to bin Laden, October 18, 2004, Abbottabad documents.

13 Thomas Hegghammer, "Global Jihadism after the Iraq War," *Middle East Journal* 60, no. 1 (2006): 11–32.

14 For an overview of this debate, see, e.g., Truls Tønnessen, "Heirs of Zarqawi or Saddam? The Relationship between al-Qaida in Iraq and the Islamic State," *Perspectives on Terrorism* 9, no. 4 (2015): 48–60.

15 "Text of the Announcement from the Mujahidin in Iraq," October 17, 2004, reprinted in *Mu'askar al-Battar* no. 21 (Ramadan 1425 [October/November 2004]), 13.

16 Wakil Khan [Tawfiq], letter to bin Laden, October 18, 2004, Abbottabad documents.

17 *Mu'askar al-Battar* no. 21 (Ramadan 1425 [October/November 2004]); see the editorial on 4, and the article containing the full text of al-Qaida in Iraq's announcement on 13.

18 "Handwritten Letter from Hafiz to Tawfiq," n.d. [*c.* mid-2004], Abbottabad letters.

19 Abu al-Faraj refers to "Hafiz" as Abu Mus'ab al-Baluchi, who was arrested recently. See Wakil Khan [Tawfiq], letter to bin Laden, October 18, 2004, Abbottabad documents; bin Laden's answer to the "Iranian proposal" can be found in Osama bin Laden, letter to Abu Fatima and Tawfiq, December 9, 2004, Abbottabad documents.

20 "Handwritten Letter from Hafiz to Tawfiq," n.d. [*c.* mid-2004], Abbottabad letters.

21 Ibid.

22 See, for instance, US Secretary of State Colin Powell's presentation to the UN Security Council, February 5, 2003, where he describes Zarqawi as a "senior Al Qaida associate and collaborator."

23 Alex Shams, "The Politics of Arbaeen: Transcending Militarized Urbanism in Iraq's Shrine Cities," *POMEPS*, n.d., https://pomeps.org/the-politics-of-arbaeen-transcending-militarized-urbanism-in-iraqs-shrine-cities.

24 Osama bin Laden, letter to Abu Fatima and Tawfiq, December 9, 2004, Abbottabad documents.

25 There were several factors that influenced Iran's decision to release bin Laden's family members. One factor was probably that the presence of bin Laden's family members in Iran had become publically known through the media, after one of Osama bin Laden's daughters escaped from Iranian custody and sought refuge in the Saudi Embassy in Teheran. In addition, al-Qaida in Pakistan kidnapped an Iranian diplomat in Peshawar and used him to negotiate with Iran for the release of bin Laden's family. The release of a group of bin Laden's family members to Syria

in late 2010 or early 2011 was confirmed in the Abbotabad documents; see Atiyah Abd al-Rahman, letter to bin Laden, January 21, 2011, Abbottabad documents.

26 Nelly Lahoud, "Al-Qaʻida's Contested Relationship with Iran: The View from Abbottabad," *New America*, September 7, 2018, https://www.newamerica.org/future-security/reports/al-qaidas-contested-relationship-iran/; and Bergen, *The Rise and Fall*, 238.

27 "Zawahiri's Letter to Zarqawi," July 9, 2005. Harmony Database.

28 "'Atiyah's Letter to Zarqawi," December 11, 2005, Harmony Database.

29 On Jamil al-Rahman and the Kunar "Emirate," see, e.g., Alex Strick van Linschoten and Felix Kuehn, *An Enemy We Created: The Myth of the Taliban-Al-Qaeda Merger in Afghanistan* (London: Hurst, 2011), 462; Thomas Ruttig, "On Kunar's Salafi Insurgents," *Afghanistan Analysts Network*, January 14, 2010, https://www.afghanistan-analysts.org/en/reports/war-and-peace/on-kunars-salafi-insurgents/.

30 "Berlusconi to Pull Out Troops from Iraq," *The Guardian*, March 16, 2005, https://www.theguardian.com/world/2005/mar/16/italy.iraq.

31 "Jaysh al-Islam," "*daʼu ʻatiyat allah, fa-huwwa aʼlam bi-ma yaqul* [leave it to Attiyat Allah, because he knows what he is talking about]," forum post, *al-Multaqa*, February 3, 2007, author's collection.

32 "'Atiyah's Letter to Zarqawi," December 11, 2005, Harmony Database, 15.

33 "Leader of Al-Qaeda in Iraq Al-Zarqawi Declares 'Total War' on Shi'ites," September 16, 2005, Middle East Research Institute, Haverford College.

34 Ibid.

35 Ibid.

36 Abu Musʼab al-Zarqawi, quoted in "Jordan: Zarqawi's Message Confirms His Involvement in the Terrorist Operation" (in Arabic), *CNN Arabic*, May 1, 2004, http://arabic.cnn.com/2004/middle_east/5/1/jordan.zarqawi/index.html.

37 "'Atiyah's Letter to Zarqawi," December 11, 2005, Harmony Database.

38 Ibid.

39 Until mid-2004, al-Qaida was concentrated in the Shakai valley north of Wana, SW. After a Pakistani Army operation and a "Peace agreement" with local tribes, al-Qaida and other Arabs probably moved north, and ended up in North Waziristan. Between May and December 2005, at least three al-Qaida operatives were killed around Mir Ali, NW, while Hamza Rabia was killed near Miran Shah on December 1, 2005.

40 Atiyah included some points in his letter to Zarqawi that he later referred to as Sheikh Saeed's orders. See Atiyah Abd al-Rahman, letter to Hajji Uthman, n.d. [*c.* January 26, 2006], Abbottabad documents.

41 Atiyah Abd al-Rahman, letter to Hajji Uthman, n.d. [*c.* January 26, 2006], Abbottabad documents.

42 For additional analysis of the letters between al-Qaida in Pakistan to Abu Musab al-Zarqawi in Iraq in 2005, see, e.g., Assaf Moghadam and Brian Fishman, *Fault Lines in Global Jihad: Organizational, Strategic, and Ideological Fissures* (London: Routledge, 2011), 39–41.

43 Atiyah Abd al-Rahman, letter to Ansar al-Sunnah, n.d. [*c*. April 2007], Abbottabad documents.

44 Atiyah wrote that he had started preparing his trip to Iraq at the end of January 2006, shortly after the Ansar al-Sunnah delegation visited Waziristan.

45 "Stipulation of Fact," PE 39, *United States v. Abd al Hadi al Iraqi*, June 9, 2022.

46 Abu Darda' meeting, n.d. [January 2006], Tape 2.

47 Abu Darda' meeting, n.d. [January 2006], Tape 3.

48 Abu Darda' meeting, n.d. [January 2006], Tape 6.

49 Abu Darda' meeting, n.d. [January 2006], Tape 2, segment 00:14:53.

50 Abu Darda' meeting, n.d. [January 2006], Tape 2, segment 00:16:51 and segment 00:18:35.

51 Abu Darda' meeting, n.d. [January 2006], Tape 2, segment 00:16:51.

52 Tønnessen, *Al-Qaida in Iraq*, 194, 233.

53 See the Abu Anas al-Shami bio in Nir Rosen, "Thinking Like a Jihadist: Iraq's Jordanian Connection," *World Policy Journal* 23, no. 1 (Spring, 2006): 1–16.

54 Abu Darda' meeting, n.d. [January 2006], Tape 2, segment 00:20:54.

55 Abu Darda' meeting, n.d. [January 2006], Tape 4, segment 00:00:06.

56 Abu Darda' meeting, n.d. [January 2006], Tape 4, segment 00:03:08.

57 For background on al-Maqdisi, see Joas Wagemakers, *A Quietist Jihadi: The Ideology and Influence of Abu Muhammad Al-Maqdisi* (Cambridge: Cambridge University Press, 2012).

58 Abu Darda' meeting, n.d. [January 2006], Tape 16, 00:00:10.

59 Atiyah Abd al-Rahman, letter to Hajji Uthman, n.d. [*c*. January 26, 2006], Abbottabad documents.

60 Ibid.

61 Ibid.

62 We do not know when bin Laden received these files, but he finally started participating in the internal al-Qaida discussion about Iraq in August 2007, suggesting he might have been cut off for quite a while.

63 Abu Musab al-Zarqawi, audio reply to Abu Darda', February 27, 2006, Abbottabad documents.

64 Atiyah Abd al-Rahman, letter to Hafiz Sultan, March 28, 2007, Abbottabad documents.

65 "Bin Ladin Warns Iraqis against Joining Anti-Al-Qa'ida Tribal Councils, Unity Govt," December 30, 2007, Haverford College, http://hdl.handle.net/10066/4658.

66 Osama bin Laden, "A Speech from Osama bin Laden Regarding the Martyrdom
    of Abu Musab al-Zarqawi," *al-Sahab*, June 29, 2006; Osama bin Laden, "To the
    Muslim Ummah in General and the Mujahideen in Iraq and Somalia in Particular,"
    al-Sahab, July 1, 2006.

67 Ayman al-Zawahiri, letter to bin Laden, January 15, 2011, Abbottabad documents.

68 Hamid al-'Ali, *"hal man la yubaya'u (Dawlat al-'iraq al-Islamiyya) 'asa'?! wa hal
    huwwa wajib al-'asr?!* [Is he who does not pledge allegiance to the (Islamic State
    in Iraq) a sinner?! And is it the duty of the age?!]," April 4, 2007, Hamid al-'Ali
    homepage (www.h-alali.net), April 4, 2007.

69 Abu Darda' meeting, n.d. [January 2006], Tape 10.

70 The ISI Shura Council seemed to write this letter to al-Qaida to explain why
    their relationship with Ansar al-Sunnah had broken down, and they probably
    also wanted to counter the alternative narratives about ISI that were spread by
    AAS in their public propaganda, especially in an AAS publication from July 2008
    called "The Book of Truth." Shura Council of the Islamic State in Iraq, letter to
    al-Qaida, 22 Rabia al-Akhar, no year [likely 1431; i.e. April 7, 2010], Abbottabad
    documents.

71 Atiyah Abd al-Rahman, letter to Adnan [Hajji Uthman], March 15, 2007,
    Abbottabad documents.

72 Atiyah Abd al-Rahman, letter to Hafiz Sultan [Hajji Uthman], March 28, 2007,
    Abbottabad documents.

73 Bin Laden's first message to Iraq, after the establishment of ISI, came in October
    2007.

74 Abu 'Umar al-Baghdadi, "Say I Am on Clear Proof from My Lord," *Al-Furqan*,
    March 13, 2007, translation to English by Jihadi Media Battalion, author's collection.

75 Atiyah Abd al-Rahman, letter to Hafiz Sultan [Hajji Uthman], March 28, 2007,
    Abbottabad documents.

76 Anne Stenersen, *Al-Qaida's Quest for Weapons of Mass Destruction: The History
    behind the Hype* (Saarbrücken: VMD Verlag, 2008), 42–3.

77 Atiyah Abd al-Rahman, letter to Hafiz Sultan [Hajji Uthman], March 28, 2007,
    Abbottabad documents.

78 Jihad and Reform Front, letter to bin Laden, May 22, 2007, Abbottabad
    documents.

79 *"Munasiha hawla al-'amal fi-al-bilad al-islamiyya,"* n.d. [*c.* 2007], Abbottabad
    documents.

80 Abdullah Saeed, letter to Sayyid Adnan [Hajji Uthman], n.d. [*c.* mid-2007],
    Abbottabad documents.

81 Karim, letter to Atiyah, n.d. [late July 2007], Abbottabad documents.

82 Karim, letter to Atiyah, n.d. [ca. fall 2007], Abbottabad documents.

83 Fishman, *The Master Plan*, Loc. 2246.

84 Atiyah recorded a series of ten audiotapes for bin Laden, eight of them were included in the collection of Abbottabad documents that were released by the CIA in November 2017. We do not know who removed them, or for what purpose. One can guess they contained sensitive information that was either deleted by bin Laden, or they remain classified with the CIA.

85 Osama bin Laden, letter to Zawahiri, August 17, 2007, Abbottabad documents; and Osama bin Laden, letter to Hajji Uthman, August 17, 2007, with appendixes, including Osama bin Laden, "*Bayyan al-Iman*," n.d. [*c.* August 17, 2007], and Osama bin Laden, "*al-mashura lil-ikhwa fil-iraq*," n.d. [*c.* August 17, 2007], Abbottabad documents; see also Ayman al-Zawahiri, "*al-ta'liq 'ala al-mashura lil-ikhwa fil-Iraq*," n.d. [October 18, 2007], Abbottabad documents.

86 Ayman al-Zawahiri, "*al-ta'liq 'ala al-mashura lil-ikhwa fil-Iraq*," n.d. [October 18, 2007], Abbottabad documents.

87 We do not know if bin Laden was aware of Ansar al-Sunnah's advice at the time. ISI informed al-Qaida of the content in the mid-2007 discussions much later, in April 2010. Shura Council of the Islamic State in Iraq, letter to al-Qaida, 22 Rabia al-Akhar, no year [likely 1431; i.e., April 7, 2010], Abbottabad documents.

88 Ayman al-Zawahiri, "*al-ta'liq 'ala al-mashura lil-ikhwa fil-Iraq*," n.d. [October 18, 2007], Abbottabad documents.

89 Ibid., 11.

90 Ibid., 12.

91 Atiyah Abd al-Rahman, letter to Hafiz Sultan [Hajji Uthman], March 28, 2007, Abbottabad documents.

92 The threat was issued in an audio tape by Abu Omar al-Baghdadi, "Qaeda Group in Iraq Threatens to Attack Iranians," *Reuters*, August 9, 2007, https://www.reuters.com/article/us-iraq-qaeda/qaeda-group-in-iraq-threatens-to-attack-iranians-idUSL0839072420070708/.

93 Ayman al-Zawahiri, letter to Karim, October 18, 2007, Abbottabad documents.

94 "Bin Laden Issues Iraq Message," *Al-Jazeera*, October 23, 2007, https://www.aljazeera.com/news/2007/10/23/bin-laden-issues-iraq-message.

95 "Al-Sahab Media Releases Bin Ladin Statement, Says Al-Jazirah 'Counterfeiting' the Facts," October 23, 2007, Harverford College, http://hdl.handle.net/10066/4656.

96 Atiyah Abd al-Rahman, letter to bin Laden, November 3, 2007, Abbottabad documents.

97 Ibid.

98 Ibid.

99 "Bin Ladin Warns Iraqis against Joining Anti-Al-Qa'ida Tribal Councils, Unity Govt."

100 Ibid.

101 al-Zawahiri, "*al-ta'liq 'ala al-mashura lil-ikhwa fil-Iraq*," n.d. [October 18, 2007], Abbottabad documents.

102 "Bin Ladin Warns Iraqis against Joining Anti-Al-Qa'ida Tribal Councils, Unity Govt."

103 Ibid.

104 Ibid.

105 Mentioned in al-Zawahiri, "*al-ta'liq 'ala al-mashura lil-ikhwa fil-Iraq*."

106 Bin Laden confirms here that neither he nor other senior al-Qaida members in Pakistan know Abu Umar al-Baghdadi personally, but bin Laden nevertheless chooses to endorse him because he was "recommended" by Abu Musab al-Zarqawi.

107 "Bin Ladin Warns Iraqis against Joining Anti-Al-Qa'ida Tribal Councils, Unity Govt."

108 Atiyah and Sheikh Saeed sent bin Laden separate pieces of advice in November 2007, and they both recommended that bin Laden endorse the ISI. Atiyah Abd al-Rahman, letter to bin Laden, November 3, 2007, Abbottabad documents; and Hajji Uthman, letter to bin Laden, November 4, 2007, Abbottabad documents.

109 Atiyah Abd al-Rahman, letter to bin Laden, February 4, 2008, Abbottabad documents.

110 Atiyah, audio report about Iraq, Tape 2, Abbottabad documents.

111 Atiyah, audio report about Iraq, Tape 8, Abbottabad documents.

112 The date of the missing bin Laden letter is February 23, 2008, according to Zawahiri's reply. Ayman al-Zawahiri, letter to bin Laden, March 5, 2008, Abbottabad documents.

113 Shura Council of the Islamic State in Iraq, letter to al-Qaida, 22 Rabia al-Akhar, no year [likely 1431; i.e., April 7, 2010], Abbottabad documents.

114 Ibid.

115 Ayman al-Zawahiri, letter to bin Laden, March 5, 2008, Abbottabad documents.

116 Ibid.

117 Ibid.

118 Ayman al-Zawahiri, letter to Abu 'Umar al-Baghdadi, March 3, 2008, Abbottabad documents.

119 Hajji Uthman, letter to bin Laden, April 16, 2008, Abbottabad documents.

120 This note from April 16, 2008 is the earliest indication in the Abbottabad documents that Yunus al-Mauritani is present in Waziristan and member of al-Qaida. In 2010, Osama bin Laden appoints Yunus al-Mauritani to be in charge of al-Qaida's External Operations, as detailed in Chapter 6.

121 Hajji Uthman, letter to bin Laden, April 16, 2008, Abbottabad documents.

122 In the Abbottabad documents, there is at least one such letter from 2010, namely the previously mentioned letter from the Shura Council of the Islamic State in

Iraq, letter to al-Qaida, 22 Rabia al-Akhar, no year [likely 1431; i.e., April 7, 2010], Abbottabad documents.

123 *Sifru al-Haqiqa*, Al-Ansar, July 14, 2008, author's collection.

124 Shura Council of the Islamic State in Iraq, letter to al-Qaida, 22 Rabia al-Akhar, no year [likely 1431; i.e. April 7, 2010], Abbottabad documents.

125 Ayman al-Zawahiri, letter to bin Laden, May 31, 2010, Abbottabad documents.

Chapter 5

1   Hajji Uthman, letter to bin Laden, April 16, 2008, Abbottabad documents.

2   "Remarks by the President in Address to the Nation on the Way Forward in Afghanistan and Pakistan," *The White House*, December 1, 2009, https:// obamawhitehouse.archives.gov/the-press-office/remarks-president-address-nation-way-forward-afghanistan-and-pakistan.

3   The more correct term is the "Rahbari Shura"; for a discussion, see Antonio Giustozzi, *The Taliban at War, 2001–2021* (New York: Oxford University Press, 2022), 32.

4   Steve Coll, *Directorate S: The C.I.A. and America's Secret Wars in Afghanistan and Pakistan, 2001–2016* (London: Allen Lane, 2018), 217.

5   Ibid., 220.

6   Ibid., 223.

7   Giustozzi, *The Taliban at War*, 44.

8   Abdul Hai Mutma'in, *Taliban: A Critical History from Within* (Berlin: First Draft Publishing, 2019), 253.

9   Giustozzi, *The Taliban at War*, 44.

10 Ibid., 22, 88.

11 See, e.g., "Aljazeera Airs Hikmatyar Video," *Al-Jazeera*, May 4, 2006; "Afghan Warlord Urges Revolt against US, Karzai," *NBC*, May 31, 2006; "Afghan Warlord 'Aaided Bin Laden,'" *BBC*, January 11, 2007.

12 "Afghan warlord 'Aided Bin Laden.'"

13 Uthman al-Shihri, letter to bin Laden, n.d. [*c.* July 2007].

14 Ibid.

15 Ibid.

16 Uthman al-Shihri, letter to Tawfiq, August 14, 2004, Abbottabad documents.

17 Giustozzi, *The Taliban at War*, 38–9.

18 Ibid., 38, 62.

19 Ibid., 43.

20 See, e.g., Ron Moreau and Sami Yousafzai, "In the Footsteps of Zarqawi; The Taliban's Bloodthirsty Top Commander in Southern Afghanistan Scares Almost Everyone–Even His Allies and Underlings," *Newsweek*, July 3, 2006.

21   Giustozzi, *The Taliban at War*, 63.

22   Alex S. Wilner, "Targeted Killings in Afghanistan: Measuring Coercion and Deterrence in Counterterrorism and Counterinsurgency," *Studies in Conflict & Terrorism* 33, no. 4 (2010): 307–29.

23   Giustozzi, *The Taliban at War*, 71.

24   "*liqa' al-ikhwa*," *al-Sahab*, September 2007, author's collection.

25   "*liqa' ma'a al-shaykh mustafa abu al-yazid*," *al-Sahab*, May 27, 2007, author's collection.

26   "Pentagon: Top al Qaeda Leader Taken to Guantanamo," *CNN*, April 27, 2007, http://www.cnn.com/2007/US/04/27/al.qaeda.gitmo/index.html.

27   See Chapter 2 for details.

28   Atiyah Abd al-Rahman, letter to bin Laden, n.d. [*c*. March 2008], Abbottabad documents; Ayman al-Zawahiri, letter to bin Laden, March 23, 2008, Abbottabad documents.

29   Ayman al-Zawahiri, letter to bin Laden, March 23, 2008, Abbottabad documents.

30   There are examples from 2003 of independent commanders styling themselves as commanders and spokesmen of the "frontlines in Afghanistan" and similar titles, on jihadist forums. See, e.g., Abu Abd al-Rahman al-Najdi, statement on marsad.org.uk, October 10, 2003, author's collection.

31   "*muqabila ma'a za'im tandhim al-Jihad, al-duktur Fadhl*," *Sa'ud al-Mawla*, March 5, 2009.

32   "Taliban Leader Exhorts Suicide Bombers in Video," *Reuters*, October 3, 2007, https://www.reuters.com/article/afghan-taliban/taliban-leader-exhorts-suicide-bombers-in-video-idINISL3672520071003/.

33   Hajji Uthman, letter to bin Laden, November 4, 2007, Abbottabad documents.

34   Michael Smith, "SBS behind Taliban Leader's Death," *The Times*, May 27, 2007.

35   Mansour Dadullah was rumored to be arrested in Pakistan around this time. The rumor was false, but he was later arrested in February 2008.

36   Osama bin Laden, letter to Hajji Uthman, December 17, 2007, Abbottabad documents.

37   Ayman al-Zawahiri, letter to bin Laden, February 4, 2008, Abbottabad documents; "A Decision from Authority of the Islamic Emirate to Remove Mansour Dadullah from His Position," *Sawt al-Jihad* [Taliban website], December 29, 2007, author's collection.

38   Ayman al-Zawahiri, letter to bin Laden, February 4, 2008, Abbottabad documents.

39   Giustozzi, *The Taliban at War*, 43.

40   Atiyah Abd al-Rahman, letter to bin Laden, n.d. [*c*. March 2008], Abbottabad documents.

41   Ibid.

42   Ibid.

43   Ayman al-Zawahiri, letter to bin Laden, March 5, 2008, Abbottabad Documents.

44 Hajji Uthman, letter to bin Laden, April 16, 2008, Abbottabad documents.

45 Ibid.

46 Ibid.

47 Ibid.

48 See, e.g., Daud Khattak, "Contrasting the Leadership of Mullah Fazlullah and Khan Said Sajna in Pakistan," *CTC Sentinel* 7, no. 7 (July 2014): 18–20.

49 Osama bin Laden, letter to Zawahiri, May 7, 2008, Abbottabad documents.

50 Mutma'in, *Taliban: A Critical History from Within,* 86, 129–30: Mufti Rasheed Ludhianvi, *Obedience to the Amir: An Early Text on the Afghan Taliban Movement* (Berlin: First Draft Publishing, 2015).

51 Anne Stenersen, *Al-Qaida in Afghanistan* (Cambridge: Cambridge University Press, 2017).

52 Hamid, *Salib fi sama' kandahar,* 138–40.

53 Osama bin Laden, letter to Zawahiri, May 7, 2008, Abbottabad documents.

54 Osama bin Laden, letter to Mullah Omar, September 25, 2010; and Osama bin Laden, letter to Mullah Omar, December 4, 2010, Abbottabad documents.

55 Ayman al-Zawahiri, letter to bin Laden, March 12, 2009, Abbottabad documents.

56 For background on the Mujahideen Shura Council, see Carlotta Gall, "Pakistan and Afghan Taliban Close Ranks," *New York Times*, March 27, 2009, https://web.archive.org/web/20210819003725/https://www.nytimes.com/2009/03/27/world/asia/27taliban.html.

57 Hajji Uthman, letter to bin Laden, August 3, 2009, Abbottabad documents; and Ayman al-Zawahiri, letter to bin Laden, September 10, 2009, Abbottabad documents.

58 Ayman al-Zawahiri, letter to bin Laden, March 12, 2009, Abbottabad documents.

59 We do not have this letter, but we have Atiyah's description of the letter a year later, as well as Tayyib Agha's reply. Atiyah Abd al-Rahman, letter to bin Laden, June 19, 2010, Abbottabad documents; Muhammad Tayib, letter to Zawahiri, n.d. [*c.* June 19, 2010], Abbottabad documents.

60 Muhammad Tayib, letter to Zawahiri, n.d. [*c.* June 19, 2010], Abbottabad documents.

61 Tayyib Agha indicates in his letter that the "treaty" refers to a treaty with Pakistan. He says, in defense of the treaty: "If we cannot win them over, so at least they will be a safe haven." He also indicates that "the beginning was from them," in what seems to be a reference to the origin of the Taliban in Pakistan in 1994. "Letter from Muhammad Tayib," n.d. [*c.* June 19, 2010], Abbottabad documents.

62 Gareth Porter, "US Silent on Taliban's al-Qaeda Offer," *Asia Times*, December 17, 2010, https://web.archive.org/web/20091219213931/http://www.atimes.com/atimes/South_Asia/KL17Df02.html.

63 See, e.g., "*bayyan maqam imarat Afghanistan al-islamiyya,*" February 14, 2008, accessed via *al-Ikhlas,* author's collection.

64   Abu Yahya al-Libi, letter to bin Laden, January 24, 2010, Abbottabad documents.

65   Ibid.

66   Ayman al-Zawahiri, letter to bin Laden, May 16, 2010, Abbottabad documents.

67   Ibid.

68   Zawahiri did indeed move al-Qaida's global jihad operations to these affiliates after 2011, for example, by appointing the AQAP Emir, Nasir al-Wuhayshi, as his deputy, in 2013.

69   Ayman al-Zawahiri, letter to bin Laden, May 31, 2010, Abbottabad documents.

70   Ibid.

71   Atiyah Abd al-Rahman, letter to bin Laden, June 19, 2010, Abbottabad documents.

72   Atiyah Abd al-Rahman, letter to bin Laden, July 8, 2010, Abbottabad documents.

73   As many as 30,000 US troops would be deployed to Afghanistan within the summer of 2010; see "US Troop Surge and End of US Combat Mission," *Britannica*, n.d., https://www.britannica.com/event/Afghanistan-War/U-S-troop-surge-and-end-of-U-S-combat-mission.

74   Giustozzi, *The Taliban at War*, 146.

75   Mutma'in, *Taliban: A Critical History*, 255.

76   Ibid., 272–3.

77   Atiyah Abd al-Rahman, letter to bin Laden, July 17, 2010, Abbottabad documents.

78   Ibid.

79   Ibid.

80   Ibid.

81   Osama bin Laden, letter to Atiyah, August 7, 2010.

82   [Mullah Omar?], letter to Osama bin Laden, n.d. [*c.* August 28, 2010], Abbottabad documents. Released by ODNI as "Undated letter re Afghanistan" on May 20, 2015.

83   Ibid.

84   Osama bin Laden, letter to Mullah Omar, September 25, 2010, Abbottabad documents.

85   The Jihadi Video Database at FFI only contained two videos from 2010, and they were both issued before August. Video no. 831, "Suicide operation against the headquarters of the US Command in Khost province," posted February 22, 2010, and Video no. 834, "Ambush on a crusader coalition base in Kunar Province," posted June 2, 2010.

86   Atiyah Abd al-Rahman, letter to bin Laden, June 19, 2010, Abbottabad documents; and Yassin Musharbash, "Bonner Qaida-Kämpfer soll bei Gefecht gestorben sein," *Der Spiegel*, January 18, 2011, https://www.spiegel.de/politik/deutschland/dschihadist-abu-talha-bonner-qaida-kaempfer-soll-bei-gefecht-gestorben-sein-a-740140.html.

87   Osama bin Laden, letter to Mullah Omar, November 5, 2010, Abbottabad documents.

88 See, e.g., Niaz Shah, "The Islamic Emirate of Afghanistan: A Layeha [Rules and Regulations] for Mujahidin," *Studies in Conflict and Terrorism* 35, no. 6 (2012): 456–70.

89 Ayman al-Zawahiri, letter to bin Laden, November 18, 2010, Abbottabad documents.

90 Ayman al-Zawahiri, letter to bin Laden, December 12, 2010, Abbottabad documents.

91 Ibid.

92 [Mullah Omar?], letter to Osama bin Laden, n.d. [*c.* August 28, 2010], Abbottabad documents. Released by ODNI as "Undated letter re Afghanistan" on May 20, 2015.

93 Ayman al-Zawahiri, letter to bin Laden, November 18, 2010, Abbottabad documents.

94 Osama bin Laden, draft of letter to Zawahiri, n.d. [*c.* January 2011], Abbottabad documents.

95 Ibid.

Chapter 6

1 Ayman Zawahiri, letter to bin Laden, May 31, 2010, Abbottabad documents.

2 Ibid.

3 Ibid.

4 Quirine Eijkman, "The German Sauerland Cell Reconsidered," *Perspectives on Terrorism* 8, no. 4 (August 2014): 82–90; Petter Nesser, *Islamist Terrorism in Europe* (Oxford: Oxford University Press, 2015), 226–33.

5 For background on the Islamic Jihad Union, see Einar Wigen, *Islamic Jihad Union—al-Qaida´s Key to the Turkic World* (Kjeller: FFI, 2009), https://www.ffi.no/en/publications-archive/islamic-jihad-union-al-qaidas-key-to-the-turkic-world; Hajji Uthman, letter to bin Laden, April 14, 2010, Abbottabad documents.

6 Atiyah Abd al-Rahman, letter to bin Laden, June 9, 2010, Abbottabad documents; Hajji Uthman, letter to bin Laden, April 14, 2010, Abbottabad documents.

7 Ayman al-Zawahiri, who had known "Tufan" for years, had a rather negative view of his personality and skills, as expressed in a letter he wrote to Atiyah, parts of which were later copied and pasted into Atiyah Abd al-Rahman, letter to bin Laden, August 28, 2010, Abbottabad documents.

8 Al-Somali described this new methodology to bin Laden *c.* April 2009: "Guide the brothers towards new methods using the simplest things, such as household knives, gas tanks, fuel, diesel and others like airplanes, trains and cars as killing tools." Saleh al-Somali, letter to bin Laden, n.d. [*c.* April 2009], Abbottabad documents.

9 Atiyah Abd al-Rahman, letter to bin Laden, August 22, 2009, Abbottabad documents.

10 For a backgrounder, see Peter L. Bergen and Daniel Rothenberg (eds.), *Drone Wars: Transforming Conflict, Law, and Policy* (Cambridge: Cambridge University Press, 2015).

11 Hajji Uthman, letter to bin Laden, April 14, 2010, Abbottabad documents.

12 Abd al-Hafiz al-Muhajir [Saleh al-Somali], letter to bin Laden, March 6, 2008, Abbottabad documents.

13 Ibid.

14 Saleh al-Somali, "*taqrir ʿan al-ʿamal al-khariji*," n.d. [*c.* April 2009], Abbottabad documents.

15 On bin Laden's internal order to target Denmark and how it was distributed to the regions, see Ayman al-Zawahiri, letter to bin Laden, March 5, 2008; Ayman al-Zawahiri, letter to Abu Umar al-Baghdadi, March 6, 2008; Abu Musʿab Abd al-Wudud, letter to Zawahiri, March 28, 2008; Hajji Uthman, letter to bin Laden, April 16, 2008, Abbottabad documents.

16 Saleh al-Somali, "*taqrir ʿan al-ʿamal al-khariji*," n.d. [*c.* April 2009], Abbottabad documents.

17 Atiyah Abd al-Rahman, letter to bin Laden, August 22, 2009, Abbottabad documents.

18 Mohammad Asghar, "Rauf's Escape Case of 'Criminal Collusion': Report," *Dawn*, December 20, 2007, https://www.dawn.com/news/281198/newspaper/column.

19 For an overview, see Raffaello Pantucci, "A Biography of Rashid Rauf: Al-Qaʿida's British Operative," *CTC Sentinel* 5, no. 7 (July 2012): 12–16.

20 Yassin Musharbash, "Al-Kaida: In ihren eigenen Worten," *Die Zeit*, March 15, 2012.

21 "Seeking Information: Adnan G. El Shukrijumah," *Rewards for Justice Program*, https://web.archive.org/web/20161222183957/https://www2.fbi.gov/terrorinfo/elshukrijumah.htm.

22 Osama bin Laden, letter to Abu Fatima and Tawfiq, December 9, 2004, Abbottabad documents.

23 *USA v. Najibullah Zazi*, United States District Court, Eastern District of New York, Case 1:09-cr-00663-RJD-SMG, Document 71, 4–5; see also *USA v. Adis Medunjanin et al.*, United States District Court, Eastern District of New York, Case 1:10-cr-00019-RJD.

24 Atiyah Abd al-Rahman, letter to bin Laden, August 22, 2009, Abbottabad documents.

25 Atiyah Abd al-Rahman, letter to bin Laden, August 28, 2010, Abbottabad documents.

26 Zawahiri's words about Tufan are pasted into a letter from Atiyah to bin Laden. Atiyah Abd al-Rahman, letter to bin Laden, August 28, 2010, Abbottabad documents.

27 Atiyah Abd al-Rahman, letter to bin Laden, August 28, 2010, Abbottabad documents.

28 Osama bin Laden, letter to Atiyah, September 26, 2010, Abbottabad documents.

29 *USA v. Najibullah Zazi,* United States District Court, Eastern District of New York, Case 1:09-cr-00663-RJD-SMG.

30 Saleh al-Somali, letter to bin Laden, n.d. [*c.* April 2009], Abbottabad documents.

31 We do not have the original letter from the Iranians, but its contents were described in correspondence between Zawahiri and bin Laden in May 2010. Ayman al-Zawahiri, letter to bin Laden, May 16, 2010, Abbottabad documents; see also Hajji Uthman, letter to bin Laden, April 14, 2010, Abbottabad documents; and Atiyah Abd al-Rahman, letter to bin Laden, June 19, 2010, Abbottabad documents.

32 Atiyah referred to this project as the "Germany program," and said that it " … aimed to put pressure on Germany and conduct psychological warfare, etc." Atiyah Abd al-Rahman, letter to bin Laden, June 9, 2010, Abbottabad documents.

33 The party most clearly in favor of pulling German troops out of Afghanistan in 2009 was the liberal Free Democratic Party (FDP). The FDP did very well in the 2009 Federal elections and entered Angela Merkel's ruling coalition, but in the end, this did not change Merkel's policy on Afghanistan. "Afghanistan Exit," *DW*, August 19, 2009, https://www.dw.com/en/german-liberal-party-calls-for-exit-timetable-for-afghanistan-troops/a-4582559.

34 Saleh al-Somali, letter to bin Laden, n.d. [*c.* April 2009], Abbottabad documents.

35 The editor of *Inspire* was the naturalized US citizen Samir Khan, who started the magazine *Jihad Recollections* in 2009. Both magazines dedicated articles to Abu Musab al-Suri. See, e.g., *Jihad Recollections,* Issue 2 (May 2009), 31–4; *Inspire Magazine*, Issue 1 (Summer 2010), 48–53.

36 Sheikh Saeed wrote that if al-Qaida does not have a secure geographical base from where to confront the United States, al-Qaida might instead fight "a war of individual resistance (*al-muqawama al-fardiyya*) as Abu Musab al-Suri wrote." Hajji Uthman, letter to bin Laden, February 17, 2010, Abbottabad documents.

37 Lia, *Architect of Global Jihad*, 7–8; 363–8.

38 As paraphrased in Atiyah Abd al-Rahman, letter to bin Laden, August 22, 2009, Abbottabad documents.

39 Atiyah Abd al-Rahman and Hajji Uthman, letter to bin Laden, January 25, 2010, Abbottabad documents.

40 Yunus al-Mauritani, letter to bin Laden, n.d. [*c.* January 25, 2010], Abbottabad documents.

41 Atiyah Abd al-Rahman and Hajji Uthman, letter to bin Laden, January 25, 2010, Abbottabad documents.

42 Ibid.

43 Ibid.

44 Ibid.

45 Yunus al-Mauritani, letter to bin Laden, March 28, 2010, Abbottabad documents.

46 Osama bin Laden, letter to Shaykh Yunus, with addendum, n.d. [*c.* February 15, 2010], Abbottabad documents.

47 Ibid.

48 Ibid.

49 Osama bin Laden, letter to Hajji Uthman, February 15, 2010, Abbottabad documents.

50 Osama bin Laden, letter to Shaykh Yunus, with addendum, n.d. [*c.* February 15, 2010], Abbottabad documents.

51 Osama bin Laden, "Oh People of Islam," *al-Sahab*, April 2006.

52 "'The Word Is the Word of the Sword 1: The Raid of the Muezzin, Abu al-Gharib al-Makki," *al-Sahab*, September 2008.

53 Osama bin Laden, letter to Shaykh Yunus, with addendum, n.d. [*c.* February 15, 2010], Abbottabad documents.

54 Hajji Uthman, letter to bin Laden, February 17, 2010, Abbottabad documents.

55 Ibid.

56 Ibid.

57 Yunus al-Mauritani, letter to bin Laden [answer to the first letter], March 28, 2010, Abbottabad documents.

58 Yunus al-Mauritani, letter to bin Laden [answer to the second letter], March 28, 2010, Abbottabad documents.

59 Yassin Musharbash, "Al-Kaida: In ihren eigenen Worten," *Die Zeit*, March 15, 2012.

60 Florian Flade, "Abbottabad und die Düsseldorfer Zelle," *Verschlusssache*, March 20, 2013, https://ojihad.wordpress.com/tag/mauritani/.

61 Flade, "Abbottabad und die Düsseldorfer Zelle."

62 "Alleged Terrorist Charged with Conspiracy to Provide Material Support to Al-Qaeda," *The US Attorney's Office, Eastern District of New York*, November 10, 2011, https://www.justice.gov/archive/usao/nye/pr/2011/2011nov10.html.

63 Hajji Uthman, letter to bin Laden, April 14, 2010, Abbottabad documents.

64 Yunus al-Mauritani, letter to bin Laden [answer to the first letter], March 28, 2010, Abbottabad documents.

65 Hajji Uthman, letter to bin Laden, April 14, 2010, Abbottabad documents.

66 Ayman al-Zawahiri, letter to bin Laden, May 31, 2010, Abbottabad documents.

67 This observation was made, for example, in Vidar B. Skretting, "Al-Qaida in the Islamic Maghrib's Expansion in the Sahara: New Insights from Primary Sources," *Studies in Conflict & Terrorism* 46, no. 8 (2020): 1382.

68 Osama bin Laden, letter to Shaykh Yunus, July 6, 2010, Abbottabad documents.

69 Osama bin Laden, letter to Bashir al-Madani [Shaykh Yunus], September 26, 2010, Abbottabad documents.

70 Atiyah Abd al-Rahman, letter to bin Laden, April 5, 2011, Abbottabad documents.

71 Ayman al-Zawahiri, "For Incitement and Publishing: You Are Held Responsible Only for Yourself," *al-Sahab*, June 2011, author's collection.

Chapter 7

1   Osama bin Laden, draft letter to Atiyah, n.d. [*c.* August 7, 2010], Abbottabad documents.

2   Ibid.

3   Osama bin Laden, letter to Atiyah, July 6, 2010, Abbottabad documents.

4   Osama bin Laden, draft letter to Atiyah, n.d. [*c.* August 7, 2010], Abbottabad documents.

5   Osama bin Laden, letter to Atiyah, July 6, 2010, Abbottabad documents.

6   Basir [Nasir al-Wuhayshi], letter to Abu Uthman, n.d. [*c.* 2009], Abbottabad documents, published by ODNI as "Letter from Basir to the Brother in Command," on March 1, 2016.

7   Osama bin Laden, '*i'lan al-jihad "ala al-amrikiyyin al-muhtallin li-bilad al-haramayn* [Declaration of jihad against the Americans occupying the land of the two holiest sites]," August 23, 1996, Combating Terrorism Center at West Point, Harmony Program, AFGP-2002-003676.

8   For background on the Sahwa, see, e.g., Stéphane Lacroix, *Awakening Islam: The Politics of Religious Dissent in Contemporary Saudi Arabia* (Cambridge, MA: Harvard University Press, 2011).

9   Abu al-Zubayr and Ayman al-Zawahiri, "*bushra sarra* [Glad Tidings]," *al-Sahab*, February 2012.

10 Atiyah Abd al-Rahman, letter to bin Laden, January 21, 2010, Abbottabad documents.

11 Ibid.

12 Osama bin Laden, letter to Atiyah, July 6, 2010, Abbottabad documents.

13 Atiyah Abd al-Rahman and Hajji Uthman, letter to bin Laden, January 25, 2010, Abbottabad documents.

14 Basir [Nasir al-Wuhayshi], letter to Abu Uthman, n.d. [*c.* 2009], Abbottabad documents, published by ODNI as "Letter from Basir to the Brother in Command," on March 1, 2016.

15 The dates of bin Laden's various letters are referred to in Ayman al-Zawahiri, letter to bin Laden, May 31, 2010, Abbottabad documents.

16 Atiyah Abd al-Rahman and Hajji Uthman, letter to bin Laden, January 25, 2010, Abbottabad documents.

17 Ayman al-Zawahiri, letter to bin Laden, May 16, 2010, Abbottabad documents.

18 For a complete history of al-Qaida in Saudi Arabia, see Hegghammer, *Jihad in Saudi Arabia.*

19 Osama bin Laden, draft letter entitled "very very important_some points," n.d. [*c.* 2010], Abbottabad documents.

20 Hajji Uthman, letter to bin Laden, February 17, 2010, Abbottabad documents.

21 Ibid.

22 Ayman al-Zawahiri, letter to bin Laden, May 31, 2010, Abbottabad documents.

23 Mukhtar Abu al-Zubayr, letter to al-Qaida, March 5, 2010, Abbottabad documents.

24 Atiyah Abd al-Rahman, letter to bin Laden, March 5, 2010, Abbottabad documents.

25 Osama bin Laden, letter to Zawahiri, March 17, 2010, Abbottabad documents; Hajji Uthman, letter to bin Laden, April 14, 2010, Abbottabad documents.

26 Hajji Uthman, letter to bin Laden, April 14, 2010, Abbottabad documents.

27 "*mulakhkhas al-nuqat al-matruha fi al-jalsa*," n.d. [*c.* April 2010], Abbottabad documents.

28 Ibid.

29 Ibid.

30 Ibid.

31 Ayman al-Zawahiri, letter to bin Laden, May 16, 2010, Abbottabad documents.

32 Ibid.

33 Ayman al-Zawahiri, letter to bin Laden, May 31, 2010, Abbottabad documents.

34 Abu Miqdad al-Masri, letter to Atiyah and bin Laden, n.d. [mid-2010], Abbottabad documents.

35 Ibid.

36 Al-Shabaab in Somalia sent a formal pledge of allegiance to bin Laden in December 2009, but internal documents suggest al-Shabaab was already treated as an "affiliate" from at least May 2009, when bin Laden had asked Sheikh Saeed to send directions to "our brothers in Iraq, Maghrib, Somalia, and Yemen." See Hajji Uthman, letter to bin Laden, May 6, 2009, Abbottabad documents.

37 Abu Yahya al-Libi, letter to Al-Qaida in the Islamic Maghreb, December 5, 2009, Abbottabad documents.

38 "FOIA Declassified documents on Anwar Awlaki (2019 release)," obtained via J.M. Berger at INTELWIRE.com, https://www.jmberger.com/documents.

39 Osama bin Laden, letter to Atiyah, July 6, 2010, Abbottabad documents.

40 Osama bin Laden, letter to Abu Basir, n.d. [August 2010], Abbottabad documents; and Atiyah Abd al-Rahman, letter to Abu Basir, July 18, 2010, Abbottabad documents.

41 Osama bin Laden, letter to Atiyah, July 6, 2010, Abbottabad documents.

42 See, e.g., Atiyah Abd al-Rahman, letter to Abu Basir, July 18, 2010, Abbottabad documents.

43 Osama bin Laden, letter to Atiyah, July 6, 2010, Abbottabad documents.

44 CIA Director George Tenet used the term "Al-Qaida Central" in a Senate hearing in February 2004. Before that, and since at least 2002, Western media had used similar terms, like "al-Qaeda's central organization" and "al Qaeda's central leadership," when referring to al-Qaida's senior leaders in Afghanistan-Pakistan. See, e.g., Michael Elliott, "Al-Qaeda: Reeling Them In," *TIME*, September 23, 2002, https://time.com/archive/6667248/al-qaeda-reeling-them-in/; "Wolfowitz: 'We Are Moving to Victory,'" *CNN*, September 11, 2003, https://edition.cnn.com/2003/ALLPOLITICS/09/09/sprj.irq.wolfowitz.cia/index.html; and finally, "Statement of the honorable George J. Tenet, Director of Central Intelligence," in "Hearing

before the Select Committee on Intelligence of the United States Senate, 108th Congress, Second Session: Current and projected national security threats to the United States," Transcript, Senate Hearing 108–588, US Government Printing Office, February 24, 2004, https://www.intelligence.senate.gov/hearings/current-and-projected-national-security-threats-united-states-february-24-2004.

45 Atiyah Abd al-Rahman, letter to Abu Basir, July 18, 2010, Abbottabad documents.

46 Atiyah Abd al-Rahman, letter to bin Laden, July 17, 2010, Abbottabad documents.

47 Atiyah Abd al-Rahman, letter to Abu Basir, July 18, 2010, Abbottabad documents.

48 Osama bin Laden, letter to Abu Yahya al-Libi, August 7, 2010, Abbottabad documents.

49 Atiyah Abd al-Rahman, letter to bin Laden, August 28, 2010, Abbottabad documents.

50 Ibid.

51 Ibid.

52 Atiyah Abd al-Rahman, letter to bin Laden, October 6, 2010, Abbottabad documents.

53 Osama bin Laden, letter to Abu Musab Abd al-Wudud, October 17, 2010, Abbottabad documents.

54 "Two French Journalists Freed in Afghanistan after 547 Days," *France 24*, June 29, 2011, https://www.france24.com/en/20110629-french-journalists-kidnapped-taliban-have-been-freed.

55 Abu Basir, letter to Atiyah, February 9, 2011, Abbottabad documents.

56 Ibid.

57 Brynjar Lia, "Understanding Jihadi Proto-States," *Perspectives on Terrorism* 9, no. 4 (2015): 35.

Conclusion

1 Atiyah Abd al-Rahman, letter to Hafiz Sultan [Hajji Uthman], March 28, 2007, Abbottabad documents.

Appendix

1 The tables were compiled from the following sources: Thomas Hegghammer, "Al-Qaida Statements 2003–2004—A Compilation of Translated Texts by Usama bin Ladin and Ayman al-Zawahiri," FFI Report-2005/01428; Thomas Hegghammer, "Dokumentasjon om al-Qa'ida—Intervjuer, kommunikéer og andre primærkilder, 1990–2002," FFI Report-2002/01393; "Al-Qaeda Statements Index," Harverford College, https://gtrp.haverford.edu/aqsi/ [now defunct; mirrored at TriCollege Libraries Institutional Scholarship, http://hdl.handle.net/10066/4022]; *BBC*; *Al-Jazeera,* and *Associated Press.*

Bibliography

"Afghan Warlord 'Aided Bin Laden,'" *BBC*, January 11, 2007, http://news.bbc.co.uk/2/hi/south_asia/6252975.stm.

"Afghan Warlord Urges Revolt against US, Karzai," *NBC*, May 31, 2006, https://www.nbcnews.com/id/wbna13068608.

"Afghanistan Exit," *DW*, August 19, 2009, https://www.dw.com/en/german-liberal-party-calls-for-exit-timetable-for-afghanistan-troops/a-4582559.

Ali, Obaid, Sayed Asadullah Sadat and Christian Bleuer. "One Land, Two Rules (8): Delivering Public Services in Insurgency-Affected Insurgent-Controlled Zurmat District," *Afghanistan Analysts Network,* September 4, 2019, https://www.afghanistan-analysts.org/en/reports/war-and-peace/one-land-two-rules-8-delivering-public-services-in-insurgency-affected-insurgent-controlled-zurmat-district/.

al-Bahri, Nassar. *Guarding Bin Laden: My Life in al-Qaeda* (Great Britain: TMP, 2013).

"Aljazeera Airs Hikmatyar Video," *Al-Jazeera*, May 4, 2006, https://web.archive.org/web/20060517002958/http://english.aljazeera.net/NR/exeres/4DB6529A-F1FC-43FC-8DB4-482F406D1DCE.htm.

Anas, Abdallah and Tam Hussein. *To the Mountains: My Life in Jihad, from Algeria to Afghanistan* (London: Hurst, 2019).

Asghar, Mohammad. "Rauf's Escape Case of 'Criminal Collusion': Report," *Dawn*, December 20, 2007, https://www.dawn.com/news/281198/newspaper/column.

Bergen, Peter L. "The Account of How We Nearly Caught Osama bin Laden in 2001," *The New Republic*, 2009, https://newrepublic.com/article/72086/the-battle-tora-bora.

Bergen, Peter L. *The Rise and Fall of Osama bin Laden* (New York: Simon & Schuster, 2021).

Bergen, Peter L. and Daniel Rothenberg (eds.), *Drone Wars: Transforming Conflict, Law, and Policy* (Cambridge: Cambridge University Press, 2015).

Bergen, Peter L. (ed.) and Katherine Tiedemann (contributor). *Talibanistan: Negotiating the Borders between Terror, Politics, and Religion* (Oxford: Oxford University Press, 2013).

"Berlusconi to Pull Out Troops from Iraq," *The Guardian*, March 16, 2005, https://www.theguardian.com/world/2005/mar/16/italy.iraq.

Bernsten, Gary. *Jawbreaker: The Attack on Bin Laden and Al-Qaeda: A Personal Account by the CIA's Key Field Commander* (New York: Random House, 2005).

Blaber, Pete. *The Mission, the Men, and Me: Lessons from a Former Delta Force Commander* (New York: Berkley Caliber, 2008).

Brachman, Jarret. "The Next Osama," *Newsweek*, September 10, 2009, https://foreignpolicy.com/2009/09/10/the-next-osama/.

Byman, Daniel and Asfandyar Mir. "How Strong Is al-Qaeda? A Debate," *War on the Rocks*, May 20, 2022, https://warontherocks.com/2022/05/how-strong-is-al-qaeda-a-debate/.

Coll, Steve. *Directorate S: The C.I.A. and America's Secret Wars in Afghanistan and Pakistan, 2001–2016* (London: Allen Lane, 2018).

Della Porta, Donatella. *Clandestine Political Violence: A Social Movements Perspective* (Cambridge: Cambridge University Press, 2013).

"Doubts Cloud Pakistani Cleric's Death," *Al-Jazeera*, August 21, 2004, https://www.aljazeera.com/news/2004/8/21/doubts-cloud-pakistani-clerics-death.

Eckholm, Erik. "Kandahar Hospital Was Unhappy Host to 18, Not 11, Armed Unholy Warriors," *New York Times*, December 18, 2001, https://www.nytimes.com/2001/12/18/world/nation-challenged-wounded-kandahar-hospital-was-unhappy-host-18-not-11-armed.html.

Edwards, Lucy Morgan. *The Afghan Solution: The Inside Story of Abdul Haq, the CIA and How Western Hubris Lost Afghanistan* (London: Pluto Press, 2011).

Eijkman, Quirine. "The German Sauerland Cell Reconsidered," *Perspectives on Terrorism* 8, no. 4 (August 2014): 82–90.

El Zalaf, Ahmed Abou. "The Special Apparatus (al-Niẓām al-Khāṣṣ): The Rise of Nationalist Militancy in the Ranks of the Egyptian Muslim Brotherhood," *Religions* 13, no. 1 (2022): 77.

Evans, Duane. *Foxtrot in Kandahar: A Memoir of a CIA Officer in Afghanistan at the Inception of America's Longest War* (El Dorado, CA: Savas Beatie, 2017).

"Excerpts from Purported Bin Laden Tape," *Associated Press*, April 8, 2003.

"FACTBOX-Assassination Attempts against Pakistan's Musharraf," *Reuters*, August 9, 2007, https://www.reuters.com/article/economy/factbox-assassination-attempts-against-pakistans-musharraf-idUSL06499787/.

Fishman, Brian. "Revising the History of al-Qaʻida's Original Meeting with Abu Musab al-Zarqawi," *CTC Sentinel* 9, no. 6 (October 2016): 28–33.

Fishman, Brian. *The Master Plan: ISIS, Al-Qaeda, and the Jihadi Strategy for Final Victory* (New Haven, CT: Yale University Press, 2016).

Flade, Florian. "Abbottabad und die Düsseldorfer Zelle," *Verschlusssache*, March 20, 2013, https://ojihad.wordpress.com/tag/mauritani/.

Fouda, Yosri and Nick Fielding. *Masterminds of Terror: The Truth behind the Most Devastating Terrorist Attack the World Has Ever Seen* (London: Penguin, 2003).

Gall, Carlotta. "Kabul Bombing Kills 4 German Soldiers and Wounds 29," *New York Times*, June 8, 2003, https://www.nytimes.com/2003/06/08/world/threats-responses-afghanistan-kabul-bombing-kills-4-german-soldiers-wounds-29.html.

Gall, Carlotta. "Pakistan and Afghan Taliban Close Ranks," *New York Times*, March 27, 2009, https://web.archive.org/web/20210819003725/https://www.nytimes.com/2009/03/27/world/asia/27taliban.html.

Gannon, Kathy. "Purported Bin Laden Tape Urges Attacks," *Associated Press*, April 8, 2003.

Gerges, Fawaz A. *The Far Enemy: Why Jihad Went Global* (Cambridge: Cambridge University Press, 2009).

Giustozzi, Antonio. *The Taliban at War, 2001–2021* (New York: Oxford University Press, 2022).

Grenier, Robert L. *88 Days to Kandahar: A CIA Diary* (New York: Simon & Schuster, 2015).

Hamid, Mustafa and Leah Farrall. *The Arabs at War in Afghanistan* (London: Hurst, 2015).

Harnden, Toby. *First Casualty: The Untold Story of the CIA Mission to Avenge 9/11* (New York: Little, Brown and Company, 2021).

Harnisch, Chris. "Question Mark of South Waziristan: Biography and Analysis of Maulvi Nazir Ahmad," *AEI*, July 17, 2009, https://www.aei.org/articles/question-mark-of-south-waziristan-biography-and-analysis-of-maulvi-nazir-ahmad/.

Hastert, Paul L. "Operation Anaconda: Perception Meets Reality in the Hills of Afghanistan," *Studies in Conflict & Terrorism* 28, no. 1 (2005): 11–20.

Hegghammer, Thomas. "Dokumentasjon om al-Qaʻida—Intervjuer, kommunikéer og andre primærkilder, 1990–2002," FFI Report-2002/01393.

Hegghammer, Thomas. "Al-Qaida Statements 2003–2004—A Compilation of Translated Texts by Usama bin Ladin and Ayman al-Zawahiri," FFI Report-2005/01428.

Hegghammer, Thomas. "Global Jihadism after the Iraq War," *Middle East Journal* 60, no. 1 (Winter, 2006): 11–32.

Hegghammer, Thomas. *Jihad in Saudi Arabia: Violence and Pan-Islamism since 1979* (Cambridge: Cambridge University Press, 2010).

Hegghammer, Thomas. *Jihadi Culture: The Art and Social Practices of Militant Islamists* (Cambridge: Cambridge University Press, 2017).

Hegghammer, Thomas. *The Caravan: Abdallah Azzam and the Rise of Global Jihad* (Cambridge: Cambridge University Press, 2020).

Hicks, David. *Guantanamo: My Journey* (Sydney: Random House Australia, 2010).

Hoffman, Bruce. "Al-Qaeda's Resurrection," *Council on Foreign Relations*, March 6, 2018, https://www.cfr.org/expert-brief/al-qaedas-resurrection.

Jackson, Kévin. "Abu Al-Layth Al-Libi," *CTC West Point*, 2015, https://ctc.westpoint.edu/wp-content/uploads/2015/03/CTC_Abu-al-Layth-al-Libi-Jihadi-Bio-February2015-1.pdf.

Khan, M. Ilyas. "Profile of Nek Muhammad," *Dawn*, June 19, 2004.

Khattak, Daud. "Contrasting the Leadership of Mullah Fazlullah and Khan Said Sajna in Pakistan," *CTC Sentinel* 7, no. 7 (July 2014): 18–20.

Lacroix, Stéphane. *Awakening Islam: The Politics of Religious Dissent in Contemporary Saudi Arabia* (Cambridge, MA: Harvard University Press, 2011).

Lahoud, Nelly. *The Bin Laden Papers: How the Abbottabad Raid Revealed the Truth about al-Qaeda, Its Leader and His Family* (New Haven, CT: Yale University Press, 2023).

Lefèvre, Raphaël. *Jihad in the City: Militant Islam and Contentious Politics in Tripoli* (Cambridge: Cambridge University Press, 2021).

Levy, Adrian and Kathy Scott-Clark. *The Exile: The Flight of Osama bin Laden* (New York and London: Bloomsbury, 2017).

Lia, Brynjar and Thomas Hegghammer. "Jihadi Strategic Studies: The Alleged Al Qaida Policy Study Preceding the Madrid Bombings," *Studies in Conflict & Terrorism* 27, no. 5 (2004): 355–75.

Lia, Brynjar. *Architect of Global Jihad: The Life of al-Qaida Strategist Abu Mus'ab al-Suri* (London: Hurst, 2014).

Lia, Brynjar. "Understanding Jihadi Proto-States," *Perspectives on Terrorism* 9, no. 4 (2015): 31–41.

Lia, Brynjar. "A Kurdish al-Qaida? Making Sense of the Ansar al-Islam Movement in Iraqi Kurdistan in the Early 2000s," *Religions* 13, no. 3 (2022): 203.

Liebl, Vernie. "Al Qaida on the US Invasion of Afghanistan in Their Own Words," *Small Wars & Insurgencies* 23, no. 3 (2012): 542–68.

Linschoten, Alex Strick van and Felix Kuehn. *An Enemy We Created: The Myth of the Taliban-Al-Qaeda Merger in Afghanistan* (London: Hurst, 2011).

Ludhianvi, Mufti Rasheed. *Obedience to the Amir: An Early Text on the Afghan Taliban Movement* (Berlin: First Draft Publishing, 2015).

Mabon, Simon. *The Struggle for Supremacy in the Middle East: Saudi Arabia and Iran* (Cambridge: Cambridge University Press, 2023).

Mahsud, Mansur Khan. "The Taliban in South Waziristan," in Peter Bergen (ed.), Katherine Tiedemann (contributor), *Talibanistan: Negotiating the Borders between Terror, Politics, and Religion* (Oxford: Oxford University Press, 2013): 164–201.

Meijer, Roel. "Yusuf al-Uyairi and the Making of a Revolutionary Salafi Praxis," *Die Welt des Islams* 47, no. 3–4 (2007): 422–59.

Mendelsohn, Barak. *The al-Qaeda Franchise: The Expansion of al-Qaeda and Its Consequences* (Oxford: Oxford University Press, 2016).

Mir, Hamid. "How Osama bin Laden Escaped Death 4 Times after 9/11," *Canada Free Press*, September 8, 2007, https://canadafreepress.com/2007/mir090907.htm.

Moghadam, Assaf and Brian Fishman. *Fault Lines in Global Jihad: Organizational, Strategic, and Ideological Fissures* (London: Routledge, 2011).

Moreau, Ron and Sami Yousafzai, "In the Footsteps of Zarqawi; The Taliban's Bloodthirsty Top Commander in Southern Afghanistan Scares Almost Everyone– Even His Allies and Underlings," *Newsweek*, July 3, 2006.

Morgan, Wesley. *The Hardest Place: The American Military Adrift in Afghanistan's Pech Valley* (New York: Random House, 2021).

Musharbash, Yassin. "Bonner Qaida-Kämpfer soll bei Gefecht gestorben sein," *Der Spiegel*, January 18, 2011, https://www.spiegel.de/politik/deutschland/dschihadist-abu-talha-bonner-qaida-kaempfer-soll-bei-gefecht-gestorben-sein-a-740140.html.

Musharbash, Yassin. "Al-Kaida: In ihren eigenen Worten," *Die Zeit*, March 15, 2012, https://www.zeit.de/2012/12/Al-Kaida-Deutschland.

Mutma'in, Abdul Hai. *Taliban: A Critical History from Within* (Berlin: First Draft Publishing, 2019).

Naylor, Sean. *Not a Good Day to Die: The Untold Story of Operation Anaconda* (New York: Berkley Books, 2005).

Nesser, Petter. *Islamist Terrorism in Europe* (Oxford: Oxford University Press, 2015).

"Pakistan: Top Terror Suspect Arrested," *Voice of America News*, July 29, 2004, https://www.voanews.com/a/a-13-a-2004-07-29-11-pakistan-66890537/261768.html.

Pantucci, Raffaello. "A Biography of Rashid Rauf: Al-Qa`ida's British Operative," *CTC Sentinel* 5, no. 7 (July 2012): 12–16.

Paterson, James. "Al-Qaeda as a Spatial Orientated Movement: Interactions between Transnational and Local Jihadism," *Small Wars & Insurgencies*, DOI: 10.1080/09592318.2024.2314653 February 15, 2024.

"Pentagon: Top al Qaeda Leader Taken to Guantanamo," *CNN*, April 27, 2007, http://www.cnn.com/2007/US/04/27/al.qaeda.gitmo/index.html.

Porter, Gareth. "US Silent on Taliban's al-Qaeda Offer," *Asia Times*, December 17, 2010, https://web.archive.org/web/20091219213931/http://www.atimes.com/atimes/South_Asia/KL17Df02.html.

"Presidential Address to the Nation," *The White House*, October 7, 2001, https://georgewbush-whitehouse.archives.gov/news/releases/2001/10/20011007-8.html.

"Qaeda Group in Iraq Threatens to Attack Iranians," *Reuters*, August 9, 2007, https://www.reuters.com/article/us-iraq-qaeda/qaeda-group-in-iraq-threatens-to-attack-iranians-idUSL08390724200707708/.

Reinares, Fernando. *Al-Qaeda's Revenge: The 2004 Madrid Train Bombings* (Washington, DC: Woodrow Wilsom Center Press, 2016).

"Remarks by the President in Address to the Nation on the Way Forward in Afghanistan and Pakistan," *The White House*, December 1, 2009, https://obamawhitehouse.archives.gov/the-press-office/remarks-president-address-nation-way-forward-afghanistan-and-pakistan.

Robertson, Nic, Paul Cruickshank, and Tim Lister, "Documents Give New Details on al Qaeda's London Bombings," *CNN*, April 30, 2012.

Rosen, Nir. "Thinking Like a Jihadist: Iraq's Jordanian Connection," *World Policy Journal* 23, no. 1 (Spring, 2006): 1–16.

Ruttig, Thomas. "On Kunar's Salafi Insurgents," *Afghanistan Analysts Network*, January 14, 2010, https://www.afghanistan-analysts.org/en/reports/war-and-peace/on-kunars-salafi-insurgents/.

Sageman, Marc. *Misunderstanding Terrorism* (Philadelphia, PA: University of Pennsylvania Press, 2017).

Sageman, Marc. *The London Bombings* (Philadelphia, PA: University of Pennsylvania Press, 2019).

Schroen, Gary. *First In: An Insider's Account of How the CIA Spearheaded the War on Terror in Afghanistan* (New York: Presidio Press, 2005).

Scott-Clark, Cathy and Adrian Levy. *The Siege: 68 Hours inside the Taj Hotel* (New York: Penguin, 2013).

"Seeking Information: Adnan G. El Shukrijumah," *Rewards for Justice Program*, https://web.archive.org/web/20161222183957/https://www2.fbi.gov/terrorinfo/elshukrijumah.htm.

Senate Select Committee on Intelligence, "Committee Study of the Central Intelligence Agency's Detention and Interrogation Program," *United States Senate*, April 3, 2014.

Serrano, Richard A., "Driven by a Son's Sacrifice," *Los Angeles Times*, April 7, 2005, https://www.latimes.com/archives/la-xpm-2005-apr-07-na-spann7-story.html.

Shah, Niaz. "The Islamic Emirate of Afghanistan: A Layeha [Rules and Regulations] for Mujahidin," *Studies in Conflict and Terrorism* 35, no. 6 (2012): 456–70.

Shahzad, Syed Saleem. "Pakistan Gets Its Man … Sort of," *Asia Times*, September 29, 2004.

Shams, Alex. "The Politics of Arbaeen: Transcending Militarized Urbanism in Iraq's Shrine Cities," *POMEPS*, n.d., https://pomeps.org/the-politics-of-arbaeen-transcending-militarized-urbanism-in-iraqs-shrine-cities.

Skretting, Vidar B. "Al-Qaida in the Islamic Maghrib's Expansion in the Sahara: New Insights from Primary Sources," *Studies in Conflict & Terrorism* 46, no. 8 (2020): 1368–92.

Smith, Michael. "SBS behind Taliban Leader's Death," *The Times*, May 27, 2007.

Smucker, Philip. *Al Qaeda's Great Escape: The Military and the Media on Terror's Trail* (Washington, DC: Potomac Books, 2004).

Soufan, Ali H. *The Black Banners: Inside the Hunt for Al Qaeda* (London: Penguin, 2011).

Stanton, Doug. *Horse Soldiers: The Extraordinary Story of a Band of US Soldiers Who Rode to Victory in Afghanistan* (New York: Simon & Schuster, 2009).

Stenersen, Anne. *Al-Qaida's Quest for Weapons of Mass Destruction: The History behind the Hype* (Saarbrucken: VMD Verlag, 2008).

Stenersen, Anne. "A History of Jihadi Cinematography," in Thomas Hegghammer (ed.), *Jihadi Culture: The Art and Social Practices of Militant Islamists* (Cambridge: Cambridge University Press, 2017): 108–27.

Stenersen, Anne. *Al-Qaida in Afghanistan* (Cambridge: Cambridge University Press, 2017).

Stewart, Richard W. "The US Army in Afghanistan: Operation Enduring Freedom, October 2001-March 2002," *Center of Military History*, CMH Pub 70-83-1.

"Taliban Leader Exhorts Suicide Bombers in Video," *Reuters*, October 3, 2007, https://www.reuters.com/article/afghan-taliban/taliban-leader-exhorts-suicide-bombers-in-video-idINISL3672520071003/.

Tawil, Camille. *Brothers in Arms: The Story of al-Qa'ida and the Arab Jihadists*, trans. Robin Bray (Lodon: Saqi Books, 2011).

"Two French Journalists Freed in Afghanistan after 547 Days," *France 24*, June 29, 2011, https://www.france24.com/en/20110629-french-journalists-kidnapped-taliban-have-been-freed.

Tyson, Ann Scott. "Going in Small in Afghanistan," *Christian Science Monitor*, January 14, 2004, https://www.csmonitor.com/2004/0114/p01s04-wosc.html.

Tønnessen, Truls. *Al-Qaida in Iraq: The Rise, the Fall and the Comeback*, PhD Thesis, Faculty of Humanities, Univeristy of Oslo, 2015.

Tønnessen, Truls. "Heirs of Zarqawi or Saddam? The Relationship between al-Qaida in Iraq and the Islamic State," *Perspectives on Terrorism* 9, no. 4 (2015): 48–60.

UNAMA, "Suicide Attacks in Afghanistan (2001–2007)," *United Nations Assistance Mission to Afghanistan*, September 1, 2007, Available: https://www.refworld.org/reference/countryrep/unama/2007/en/68699.

"US Troop Surge and End of US Combat Mission," *Britannica*, n.d., https://www.britannica.com/event/Afghanistan-War/U-S-troop-surge-and-end-of-U-S-combat-mission.

Wagemakers, Joas. *A Quietist Jihadi: The Ideology and Influence of Abu Muhammad al-Maqdisi* (Cambridge: Cambridge University Press, 2012).

Wigen, Einar. "Islamic Jihad Union—al-Qaida´s Key to the Turkic World," FFI-Report 2009/00687, https://www.ffi.no/en/publications-archive/islamic-jihad-union-al-qaidas-key-to-the-turkic-world.

Wilner, Alex S. "Targeted Killings in Afghanistan: Measuring Coercion and Deterrence in Counterterrorism and Counterinsurgency," *Studies in Conflict & Terrorism* 33, no. 4 (2010): 307–29.

Yusufzai, Rahimullah. "Battle Creates a New Taliban Legend," *TIME Magazine*, March 7, 2002.

Primary Source Archives

"Al-Qaeda Statements," Haverford College, Department of Political science, http://hdl.handle.net/10066/4022.

"Bin Laden's Bookshelf," *Office of the Director of National Intelligence (ODNI)*, https://www.dni.gov/index.php/features/bin-laden-s-bookshelf.

"FFI's archive of jihadist primary sources," offline, located at the Norwegian Defence Research Establishment (FFI), Kjeller, Norway.

"Harmony Program," *Combating Terrorism Center at West Point*, https://ctc.westpoint.edu/harmony-program/.

"November 2017 Release of Abbottabad Compound Material," *Central Intelligence Agency*, https://www.cia.gov/library/abbottabad-compound/index.html.

Index